Europe
Since 1945
A Concise History

J. Robert Wegs

ST. MARTIN'S PRESS
New York

To Joyce and Alison

Cover design: Vickie Peslak

Library of Congress Catalog Card Number: 76-05543
Copyright © 1977 by St. Martin's Press, Inc.
All Rights Reserved.
Manufactured in the United States of America.
0987
fedcba
For information, write: St. Martin's Press, Inc.,
175 Fifth Avenue, New York, N.Y. 10010

cloth ISBN: 312-27020-8
paper ISBN: 312-27055-0

Preface

Europe Since 1945: A Concise History provides comprehensive yet succinct coverage of a period that is often neglected in historical studies of twentieth-century Europe. In teaching the history of Europe since 1945 for the past six years, I have found that the few studies that do concentrate on the post-1945 period are either too encyclopedic, burying stimulating theses under mountains of facts, or too brief. Other objections often voiced by my students are that existing studies are too narrowly political or too exclusively concentrated on developments in the major Western European states. The search for a broader thematic approach to postwar European history, one that paid greater attention to Eastern Europe and the minor states of Western Europe, led me to write this survey.

The book is organized both chronologically and thematically. The chapters on politics provide the basic chronological structure. Other chapters, primarily thematic, are located at points where comprehension of their arguments will enhance the understanding of the chapters that follow. For example, the chapters on a bipolar world and on the Cold War and the Sovietization of Eastern Europe are fundamental to an understanding of the chapter on European politics from 1945 to 1948. The chapters on politics are tied to the other chapters by an underlying socioeconomic theme that is viewed as the major determinant of political change or continuity.

Throughout the study, I have favored conciseness over excessive attention to detail in order to highlight significant patterns and theses. Much of the statistical material is incorporated in the many tables located throughout the book. Six maps help students to fully grasp the significance of political and economic developments. An annotated list of selected readings at the end of each chapter guides students in research and further study.

I have viewed developments in postwar Europe as the culmination of a chain of events stretching back to the turn of the century. However, I have not overlooked the enormous impact of World War II in shaping the postwar world. For example, I explain the Cold War confrontation between the Soviet Union and the United States as resulting in part from the growth of non-European power centers beginning with the emergence of Japan and the United States in the late nineteenth century, and from the struggle between communism and capitalism that had been at work in domestic and international politics since 1917. The incorporation of Europe within a bipolar world after 1945 is, according to this interpretation, primarily the result of the attainment of superpower status by the United States and the U.S.S.R. during the century. But I do not neglect the importance of the lessening of German power in creating a power vacuum in central Europe that could only be filled by the two superpowers. Similarly, the emergence of independent third-world countries in the postwar period is explained by a three-stage revolutionary pattern stretching over nearly a century and by the economic and military weaknesses suffered by the European powers during World War II.

In the chapters on economic and social developments, demographic and statistical data are interwoven with theories that have been advanced to explain postwar European society. Such phenomena as changing occupational structures, the spread of affluence, and the persistence of distinct social classes and governing elites are treated in depth. In dealing with these themes, I have given special attention to the smaller European states, as they have often been forerunners in the development of the postwar welfare state. It is, for example, to Scandinavia that one must look in order to understand the impact of socioeconomic policies that have been pursued by most Western European states since World War II. I have also examined the effect of economic modernization and communism on Soviet and Eastern European societies.

I wish to thank Professor Richard Hull of New York University for reviewing chapter 6 (The End of European Empire), and Anita Samen and Ellen Wynn of St. Martin's Press for their suggestions and expeditious handling of the book.

J. ROBERT WEGS

Contents

Preface   v

1   A Bipolar World   1

2   The Cold War and the Sovietization of Eastern Europe   26

3   From Left to Right: European Politics, 1945–1948   44

4   Economic Recovery in Western Europe   63

5   Western European Politics, 1948–1965   79

6   The End of European Empire   98

7   From Stalin to Khrushchev: The New Course and Polycentrism   119

8   European Unity   136

9   European Society in the 1960s: The Managed   151

10   European Society in the 1960s: The Managers   171

11   Economics and Society in the Communist World   188

12   1968: Year of Crisis   206

13   To the 1970s and Beyond   222

Index   239

1 A Bipolar World

> There are on earth today two great peoples, who, from different points of departure seem to be advancing towards the same end. They are the Russians and the Anglo-Americans.
>
> Alexis de Tocqueville, *Democracy in America*

Contemporary history tends to exaggerate the influence of recent events — the impact of World War II on Europe's role in world affairs, for example. Long-term factors — the growing economic and political importance of the United States, Japan, and the Soviet Union, or the demographic patterns that began to reduce Europe's proportion of the world's population after 1930 — do not receive the attention given to a recent cataclysmic event such as World War II.

The Emergence of the Superpowers

This is not to minimize the enormous consequences of World War II. But it was only one of many factors that led to the polarization of world affairs around the activities of the United States and the Soviet Union, which emerged as superpowers after the war. The eclipse of the European balance of power system seems on the surface to be primarily a result of the war. But in fact the origin of that eclipse can be traced to the prewar emergence of power centers outside Western Europe. Even before the war, the countries rimming the Pacific Ocean had begun to shift the power balance away from Europe and usher in an era of global politics.

The meeting of the American and Soviet armies on the Elbe River in 1945 merely symbolized the changes that had been going on in the world's power relationships for over half a century. In World War I, Great Britain and France had already had to call on the United States to restore the power equilibrium in Europe. In the interwar period, the growing economic strength and political importance of the United States and the Soviet Union were for the most part unobserved because of the American policy of isolation from European affairs and the Soviet concentration on internal problems.

As indicated in Table 1-1, the United States had overtaken Western Europe in industrial production in the interwar years. By 1939 the United States was producing one-third of the world's most important metals, one-third of its coal and electrical energy, two-thirds of its oil, and three-quarters of its automobiles.

Despite this rapid growth, between 1929 and 1938 the U.S. share of the world's industrial output had actually declined from 42.2 to 32.2 percent. This decline resulted from the Great Depression of 1929 and the growth in the Soviet share of world production from 4.3 to 18.3 percent during the same period.

That such accelerated growth would ultimately have a far-reaching impact on world affairs did not escape the attention of some Europeans. It apparently convinced Adolf Hitler that Germany had only a short time to secure the territorial basis for competing in a world of superpowers. In 1928 Hitler wrote, "With the American Union a new power of such dimensions has come into being as threatens to upset the whole former power and order of rank of the states." The defeat of Germany and Japan in 1945 and the switchover to the production of war materiel in the United States and the Soviet Union brought about the concentration of power in the hands of the superpowers that Hitler had feared.

Although many had predicted the awesome military power exercised by the Soviet Union and the United States in 1945, few foresaw the collapse of power in Europe that brought about the Soviet–American confrontation. The Allied policy of unconditional surrender made it impossible for Germany or Japan to seek a compromise peace. Leaders in both countries realized what fate awaited them and therefore exhausted their countries'

Table 1-1   Growth of Industrial Production in Western Europe and the United States, 1901-1955

	Index of Industrial Production (volume) (W.E. 1938 = 100)		Index of Industrial Production (per capita) (W.E. 1955 = 100)	
	WESTERN EUROPE	UNITED STATES	WESTERN EUROPE	UNITED STATES
1901	44	35	37	74
1913	69	66	51	109
1929	86	124	60	165
1937	102	127	67	160
1955	177	291	100	285

SOURCE: Carlo M. Cipolla, *The Economic History of World Population*, 3rd ed. (Baltimore: Penguin Books, 1965), p. 69. Reprinted by permission of Penguin Books Ltd.

resources in the hope that a last-minute miracle might avert defeat. Hitler put his hopes in German rockets, jet planes, and the possibility that the United States and the Soviet Union might come to blows before the defeat of Germany. With German resistance continuing until the fall of Berlin in May 1945, Germany lay in ruins. France, weakened by defeat and internal divisions, was incapable of assuming leadership in Europe. Only Great Britain seemed to offer an alternative power center.

But World War II had in an economic sense been a hollow victory for the British. The nation that had ruled a quarter of the human race in 1914 was no match for the superpowers in 1945. The second largest creditor nation in the world in 1939, Britain became the largest debtor as a result of World War II. While expenditures increased fivefold during the war, exports were reduced to only 60 percent of the prewar total. To meet its wartime obligations, Britain had to liquidate more than a billion pounds in foreign assets.

The relative decline of Britain had begun even before the war. Its territorial base shrank as its colonies and territories gained independence or became autonomous members of the empire. Nor could it any longer tap the resources of colonies as it had done in the nineteenth century. As the empire was transformed into a commonwealth of nations in the two decades after the war, Britain was reduced to a small island nation whose population and resources were inadequate to compete with the superpowers. British foreign policy in the postwar years became increasingly dependent upon U.S. economic and military power and the American view of world affairs. When Britain tried to act independently, as it did at Suez in 1956, American disapproval and limited British resources thwarted the attempt.

With no possibility of restoring a European power equilibrium because of the military preponderance of the Soviet Union, Western leaders were fearful that all of Europe would be at the mercy of what they saw as Soviet expansionism. A prostrate Europe offered Soviet expansionists tempting bait. Yet did Soviet leaders actually desire an extension of Soviet hegemony over all Europe? Or, as American radical revisionists such as Gabriel Kolko and William A. Williams believe, were Soviet actions a response to the United States' attempt to use its economic and military superiority as a basis for global hegemony? Or are these positions extremist and unsupported by the evidence? The answers to these questions are to be found in Soviet and American objectives and actions.

The Soviet Union at War's End

At the end of World War II, the Soviet Union controlled most of Eastern Europe, Manchuria, and northern Korea and threatened to expand into Iran and Turkey. Despite Soviet military preponderance in these areas, which was soon to be of fundamental importance in determining postwar spheres of influence, Josef Stalin, as leader of the victorious Soviet forces, was awed by the enormous economic and military might of the United States and anxious about his role at home.

Stalin's fears for Soviet security, bolstered by serious weaknesses in the Soviet economy and growing suspicion and hostility abroad, were not unfounded. Twice within the previous twenty-five years Russia had suffered extensively from foreign invasions. Nearly 25 million Soviet citizens died as a direct or indirect result of World War II. Large sections of the country were laid waste by German and Soviet armies. Cities such as Kiev and Minsk had been devastated and had to be completely rebuilt; Leningrad suffered severe damage during two years of siege and bombardment, and 1 million of its in inhabitants — half the city's population — perished during the siege. In many industries, production had been halved because of the shortage of manpower and raw materials and the war damage to factories.

On the other hand, Stalin was keenly aware of American economic strength because of the vast amounts of U.S. material shipped to Europe and the Soviet Union during the war and used by U.S. forces in both the Pacific and the European war zones. Equally disturbing to him was the size of American military forces, numbering 12 million men as compared to the Soviet Union's 11 million. Stalin was aware that in an economic sense his country was not a superpower at the end of the war. To restore its economic strength, he hoped to obtain American aid and expected to acquire indispensable industrial equipment and raw materials from Germany and the countries of Eastern Europe. U.S. opposition to these goals was to be one of the major causes of the Cold War between East and West.

Stalin's feelings of insecurity both at home and elsewhere in the Communist world had a direct impact on his foreign policy. His opposition to Communist revolutionary movements, such as those in China and Yugoslavia, revealed his fear of outside rivals. His opposition to the leftist forces in the Greek civil war and to Yugoslav support of the rebels reflected his fear that President Tito of Yugoslavia might establish a Balkan Communist confederation big enough to challenge Stalin's preeminence in Eastern Europe and his domination over the Eastern European Communist parties. It was his dislike of Tito's independent course that led to Yugoslavia's ostracism from the Soviet-dominated Communist bloc (see chapter 2).

Within the Soviet Union, Stalin had been excessively concerned with the possible ideological contamination of Soviet citizens because of their contacts with Western Europe during the war. After the war, his desire to keep the West unaware of Soviet economic weakness and to avoid further "contamination" from Western ideas led to the curtailment of contacts with the West for all but a few Soviet nationals. By preventing Western knowledge of Soviet domestic affairs, Stalin only increased the mystery concerning life in the Soviet Union and promoted Western abhorrence of what came to be known as Stalinism. Widespread fear among nations of the

During World War II cities on both sides were ravaged by bombing raids. However, Leningrad, which was under siege for two years, suffered especially severe damage and loss of life. In this photo, taken in 1942, fire has broken out following bombardment of the city by the Germans.

Novosti from Sovfoto

West that such a system might spread beyond the Soviet sphere of influence provided considerable support for the eventual United States policy of containment of communism.

It was in order to achieve the national security against a resurgent Germany which he felt the West was not willing to provide that Stalin tried during the war and after to gain control over Eastern Europe. He had become convinced of the West's hostility toward the Soviet Union long before the Cold War. He well remembered the West's attempts to defeat bolshevism after World War I, the sellout of Czechoslovakia in 1938 at the Munich Conference, and the failure to side with the Soviet Union against Germany before the war. In order to avoid war with Germany, Stalin felt compelled to sign the Nazi–Soviet Nonaggression Pact in 1939. This pact gave the Soviet Union two more years to prepare its armies for the conflict with Hitler.

East–West Relations During World War II

Stalin's suspicions concerning Western intentions were not allayed by Western actions during the war. His actions were therefore determined by traditional balance of power considerations aimed at obtaining strategic and economic benefits for the Soviet Union after the war. As early as the Moscow Conference in December 1941, Stalin offered Great Britain whatever security arrangements it wanted in France, the Low Countries, Norway, and Denmark if the Western Allies would grant the Soviet Union similar rights in Eastern Poland, Finland, and Romania.

British Foreign Minister Anthony Eden later wrote of that conference, "Russian ideas were already starkly definite. They changed little during the next three years, for their purpose was to secure the most tangible physical guarantees for Russia's future safety." Only because of President Franklin D. Roosevelt's objections — British Prime Minister Winston Churchill had already accepted — were the East European riders excluded from the subsequent Anglo–Soviet Treaty of Alliance of May 1942.

Serious rifts began to develop between the Allies in 1943. Since Stalin was bearing the brunt of the German attack, he wanted his Western allies to open a second front in Western Europe to divert some German forces from the Russian front. The refusal to launch the Normandy invasion until June 1944 fed Stalin's suspicion that the West hoped to weaken Soviet forces in order to reduce Soviet strength in the postwar period.

Stalin viewed the Anglo–American invasion of Italy as militarily insignificant. The fact that German troops held out in Italy against vastly superior Western forces until the fall of Berlin in 1945 must have convinced him that his judgment had been accurate.

Stalin's suspicions of Western intentions were further borne out, in his mind, when the United States and Great Britain tried to exclude the Soviet Union from any control over liberated southern Italy. Stalin's demands to be given a voice in Italian affairs prompted the Western Allies to form an Advisory Council for Italy with French as well as Soviet participation. However, this council proved to be powerless. Real jurisdiction in Italy was lodged in an Anglo–American Control Commission. A noted American historian, W. H. McNeill, astutely observed, "Having excluded Russia from any but nominal participation in Italian affairs, the Western Allies prepared the way for their own exclusion from any but a marginal share in the affairs of Eastern Europe."

Teheran, Yalta, and Potsdam

Since Soviet domination of Eastern Europe eventually became one of the major reasons for East–West hostility, an understanding of the wartime diplomacy that facilitated Soviet control sheds much light on later Soviet actions in Eastern Europe. Even before the Big Three meetings of U.S.,

Soviet, and British leaders at Yalta and Potsdam — often viewed as the meetings that led to Soviet control of Eastern Europe — three factors had led Stalin to believe he would have a free hand in that area: The first factor was the Soviet military occupation of Eastern Europe. The second was the Anglo–American decision not to invade Germany through the Balkans. This decision, reached by the Big Three at the Teheran Conference in November 1943, left only Soviet forces and troops from Balkan nations to clear Eastern Europe of Axis troops.

Churchill wanted to invade Europe through Greece and the Balkans for political reasons: to prevent Soviet domination of Eastern Europe. But his proposal was considered militarily inappropriate by U.S. military experts at Teheran, who felt that a single concerted attack across the English Channel would achieve much faster results.

By recognizing Soviet supremacy in an eastern zone of operations, the Teheran meeting limited the West's participation in the postwar political affairs in that area. But when Soviet troops liberated Romania and Bulgaria in August–September 1944, Churchill decided to head off further Soviet expansion into Greece and Yugoslavia by reaching a *modus vivendi* with Stalin. This was the background for the October 1944 agreements between Churchill and Stalin in Moscow that were the third factor in convincing Stalin he would have a free hand in the Balkans. At this meeting Churchill and Stalin agreed that the Soviet Union should have 90 percent control over Romania and 75 percent control over Bulgaria. With Soviet armies firmly in control of both countries, Churchill felt he was sacrificing little. Yugoslavia and Hungary were to be controlled equally. In return, Churchill got what he wanted — 90 percent Western jurisdiction over Greece.

Although Churchill has been severely criticized for such horse trading, the Western Allies could have expected little more in the Balkans. Even though President Roosevelt never approved these agreements, Churchill's acquiescence apparently convinced Stalin that the West would accept Soviet predominance in these areas. Moreover, Churchill believed Stalin had upheld the agreement when the latter permitted the British to defeat the Communist forces in Greece during the first stage of the Greek Civil War in 1944. But it is also true that Stalin realized that the power balance in Greece favored Britain and the United States and that Greece was hardly essential to Soviet security. As Milovan Djilas related in *Conversations with Stalin,* Stalin told a Yugoslav delegation, "What do you think, that Great Britain and the U.S. — the U.S., the most powerful state in the world — will permit you to break their line of communication in the Mediterranean Sea! Nonsense. And we have no navy. The uprising in Greece must be stopped, and as quickly as possible."

The Yalta Declaration and the United Nations During the Yalta Conference in February 1945, Stalin's *realpolitik* confronted Roosevelt's utopian view of postwar politics across an unbridgeable gulf. Stalin wanted to resolve issues before the war ended, but Roosevelt wanted to put off making decisions in order to avoid East–West acrimony that might doom his pet scheme of a postwar worldwide organization. By postponing final decisions on such issues as German borders and reparations, and by making some concessions to Stalin over Eastern Europe, Roosevelt avoided a direct confrontation that might in his opinion have led to a Soviet refusal to join the United Nations.

Roosevelt was convinced that, having obtained Soviet approval for the formation of the United Nations at Yalta, he could assure the world's nations that they would have a forum for the resolution of all postwar problems. After returning from the Yalta Conference, he told a joint session of Congress that the agreements at Yalta

> ought to spell the end of the system of unilateral action, the exclusive alliances, the spheres of influence, the balances of power, and all the expedients that have been tried for centuries and have always failed. We propose to substitute for all these, a universal organization in which all peace-loving nations will finally have a chance to join.

When Stalin agreed to the Yalta Declaration on Liberated Europe that would provide governments responsive to the will of the people, he thought it an American propaganda weapon. The 1944 agreements with Churchill and the presence of Soviet armies in Eastern Europe reassured him that the declaration was only for public consumption. He believed foreign affairs should be settled in private among government leaders, not decided in open forum. One month after signing the declaration, Stalin forced Romania and Bulgaria to accept governments "friendly" to the Soviet Union.

In retrospect, the Yalta Declaration must be seen as a rather naïve document. To expect the Soviet Union to withdraw its troops from Eastern Europe and permit free elections was unrealistic. Yet perhaps Roosevelt expected that world opinion, centered in the United Nations, could actuate the Soviet Union to carry out the agreements reached in the declaration. Roosevelt was surely aware the West would have a majority in the U.N. Security Council (in which the five permanent members could exercise a veto) since Great Britain, France, and China could at that time be expected to support the American viewpoint.

Stalin obviously viewed the United Nations with great suspicion. After having long been denied membership in a similar world organization, the League of Nations, and then having been expelled from it in 1939 for invading Finland, the Soviet Union could not be expected to view the United Nations, where the West would have a four-to-one majority in the Security Council, as a guarantor of Soviet security. So Stalin continued to strengthen Soviet control over Eastern Europe and at the same time reluctantly permitted his foreign minister, Vyacheslav Molotov, to sign the United Nations charter in April 1945.

Germany: Reparations or Dismemberment?   Disagreements among the Allies over Germany also originated before the wartime conferences at Yalta and Potsdam. Allied failure to reach firm commitments on postwar German reparations and boundaries before the end of the war led to Germany's division and contributed mightily to the development of the Cold War. The Allies' inability to resolve the German problem had its immediate cause in differing Soviet and Western attitudes toward reparations. But the reparations question stemmed from the earlier disagreement over Germany's future. The Soviet Union desired not only the destruction of Germany's warmaking potential but also the dismemberment of Germany. On the other hand, the United States and Great Britain wanted to destroy Germany's warmaking potential but retreated from the idea of dismemberment when it was discussed at the Quebec Conference in September 1944.

At Quebec U.S. Secretary of the Treasury Henry Morgenthau presented his plan to dismember Germany, to eliminate all heavy industry in the newly constituted areas, and to leave Germany under the occupation of the Soviet Union and France. The plan was the major topic of discussion. Stalin already suspected that the West's late opening of a second front against the Germans was a prelude to the establishment of a German bulwark against the Soviet Union. To reassure him that they were not going to adopt a lenient policy toward Germany, Roosevelt and Churchill did not reject the Morgenthau Plan outright.

Soon after the Quebec Conference, Western actions and statements indicated that the West was indeed going to adopt a policy of leniency. To avoid specific guarantees to the Soviet Union on the amount of reparations it would receive, the British and American leaders now sought to postpone any discussion of Germany's future until after the war.

Roosevelt seemed to repudiate the Morgenthau Plan completely in December 1944 when he told Secretary of State Edward Stettinius that Germany should be permitted to "come back industrially to meet her own needs" after the war and that the United States would not allow the imposition of reparations. Roosevelt was apparently able to overcome his fear of a resurgent Germany when confronted by the specter of an all-powerful Soviet Union. He also believed that support of the Morgenthau Plan would steel German resistance, lengthen the war, and possibly cost him some support in the coming presidential elections.

At the Yalta Conference in February 1945, Stalin directly challenged Western attempts to avoid specific agreement over reparations or dismemberment. Stalin wanted to have a specific dismemberment clause in the German surrender terms. He was opposed by Churchill and circumvented by Roosevelt, who was against such a clause but wanted Soviet help against Japan after victory was achieved in Europe. The only agreement reached was that the Allies would undertake the "complete disarmament, demilitarization and the dismemberment of Germany as they deem requisite for future peace and security.'' In other words, each ally could interpret the clause as it wished once Germany was defeated. An Allied Control Council agreed to at Yalta to provide and implement uniform policies throughout the separate zones of occupation proved to be ineffective.

When the topic of discussion at Yalta switched to reparations, the impasse between the Soviet and Anglo–American views was even more readily discernible. Stalin wanted to set specific reparation sums; Churchill and Roosevelt opposed the idea. Roosevelt maintained that no precise amounts could be agreed on until after the war, when it could be determined how much Germany could pay. Churchill agreed with Roosevelt that no specific sums could be decided and that no specific percentage of total reparations for the Soviet Union could be set. Ultimately, it was decided at Yalta to instruct a Reparations Commission, to be set up in Moscow, that a total reparations bill of $20 billion — of which 50 percent should go to the Soviet Union — should serve as a basis for discussion after the war. Underlying the practical obstacles to reaching specific reparations figures was the Anglo–American desire not to weaken Germany to the extent that central Europe would be easy prey to Soviet expansion into the heart of Europe. Immediately after the Yalta Conference Churchill said he wanted to postpone the question of ''dismembering Germany until my doubts about Russian intentions have been cleared away.''

Equally indecisive were the discussions concerning Germany's postwar borders. At Moscow in October 1944, Churchill had acceded to the Soviet desire to internationalize the Saar and Ruhr areas. Now, more concerned about Moscow's intentions, he sought to delay any agreements that would be binding after the war. Concerning Germany's eastern borders, the most the conference could agree on was that Poland had the right to expand north and west but that the final borders should not be established until a postwar peace conference was held. Stalin was willing to accept postponement of the Polish–German border issue since he knew his armies would control that territory at the war's end. Moreover, the division of Germany into occupation zones, agreed to at Quebec by Churchill and Roosevelt and at Yalta by the Big Three, put eastern Germany and thus the Polish–German border area under Soviet jurisdiction.

Since no major postwar peace conference was held because of the animosity among the Allies, both Germany's borders and the reparations issue were finally determined by the occupation zones set up at Yalta and confirmed at the Potsdam Conference in July 1945. At Potsdam the Big Three agreed to permit each occupying power to remove German property from its own zone but not so much as to jeopardize a tolerable German standard of living. In addition, the Soviet Union was to get 25 percent of the dismantled industrial equipment from the Western zones, since most German industry was located there, in exchange for food and raw materials from the Soviet zone. The conference participants also agreed to establish the Polish–German border along the Oder and western Neisse rivers, thus moving Poland 200 miles to the west. Little else was achieved at Potsdam owing to the growing intransigence between Stalin and Western leaders.

President Harry Truman, who had replaced Roosevelt at the conference table, was emboldened by America's explosion of the first atomic bomb in July 1945 and angry at what he considered to be Soviet betrayal of the Yalta agreements over Eastern Europe. He therefore decided to shift from compromise to a policy of confrontation. Churchill was equally convinced that this new atomic weapon gave the West irresistible power. But the bomb never became as significant a factor in East–West negotiations as Churchill or Truman expected. Stalin was well aware that the United States would have few atomic bombs and would permit their use against the Soviet Union only under the most extraordinary provocation. He told a United Press correspondent, "Atom bombs are designed to scare those with weak nerves, but they cannot decide wars because there are not enough of them." Although only the threat of the bomb was used in diplomatic negotiations, its existence did significantly inhibit the actions of both East and West because of its destructive potential. As we shall see, it was instrumental in restraining both the Soviet Union and the West during the Berlin crisis of 1948–1949.

The Occupation of Germany

At the war's end, France and the Soviet Union hoped to rebuild their own economies and destroy Germany's warmaking potential. To do so they immediately began to strip their zones of industrial plants and materiel. But the exchange of industrial equipment for food and raw materials between the Soviet and Western zones led to endless acrimony because the Soviet Union and the West put different values on those goods and arrived at different estimates of a minimum tolerable level of industrial capacity for Germany. The United States maintained that the permissible industrial capacity would have to be raised in the American zone because of the influx of refugees from the Soviet zone. The Soviets refused to ship stipulated quantities of food from their zone to the Western zones because, they maintained, insufficient industrial equipment was being sent from the Western zones. This led the Western Allies to refuse, in May 1946, to continue dismantling and shipping industrial materiel from their zones to the Soviet Union. Only if both sides had been completely trusting and cooperative could an amicable settlement have been reached over the exchange of goods. Great Britain and the United States, faced with severe food shortages and economic chaos in their zones, stopped sending reparations out and began bringing food in.

Soviet policy in the Soviet zone had contributed to the political impasse.

East German Communist party leader Walter Ulbricht, who had been in exile in Moscow since Hitler's destruction of the Communist party in Germany, returned to the Soviet zone even before the war ended. After the war the Soviet Union permitted other parties to exist, although the Communist party was clearly favored. But when local elections went against the Communists in early 1946, the Soviet Union decided to eliminate all other political parties; even the Socialist party was forced to unite with the Communists in a new socialist unity party (Sozialistische Einheitspartei Deutschlands, or SED) in April 1946. Stalin's policy toward the Soviet zone was guided by his threefold desire to keep it weak, to use it to help rebuild Soviet industry, and to prevent the emergence of any groups, political or otherwise, that might challenge Soviet jurisdiction.

It was Western distrust of Soviet intentions as well as the economic misery in the Western zones that prompted the United States and Britain to change their occupation policies. Secretary of State James Byrnes's call for a revival of the German economy in September 1946 was soon followed by the fusion of the American and British zones into a single economic and administrative unit called Bizonia. France refused to merge its zone with the British and American zones at this time since it opposed any measures that might lead to a unitary and therefore more powerful German state. It was still possible in 1946 that some sort of amicable settlement would prevent the division of Germany. East–West opposition had not yet reached the fever pitch that marked the relationship after 1947 and prevented any diplomatic settlement.

The Iron Curtain Descends

The announcement of the Truman Doctrine and the Marshall Plan, and Stalin's reactions to them, split the world into two hostile camps in 1947. Until then, several important issues had been resolved between the superpowers. The Soviet Union withdrew its support of the Iranian separatist movement when the issue was brought before the U.N. Security Council. Determined Western opposition, epitomized in Churchill's denunciation described below, apparently convinced Stalin that the attempt to incorporate northern Iran into the Soviet Union would lead to a major East–West confrontation. Moreover, the Soviet Union accepted its failure to obtain an oil concession when the Iranian Parliament refused to ratify the withdrawal agreement. The Soviets also gave up their claim for a base in the straits connecting the Black Sea to the Mediterranean when the Turkish government, bolstered by the dispatch of an American naval contingent, rejected their demands.

While these issues were being resolved according to traditional power considerations, anti-Communism gained importance in the confrontation. In March 1946, at Westminster College in Fulton, Missouri, Churchill delivered a stinging attack on the Soviet Union. With Truman at his side,

British Prime Minister Winston Churchill (left) and American President Harry Truman in 1946 en route to Fulton, Missouri, where Churchill, receiving an honorary degree from Westminster College, warned of the danger of communism.

United Press International Photo

Churchill declared:

> A shadow has fallen upon the scenes so lately lighted by the allied victory. Nobody knows what Soviet Russia and its Communist international organization intends to do in the immediate future, or what are the limits, if any, to their expansive and proselytising tendencies. . . . From Stettin in the Baltic to Trieste in the Adriatic, an iron curtain has descended across the continent.

He warned that many nations, including Italy and France, were imperiled by Communist parties or fifth columns that constituted "a growing challenge and peril to Christian civilization."

Concern about a worldwide Communist peril increased in 1946 as the forces of Mao Tse-tung gained strength in China and economic conditions deteriorated in Europe. Communist parties in France and Italy were seen as fifth columns ready to seize power when the economic collapse came. The decisive events that propelled the United States into a worldwide struggle against communism in 1947 were Communist support for the leftists in Greece and the British announcement that economic aid could no longer be extended to Greece and Turkey. The fact that it was Yugoslavia that supported the Greek leftists against Stalin's wishes was either not known or was purposely misrepresented by the Truman administration, since it would be easier to secure congressional approval of aid to Greece and Turkey if aid from Yugoslavia was depicted as an aspect of Communist expansionism.

Since the Truman administration had previously drawn up plans for economic and military aid to Greece, Truman immediately asked Congress for $400 million in aid to Turkey and Greece "to support free peoples who are resisting subjugation by armed minorities or by outside pressures." Arthur Vandenberg, chairman of the Senate Foreign Relations Committee, advised Truman "to scare the hell out of the country" if he wanted congressional approval for American aid. Truman therefore stressed in his message to Congress that the aid was necessary to maintain freedom throughout the world. He did not mention the more legitimate foreign policy goal of protecting Western interests in the eastern Mediterranean because he realized that such an objective was unlikely to sway the public and Congress. Identifying as a Soviet aim the spread of communism, rather than traditional Russian imperialism, the Truman Doctrine committed the United States to a global crusade to stem that tide.

The military and economic might of the two superpowers and Truman's ideological campaign against "totalitarian communism" forced many nations to line up with one superpower or the other. A nation's support for either side was now equated with ideological commitment to the American or Soviet world view, irrespective of its domestic politics. Congress, now convinced of the specter of Communist subversion, overwhelmingly approved U.S. aid for Greece and Turkey. This was a turning point not only for the United States but also for Great Britain. A dominant power in 1939, Britain was now forced into dependence on the United States, for only through cooperation with the United States could Britain hope to obtain the financial aid needed to overcome its severe domestic problems and maintain its empire.

Even more alarming to Washington was the imminent economic and political collapse of Western Europe itself. Without immediate aid, many European countries faced bankruptcy. Fear that Communist parties in Italy and France would gain power in the event of economic chaos was enough to convince Americans that massive aid was necessary. The U.S. response to Europe's economic needs, unlike the Truman Doctrine, was not couched in ideological terms. Formulated by Secretary of State George Marshall and a policy planning staff directed by George F. Kennan, the Marshall Plan was, in Marshall's words, "directed not against country or doctrine, but against hunger, poverty, desperation, and chaos." But Under-Secretary of State Dean Acheson pointed out that the Marshall Plan was to provide aid to "free people who are seeking to preserve their independence and democratic institutions and human freedoms against totalitarian pressures, either internal or external."

This European Recovery Program, its official name, was formulated to help all European countries, including the Soviet Union and its so-called satellites in Eastern Europe. Marshall and Kennan had opposed the sharp ideological tone of the Truman Doctrine and did not want the United States to be responsible for the final division of Europe between East and West. If Stalin rejected the program — as he did in July 1947 — the onus of the division of Europe would be shifted to the Soviet Union.

Stalin rejected the Marshall Plan because he thought it would increase U.S. influence in Europe, including Eastern Europe, and thereby threaten Soviet hegemony in those areas it considered essential to its own security. Whatever its needs, the Soviet Union would not accede to the requirement that participating countries reveal their financial needs to an all-European conference that would determine the total amount required from the United States. Futhermore, Stalin did not expect that Europe would recover and believed it better to have a weak Western Europe that posed no threat to Soviet security than a revitalized Europe under the influence of the United States. When Stalin forbade the Eastern European satellite countries to accept Marshall Plan help, he completed the division of Europe into two antagonistic parts.

The Rift Widens

Realizing that an accommodation with the United States was impossible after the Truman Doctrine and Marshall Plan, the Soviet Union launched an offensive in 1947 to bring territories it occupied more firmly under its control (see chapter 2 for details). Beginning with Czechoslovakia, Soviet leaders instructed Eastern European Communist parties to remove all noncommunists from their governments and all national communists (those who would not follow Moscow's direction) from the Communist parties. Diversity within the Communist camp was no longer tolerated as it had been from 1945 to 1947 when Stalin thought there might be a resolution of East–West problems.

The Communist International (Comintern) had been set up by Lenin to promote Communist revolution throughout the world and had been disbanded during World War II to please Stalin's Western allies. In its place a new organization, the Cominform (Communist Information Bureau), was established in September 1947. The Cominform's principal aim was to pressure Communist countries into strict obedience to Moscow to prevent them from being seduced into cooperation with the West. Terming the Marshall Plan and Truman Doctrine "an attack on the principle of national sovereignty," A. A. Zhdanov, the major Soviet delegate to the Cominform conference, instructed Western European Communist parties to "take up the standard in defense of the national independence and sovereignty of their countries."

The Soviet Union had reversed its hands-off policy in Western Europe by instructing Communist parties in the West to "bend every effort" to defeat the Marshall Plan. Now Communist parties in Western Europe were instructed to discontinue their support of coalition governments and follow an obstructionist course. Beginning in November 1947, Western Europe was subjected to numerous strikes instigated by the Communist parties, thus lending credence to earlier U.S. assertions that the Communist parties represented a threat to Western European governments.

Several events were to intervene before Europe was divided into two extremely hostile camps. The first was the Communist coup d'état in Czechoslovakia in February 1948, which brought Czechoslovakia firmly within the Soviet camp (see chapter 2). The heated reaction in the West portrayed the Czech coup as merely another step in the worldwide expansion of communism rather than a Soviet move to strengthen its control over Eastern Europe.

Although the Czech coup convinced the United States Congress to approve the Marshall Plan, it was hardly unexpected in Washington. George Kennan, the formulator of the U.S. policy of containment of communism, supports the revisionist historians who insist that the administration knew the coup was not an indication of new Soviet aggressiveness. He wrote in his memoirs that the coup "had nothing to do with any Soviet decision to launch its military forces against the West," and that Soviet action "flowed logically from the inauguration of the Marshall Plan Program, and was confidently predicted by U.S. government observers six months in advance of the event."

Nevertheless, Truman said the Czech coup proved that the Soviet Union intended to expand "to the remaining free nations of Europe." His response to the coup and the previously formed Cominform was to introduce a bill in Congress for universal military training and a return to conscription. The foreign ministers of Great Britain, France, Belgium, Holland, and Luxembourg signed a treaty establishing the Western Union for collective defense against armed attack on any member nation. These responses led to the West's calling the London Six-Power Conference (excluding the Soviet Union) to discuss further integration of the Western occupation zones in Germany and led ultimately to the first major East–West confrontation in Berlin in June 1948.

London Conference representatives announced in a communiqué of March 6, 1948 that agreement had been reached on a plan for a federal form of government and the further economic integration of the Western zones. This provoked an angry reaction from the Soviet Union. Stalin realized that successful implementation of the London communiqué would end his hopes of keeping Germany neutralized and weak. Two weeks later Soviet Marshal Sokolovsky ended the charade of East–West cooperation concerning Germany by walking out of the Allied Control Council deliberations in Berlin. Next, Stalin ordered a meeting of the Second People's Congress in the Soviet zone of Germany in March to create a People's Council (later the People's Chamber of the German Democratic Republic) for the Soviet zone. He also began restricting access to Berlin on March 31, apparently in the belief that this would divide the Western powers and force a retreat on their plans. But France, finding no support for the plan to keep Germany dismembered and weak, and confident that the United States and Britain were going to be in Germany indefinitely because of the Soviet threat, had less reason to fear the unification of the Western zones. On June 18, 1948, France agreed to fuse its zone with Bizonia, the Anglo–American zone. Now Stalin was presented with a solid Western front.

The Berlin Blockade   When the West decided to reform Germany's currency by introducing a new deutschemark on June 20, 1948, Stalin realized that a strong German currency under Western sponsorship would destroy the weak German currency in the Soviet zone. The Soviet Union therefore responded four days later by introducing a similar currency reform in its zone. At the same time it initiated a blockade of all land traffic into and out of Berlin, which was deep inside the Soviet zone. Stalin hoped the blockade would be a bargaining weapon to prevent the establishment of a strong German state under Western auspices. But his plan was thwarted when the Western powers instituted an airlift that kept Berlin supplied with food, fuel, and medicines for nearly a year.

Stalin knew he had lost. Recognizing that a Soviet attack on Western aircraft would mean war, denied the bargaining leverage he had sought, and fast losing face in what appeared to be an attempt to starve 2.25 million residents of Berlin into submission, Stalin had to call off the blockade in May 1949. This first major East–West confrontation made vividly apparent the limits of Soviet power when faced with the West's air superiority and nuclear monopoly. Stalin could not use his massive land superiority against Berlin to force the West to bargain because of the West's ability to destroy Russian cities with airpower and nuclear weapons.

The New West German State   The Berlin blockade speeded up the West's plans for the establishment of a separate German state comprising the three Western zones. After the West founded the German Federal Republic on May 21, 1949, the Soviet Union responded by establishing the German Democratic Republic in October of the same year. The first parliamentary elections in West Germany produced a Christian Democratic (CDU) majority with Konrad Adenauer as the first chancellor. Having gained fame for his resistance to Nazism, Adenauer was a popular choice. He also represented almost everything the West desired in a German leader: cooperation with the West; rapprochement with Germany's traditional enemy, France; a federal structure rather than the highly centralized Nazi state; and, after 1948, an active anticommunist posture.

The United States distrusted the other major German party, the Social Democrats (SPD). SPD leader Kurt Schumacher's call for the nationalization of industry and banks, combined with the growing Western fear of the Soviet Union, had prompted active Western support for the CDU prior to the Berlin crisis. Although the CDU had a slim seven-seat advantage over the SPD in the legislature, Adenauer put together a

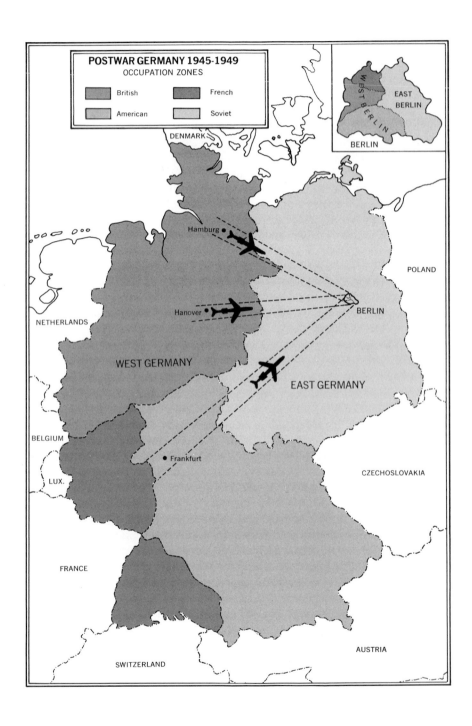

POSTWAR GERMANY 1945-1949
OCCUPATION ZONES

British   French
American   Soviet

coalition with the Free Democratic Party (FDP) that excluded the SPD from any role in the government.

U.S. Military Might in Europe   The Berlin crisis provided a powerful stimulus for the integration of Western Europe into a military alliance dominated by the United States. In April 1949 eleven European countries joined with the United States in forming the North Atlantic Treaty Organization (NATO). Thus began the return of American military might in Western Europe and the division of Europe into two armed camps.

Military cooperation among Western countries seemed even more imperative in 1949, when the Soviet Union developed its own nuclear capability. Western Europe was now economically and militarily dependent upon the United States. Economic aid from the United States was often tied to military and political cooperation (see chapter 3). Western European nations were made aware that the reduction of Communist influence in their governments was necessary if they were to achieve economic recovery. In cases such as France and Italy, United States aid was promised only after Communist parties were removed from governing coalitions. As a result of American pressure, Communist party members had already been removed from the French and Italian cabinets in May 1947.

Western Europe now moved toward integration under the auspices and encouragement of the United States. Containment of the Soviet Union became official U.S. policy. One way to achieve this goal was to restore Europe's economic vitality and integrate it further in a Western economic and military bloc. Sixteen nations of Western Europe established the Organization for European Economic Cooperation (OEEC) to dispense American aid. At the same time, the United States allocated $5.3 billion to meet the needs of OEEC members in the first year of the Marshall Plan. The economic recovery of Western Europe had begun.

By 1949 the iron curtain that Churchill had described in 1946 had become a reality. With the buildup of American strength there, a power equilibrium had been restored in Europe that could not be disrupted short of all-out war. Since both sides now portrayed the East–West conflict as an ideological struggle, there was little possibility of resolving conflicts through normal diplomatic procedures. Each side was now in a struggle to protect freedom, either from "Western imperialism" or from "Soviet communism," throughout the world.

The Korean Conflict

Because of the global nature of the Cold War and Europe's increasing dependence on the United States, events in the Far East soon had a direct impact on Europe. The triumph of the Communist forces in China in 1949 was viewed in the West as another demonstration of the threat of worldwide Communist expansion. When the Soviet-backed Communist regime in North Korea attacked the American-supported South Korean government

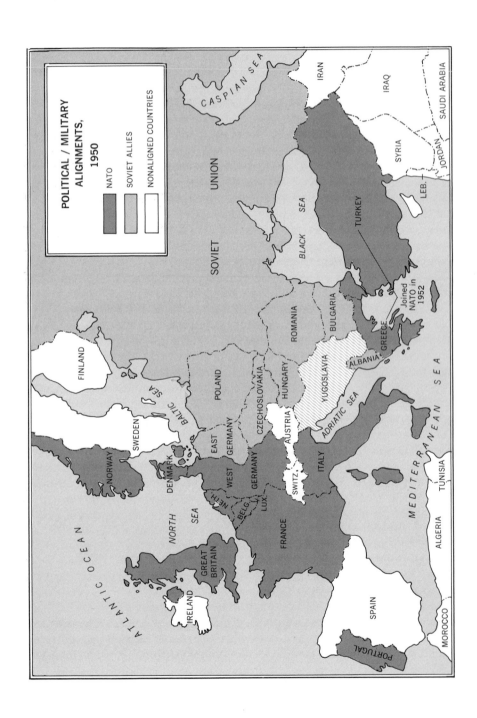

in June 1950, the United States immediately assumed that the Soviet Union was behind it. President Truman charged, "The attack upon the Republic of Korea makes it plain beyond all doubt that the international communist movement is prepared to use armed invasion to conquer independent nations." While it appears likely that the North Korean decision to invade stemmed largely from local causes, it is obvious that the invasion would not have been launched without Stalin's permission.

One possible explanation for the invasion is offered by revisionists and supported by Kennan. They suggest that the peace treaty being negotiated between the United States and Japan, providing for American naval and air bases in Japan, could have persuaded Moscow to establish a Communist government throughout Korea before the United States could bring a preponderance of power to the area.

Public statements by American leaders had led the North Koreans and the Soviet Union to believe that Korea was not essential to America's "perimeter of defense" in Asia, leading them to expect an easy victory. But the specter of Communist regimes dominating the entire Asian continent and threatening a disarmed Japan brought a sudden reversal of U.S. policy in Asia. Moreover, the United States realized that its desertion of South Korea after the North Korean attack would bring into question American commitments throughout the world. The United States, envisaging a worldwide struggle against communism, committed itself to a policy of containment in Asia as well as in Europe.

Faced with the task of mobilizing sufficient forces to both repel the North Korean invasion and maintain Western strength in Europe, the United States began a massive buildup of Western military strength that included a call for the rearmament of West Germany. In September 1950, Great Britain agreed to the re-creation of an army for the German Federal Republic. Stalin's view that Western hostility toward the Soviet Union knew no bounds was borne out, in his own mind, by the rearming of this traditional foe. Kennan's warning to the United States government that rearmament would divide Germany permanently into Soviet and Western zones was ignored.

Both the United States and the Soviet Union were now convinced that their security lay in enlarging their spheres of influence and strengthening their alliances. The United Nations decision to send a police force against the North Koreans, made possible by Soviet absence from the Security Council in protest against Nationalist Chinese representation on the Security Council, led Stalin to denounce the United Nations as an agency of "United States imperialist aggression." In reality, Stalin was surprised by the strength of the American reaction because of the mildness of the U.S. public statements concerning Korea and U.S. acquiescence to Mao's victory in China. The American public, by now convinced of the evil intentions of Soviet communism, supported a massive buildup of the NATO forces in Europe and United States military units and alliances in Asia to halt

Communist aggression. By 1951, mutual defense treaties bound the Philippines, Australia, New Zealand, and Japan to the United States.

When Communist China sent 200,000 so-called volunteers to aid North Korea in October of 1950, Americans had little doubt that the United States decision had been the proper one. Scant thought was given to the fact that the Chinese intervention came only after the United States had decided to wipe out the North Korean regime and United Nations armies were approaching the Chinese borders. Only with great difficulty did President Truman prevent the United States from becoming involved in a major land war with Communist China. He refused to permit General Douglas MacArthur to extend the war to the Chinese mainland for three reasons. For one thing, it might bring the Soviet Union into the conflict. For another thing, committing the bulk of American forces to Asia would endanger the defense of Western Europe. A third constraining force was the possibility of nuclear war, since the Soviet Union could not be expected to sit idly by while the United States used atomic weapons against China as MacArthur advocated. Yet Truman's refusal sharply reduced his support among the American public.

The impasse in Korea was ultimately resolved by Dwight Eisenhower's election to the United States presidency. His enormous popularity in the United States as a result of his leadership during World War II allowed him to accept a negotiated peace in Korea that Truman might have been denied. Although the war in Korea ended with an armistice in July 1953, the confrontation in Asia had only begun.

The War Decade Ends

Although United States–Soviet predominance in the world continued in the 1950s — as in some respects it continues even now — the early 1950s marked the beginning of the end of the bipolar world. A new power, the People's Republic of China, posed a threat to United States forces in Asia and, later in the decade, challenged Soviet domination of the Communist world. As the monolithic Communist world began to disintegrate, United States leadership in the Western world was challenged by a resurgent Western Europe, led by Charles de Gaulle, that no longer shared the U.S. fear of communism.

In retrospect, it is difficult to see how the outcome of the immediate postwar struggle between East and West could have been much different. The wartime policy of unconditional surrender had produced a power vacuum in Europe. Soviet–American hostility was inevitable, because neither side was willing to make a major concession to the other. Even revisionist historians William A. Williams and Lloyd Gardner admit that the early stages of the Cold War were perhaps unavoidable, although they maintain that the United States bore primary responsibility for the lengths to which the Cold War was carried. Some revisionists argue that the United

States, because of its superior power, should have been willing to make concessions to the Soviet Union. In particular, they say, a concession of a sphere of influence for the Soviet Union in Eastern Europe would have avoided conflict. Such concessions would have required a magnanimity on the part of American leaders that they were far from possessing in the immediate postwar period.

The revisionists have pointed out the importance of American economic objectives in the Cold War, and especially the U.S. desire to keep all areas of the world open for its trade. This recognition is fundamental to the understanding of the broadening of the Cold War into a worldwide conflict. However, the revisionists tend to overlook the ambiguity of Stalin's objectives and the fear and distrust they provoked in Washington. It now appears that Stalin may have wanted a sphere of influence only in Eastern Europe. However, Soviet actions in the postwar period in Iran and its demands for bases in Turkey led many Western leaders to believe that the Soviet Union would not limit its expansion to Eastern Europe.

FURTHER READING

The following studies contend that the Soviet Union was primarily responsible for the Cold War: Winston S. Churchill, *The Second World War* (6 vols., 1948–1953); Herbert Feis, *Between War and Peace: The Potsdam Conference* (1960); *Churchill, Roosevelt, Stalin* (1951); and *From Trust to Terror: The Onset of the Cold War, 1945–1950* (1970). Although the last-named work was written as a refutation of the left-revisionist interpretation, it combines some revisionist arguments with earlier standard views of the Cold War. Adam Ulam, *Expansion and Coexistence: The History of Soviet Foreign Policy 1917–1967* (1968); and *The Rivals: America and Russia Since World War II* (1971). Ulam's works contain keen insights concerning Stalin's motives. George Kennan's *American Diplomacy, 1900–1950* (1951) and *Memoirs, 1950–1963* contain valuable information on his personal recollections of the diplomacy of the postwar period. His *Memoirs* contains information that tends to support the revisionist as well as the orthodox interpretations of the Cold War.

It is difficult to fit the following interpretations into any precise category since they take the position that the Soviet Union was primarily responsible for the Cold War but that the United States must share some of the blame: William McNeill, *America, Britain, and Russia: Their Cooperation and Conflict, 1941–1946* (1953); and John L. Gaddis, *The United States and the Origins of the Cold War, 1941–1947* (1972). Gaddis's study is a scholarly fusing of the orthodox and revisionist views that is critical of the extreme revisionist argument. Norman A. Graebner's *Cold War Diplomacy* (1962) is a brief but important critique of American foreign policy. Graebner finds an inconsistency between the broad nature of United States foreign policy goals and the limited means Americans were willing to use to carry out those goals. Louis J. Halle in *The Cold War as History* (1967) concludes that historical circumstance, such as the power vacuum in Europe at the end of World War II, propelled both the Soviet Union and the United States into a confrontation that neither desired.

Although there are important differences in the interpretations of the revisionist studies of the Cold War, they all agree that the United Sates was primarily to blame for the global nature of the Cold War and that U.S. diplomacy was guided by its economic imperialism. Gar Alperowitz in *Atomic Diplomacy* (1965) contends that Truman's policy of confrontation represented a dramatic shift from Roosevelt's policy of compromise. He further contends that America used the atomic bomb against Japan primarily to frighten the Soviet Union rather than to win the war against Japan. Diane Shaver Clemens in *Yalta* (1970) maintains that the United States rather than the Soviet Union violated the Yalta accords.

Gabriel Kolko in *The Politics of War: The World and United States Foreign Policy 1943–1945* (1968) takes the position that President Roosevelt sought a liberal–capitalist world dominated by the United States. Kolko sees no difference in the policies of Roosevelt and Truman. Joyce and Gabriel Kolko in *The Limits of Power: The World and United States Foreign Policy, 1945–1954* (1972) contend that the United States used its enormous wealth and military power to dominate its allies, suppress social change throughout the world, and ensure the triumph of the capitalist order.

Lloyd C. Gardner's *Architects of Illusion* (1970) is a scholarly statement of the revisionist position that avoids the polemics of some revisionist studies. Gardner believes that both Roosevelt and Truman sought to maintain the open door throughout the world to ensure the triumph of American capitalism. Walter LaFeber in *America, Russia and the Cold War, 1945–1966* (1968) maintains that because of the military and economic superiority it enjoyed in the postwar period, the United States should have been more willing to seek an understanding with the Soviet Union since its security was not threatened while that of the Soviet Union was.

Martin Sherwin in *A World Destroyed: The Atomic Bomb and the Grand Alliance* (1976) believes that the American reluctance to confide in the Soviet Union during the war, including maintaining nuclear power as an Anglo-American monopoly, increased Soviet intransigence and reduced the possibility of American–Soviet cooperation in the postwar period. William A. Williams in *The Tragedy of American Diplomacy* (rev. ed. 1962) finds that U.S. expansionism was necessitated by the demands of an acquisitive capitalist society.

Critiques of the revisionist studies are Robert L. Maddox, *The New Left and the Origins of the Cold War* (1973), in which Maddox charges that the revisionists have misused and misinterpreted source materials; and Robert W. Tucker, *The Radical Left and American Foreign Policy* (1971), a scholarly, balanced criticism of the left–revisionist interpretation.

Many memoirs shed light on the debate over the Cold War. Especially important are the memoirs of George Kennan (cited above) and of W. Averell Harriman, *Special Envoy to Churchill and Stalin 1941–1946* (1976), by W. Averell Harriman and Elie Abel.

Important information and interpretations on Germany can be found in E. Davidson, *The Death and Life of Germany: An Account of the American Occupation* (1959); W. Phillips Davison, *The Berlin Blockade: A Study in Cold War Politics* (1958); J. L. Snell, *Wartime Origins of the East–West Dilemma over Germany* (1959); J. F. Golay, *The Founding of the Federal Republic of Germany* (1958); and J. P. Nettl, *The Eastern Zone and Soviet Policy in Germany, 1945–1950* (1951).

2 The Cold War and the Sovietization of Eastern Europe

> This war is not as in the past; whoever occupies a territory also imposes his own social system. Everyone imposes his own system as far as his army can reach. It cannot be otherwise.
>
> Josef Stalin, in *Conversations with Stalin* by Milovan Djilas

The modern history of Eastern Europe is a history of encirclement by more powerful empires and nations. Before and during the eighteenth century this area fell victim to the expansionist drives of the Russian, Prussian, Austrian, and Ottoman empires. Although Greece, Romania, Serbia, and Bulgaria gained independence in the nineteenth century, theirs was a perilous existence that resulted from the compromises and machinations of the major powers. Since no major power gained a decided military advantage until after World War II, conflicts in Eastern Europe tended to be limited.

World War I came about partially as a result of a changed power relationship at the turn of the century. The alliance of Germany and Austria–Hungary, combined with the military weakness of the Ottoman Empire, convinced the first two that they could dominate the Balkans and break the power equilibrium in Eastern Europe. Their failure in World War I led to the collapse of the German, Ottoman, Austro–Hungarian, and Russian empires and produced a power vacuum in East–Central Europe that permitted the establishment of independent states throughout Eastern Europe. The newly established Soviet Union, weakened by internal civil war, could not take advantage of the defeat of its former rivals to gain supremacy in East–Central Europe.

The revival of German and Soviet military power in the 1930's again placed Eastern Europe at the mercy of its stronger neighbors. With the other great powers uninterested in or incapable of intervening, the fate of Eastern Europe now rested in the hands of Hitler and Stalin. The two states resumed the collaborationist policy that had characterized their relationship to Eastern Europe in the eighteenth and nineteenth centuries.

Confronted with Western indifference to the threat of German expansion, made clear by the acquiescence of Britain and France to the dismemberment of Czechoslovakia at Munich in 1938, Stalin chose to join with Hitler in the Nazi–Soviet Pact of 1939. This agreement gave Stalin time to build up Soviet military strength to meet the German attack in 1941 and to regain territory taken by Poland in 1920 during the Russian Civil War.

Again, war was to have momentous consequences for Eastern Europe. The defeat of Germany and the exhaustion of France and Great Britain in World War II left a power vacuum in East-Central Europe that was filled immediately by Soviet armies. Roosevelt had informed Stalin at Yalta that American forces would be withdrawn from Europe after the war, and Churchill had acquiesced to Soviet domination of most of Eastern Europe in 1944, leading Stalin to expect that Soviet hegemony in Eastern Europe would not be contested.

Although the West objected to Soviet actions in Eastern Europe, Soviet military might was overwhelming. Almost all the Eastern European states reached whatever terms they could with Stalin. In 1944–1945 the terms rested on several major factors: the role those states had played in the German invasion of the Soviet Union, the Soviet assessment of the area's strategic importance, Stalin's relationship with the former leaders of the various states, the ability and willingness of the states to oppose Soviet power, and Stalin's objectives in Eastern Europe.

Soviet Goals in Eastern Europe

As summarized in chapter 1, Stalin wanted Eastern Europe to be a buffer zone between the Soviet Union and German territory. Some have criticized this goal as an expression of paranoia, considering the condition of Germany and the Soviet Union at the end of the war. But only Stalin was aware of the severe Soviet economic weaknesses in 1945, and he was distrustful of the West's intentions in Germany. By controlling Eastern Europe he could prevent those states from participating in an attack on the Soviet Union or again becoming a staging area for an attack on the Soviet Union.

In addition, Eastern Europe became an indispensable aid to Soviet economic development, an area to be exploited. States that fought against the Soviet Union were forced to pay reparations. The entire area was integrated in the Soviet economic system as a source of cheap goods, especially raw materials. Countries were forced to sell goods to the Soviet Union at low prices to keep Soviet manufacturing costs low and profits high. Many Eastern European companies were compelled to include the Soviet Union as a partner in their operations. Strict adherence to these conditions was equated with political orthodoxy. Charges of political deviation were hurled at those attempting economic independence as well as at those guilty of ideological heresies.

WHITE
SEA

NORWAY

FINLAND

from Finland

SWEDEN

SOVIET

UNION

NORTH
SEA

Estonia

Latvia

BALTIC SEA

Lithuania

**SOVIET
TERRITORIAL GAINS,
1945**

Soviet territorial gains

German territory to Poland

NETH.

BELG. LUX.

EAST

GERMANY

SILESIA

East
Prussia

POLAND

WEST

GERMANY

CZECHOSLOVAKIA

from Poland

FRANCE

from Czechoslovakia

SWITZ.

AUSTRIA

HUNGARY

from Romania

ROMANIA

YUGOSLAVIA

ITALY

ADRIATIC SEA

BLACK SEA

BULGARIA

ALBANIA

GREECE

TURKEY

In the immediate postwar years the Soviet Union permitted considerable political diversity in the East European states as long as they seemed to pose no threat to Soviet security or Soviet leadership among Communist nations and as long as they continued to cooperate economically. As a rule, coalition governments were permitted throughout the area.

Stalin opposed precipitate Communist takeovers for several reasons. First, he did not want to provoke the Western powers to intervene in Eastern Europe. Second, he wanted to avoid violent resistance to communism in Eastern Europe since it would necessitate large Soviet forces to contain the unrest and it would also destroy the Soviet argument that the Communist parties in Eastern Europe were popular. Third, he still hoped for financial aid from the United States. Stalin believed a loan to the Soviet Union might actually help the United States by putting former soldiers to work in order to meet the Soviet demands for goods, and therefore he thought that the United States might supply the desperately needed finances. Finally, Stalin believed it was still possible to resolve the conflict with the West over German reparations, and thereby gain additional funds.

As to Stalin's long-term goals in Eastern Europe, a major difference of opinion exists between orthodox and revisionist writers. The orthodox view, represented by such studies as Hugh Seton-Watson's *The East European Revolution,* discerns a three-stage pattern of conquest by Soviet-backed Communist parties. The conquest begins with a coalition government including non-Communist representatives, then proceeds to a second-stage persecution of non-Communist groups and Communist domination of the important state offices such as the premierships and interior ministries. The final stage is the elimination of all non-Communists from the governments and the inclusion of the state within a monolithic Communist bloc headed by the Soviet Union.

The revisionists reject this concept and insist that Stalin would have permitted the coalition governments to continue indefinitely and would have relaxed Soviet control in Eastern Europe if Western hostility and the Cold War had not forced him to clamp down in 1948.

Both views overlook several important factors. The orthodox view presents an overly deterministic Stalinist blueprint for Soviet domination of Eastern Europe and underestimates the impact of the Cold War on Stalin. The revisionists, in turn, fail to understand Stalin's goal of a monolithic Communist sphere of influence in which Soviet objectives prevail. In some cases, the Cold War did indeed determine the timing of the Soviet crackdown in Eastern Europe. But this does not mean that Stalin would not have acted at some other time to maintain the economic integration of the area, to halt the movement toward an independent form of national communism in the various states, or to prevent countries from endangering Soviet security by becoming too closely associated with the West. A closer examination of Soviet actions in the different East European states will clarify these points.

Poland's Coalition Government

Where Stalin felt Soviet security was seriously threatened, as in Poland, the coalition governments he allowed could only be described as shams. The Polish attack on the Soviet Union after World War I and the hostility of interwar Polish leaders convinced Stalin that Poland must be subordinated to Moscow.

East–West acrimony over Poland had been building during the war. Remnants of the Polish government and army had fled to France and finally to Britain after Poland was attacked first by German and then by Soviet armies in 1939. Throughout the war Stalin sought approval from the exiled Polish government in London of the incorporation of eastern Poland into the Soviet Union. Stalin felt that his claim to the territory was valid because the bulk of the population of eastern Poland was ethnically either Ukrainian or White Russian, and because eastern Poland had been taken from the Soviet Union during the Russian Civil War in 1920. But the London Poles were reluctant to approve the loss of eastern Poland, which the Soviet army had conquered while Poland was in the midst of a life-or-death struggle with Germany. Furthermore, the London Poles feared that their acquiescence would cost them the support of the Polish Home Army, which adamantly opposed ceding eastern Poland. Therefore, the London Poles adhered to the position of the Polish Underground, as articulated in a February 1944 resolution rejecting the Soviet incorporation of eastern Poland and expressing their determination "to fight the new Soviet aggression." However, the same resolution accepted an extensive enlargement of Poland's western boundaries at Germany's expense. This attitude undoubtedly led to Stalin's decision to destroy the Polish Underground in 1944–1945.

Stalin had already been provided with a pretext for liquidating the Polish Underground by the attitude of the London Poles concerning the massacre of 14,000 Polish officers in the Katyn Forest during the war. The London Poles called for a neutral investigation of the massacre by the International Red Cross, which implied that they felt that Soviet rather than German forces might have been responsible. This gave Stalin the opportunity to set up his own Soviet-styled Polish government. Charging that the Polish government in London had "sunk so low as to enter the path of accord with the Hitlerite government," Stalin broke off relations with the London Poles in April 1943. Then, in July 1944, he announced the creation of a Communist-dominated Lublin Committee to replace the exiled Polish government.

Stalin eliminated the other major source of opposition when Soviet forces allowed the Germans to destroy the bulk of the underground Polish Home Army when it attempted to liberate Warsaw in late 1944. As Soviet troops advanced across Poland, they vanquished most of the remnants of the Polish Home Army. Thus at the end of the war, the Soviet-backed Lublin government had no opposition inside Poland.

At the Yalta Conference in 1945 the West pressured Stalin into forming a coalition government in Poland. Stalin's response was to permit four of the London Poles to join sixteen Communists in a new government. Subsequent Western demands for a democratic government and elections met stiff Soviet resistance. Stalin judged correctly that "any freely elected government would be anti-Soviet, and that we cannot permit."

The illusion of a coalition government continued when Stalin permitted the Polish Peasant party leader, Stanislaw Mikolajczyk, to join the coalition. However, Stalin had no intention of letting the Peasant party become a viable political force. As the major non-Communist organization in Poland it had been extremely popular among the predominantly peasant population in the interwar years, and Stalin knew that it could outbid the Communists for support. Communist intimidation and Mikolajczyk's own political blunders soon splintered the Peasant party and rendered it ineffective. In the January 1947 parliamentary elections the Peasant party gained a mere 27 seats compared to 392 seats for the government bloc of Communists, Socialists, dissident Peasants, and a so-called Democratic party. Mikolajczyk was dropped from the cabinet and fled the country in October 1947.

The other rival to the Communist party, the Polish Socialist Workers party (RPPS), proved equally troublesome. In 1946 the RPPS challenged the claim that the Communists were the leading party in the government coalition and demanded a greater role in the cabinet. RPPS leaders were summoned to Moscow twice in 1946 and were forced to cooperate with the Communist party in the January 1947 elections in return for the promise that the RPPS would be allowed to retain its separate identity. However, after the Cold War events of 1947-1948, the RPPS was purged in September 1948 and then in December 1948 it was forced to merge with the Communists in the Polish United Workers' party. Since Communists filled eight of the eleven seats in the Politburo of the party, the RPPS had been rendered ineffective. Although the Cold War speeded up the pace of events in Poland, it is doubtful that Stalin would have permitted the Socialists a separate existence for much longer. He was distrustful of their independence and their contacts with Socialist parties in Western Europe.

Romania's Coalition Government

The Romanian case was similar to that of Poland in terms of its strategic importance as well as its previous hostility toward the Soviet Union, made clear by its participation in the German invasion of the Soviet Union. Stalin's insistence on a government friendly toward the Soviet Union, which initially was supported by Churchill and Roosevelt, conflicted with the later Western demand for democratic governments and free elections in Eastern Europe. But, as in the Polish case, a freely elected government in Romania would have been hostile to the Soviets.

Because King Michael had gained widespread popularity when he overthrew the pro-Nazi regime of Marshal Ion Antonescu in August 1944 and declared war on Germany, Stalin had to proceed slowly so as not to cause a massive insurrection and further exacerbate East–West relations. Not only did King Michael retain his throne but he was awarded the Soviet Order of Victory after the war.

Rightly fearing that Michael's popularity would decrease support for the Romanian Communist party, in March 1945 Stalin pressured the king to appoint a National Democratic Front Coalition, including Communist representatives. Although the Communists held only three ministries, the new government was headed by the pro-Communist leader of the Ploughman's Front, Petru Groza. The presence of Soviet occupation forces would have made it possible to enforce acceptance of a Communist government, but Stalin proceeded slowly in order to build up support for the Communist party. The popular front government was probably a temporary expedient to enhance Communist support and to end Western criticism.

The coalition immediately gained popular support by confiscating and redistributing all land holdings exceeding 120 acres. An election in November 1946, marked by considerable intimidation of noncoalition parties, gave the Democratic Front an overwhelming victory. Even though the Communist party held only one-sixth of the seats in parliament, the presence of a Soviet army of occupation gave them considerably more authority than their numbers warranted. By the spring of 1947 the Communists began to act against the opposition parties. Accused of complicity with American imperialism, opposition party members were tried and sentenced to long prison terms. The popular Peasant party leaders were imprisoned and their party disbanded. King Michael had to abdicate in December 1947, and Romania became a People's Republic the following spring. Groza continued as puppet premier, with Communists heading all the other important government offices. By March 1948 the Communist party had disbanded or absorbed all other parties into the Romanian Workers' party. Premier Gheorghe Gheorghiu-Dej assumed direction of the economy and Ana Pauker, a Communist trained in Moscow, became foreign minister. At this point, the nationalization of industry and collectivization of agriculture began in earnest.

Soviet Relations with Bulgaria

Despite the fact that Bulgaria had been allied with Germany in World War II, it had not participated in the German attack on the Soviet Union. Instead of animosity, the Bulgarian–Russian relationship had always been marked by friendship. Owing their liberation from the Turks in the nineteenth century to Czarist Russia and from the Germans in 1944 to the Soviet Union, most Bulgarians looked to their mighty northern neighbor as a benefactor. As they had built the Alexander Nevski Church in honor of Czarist armies, they now constructed monuments to Soviet forces.

The Bulgarians had overthrown their profascist government as Soviet armies were marching toward Bulgaria in 1944. But the fact that Bulgaria had been a German ally provided the Soviet Union with the pretext for invading Bulgaria and establishing a Soviet-supported Fatherland Front coalition government in September 1944. The subsequent participation of the Bulgarian army in the attack on Germany removed much of the stigma of the earlier association with Germany. In contrast to his policy toward Romania and Hungary, Stalin demanded no reparations from Bulgaria.

Although the Fatherland Front did not become openly Communist-dominated until 1947, the non-Communist members of the coalition had lost their effectiveness by the preceding year. At first, Communist domination of the important state offices was challenged by opposition groups and by the Peasant and Socialist parties, led by Nikola Petkov and Kosta Lulchev respectively. Encouraged by Anglo–American support, Petkov and Lulchev demanded that the Communists relinquish their control of the interior and justice ministries. Although a compromise was reached at the Allied Foreign Ministers' Conference in Moscow in December 1945, whereby two members of the opposition were to be admitted to the government, Petkov and Lulchev would not back down from their demand that the positions be ministers of the interior and of justice.

Confronted with a crisis that appeared to threaten Soviet domination, and with the Bulgarian Communist party already having worked out a compromise with Petkov and Lulchev, Stalin decided to eliminate the opposition groups. In July 1946, leadership of the Bulgarian army was transferred from a non-Communist member of the coalition to the entire cabinet, and the army was purged of possible opponents. A plebiscite in September 1946 changed Bulgaria from a kingdom to a republic and forced the abdication and exile of seven-year-old King Simeon. Once the United States ratified the Bulgarian Peace Treaty in June 1947, eliminating the Control Commission for Bulgaria and thus ending direct American participation in Bulgarian affairs, Stalin ordered the elimination of the political opposition. Petkov's Peasant Union was dissolved in August and he was arrested and, in September 1947, hanged.

Throughout this period the Communist party was led by Georgi Dimitrov, who had served as secretary-general of the Communist International Headquarters in Moscow and was a close friend of Stalin. Firmly in control of the country by 1948, Dimitrov ousted all non-Communists from the government, forced the Socialist party to merge with the Communist party, instituted a Soviet-style constitution, and began the nationalization of industry and the collectivization of agriculture. Bulgaria now became the most avid supporter of Stalin's attempt to overthrow Yugoslav leader Marshal Tito. On the ground that Tito wished to incorporate Bulgaria into an enlarged Yugoslavia, all pro-Yugoslav Communists were either executed or driven from the country.

Hungary's Coalition Government

Because of Hungary's strategic importance as well as its participation in the German attack on the Soviet Union Stalin wanted its government to be friendly toward the Soviet Union. However, Stalin was forced to proceed slowly because of the presence in Hungary of an Allied Control Commission and because of the Churchill–Stalin agreement to divide jurisdiction equally in Hungary. Therefore, the Provisional National Government of Democratic Hungary, set up under Soviet auspices in December 1944, was a true coalition government headed by a former member of the interwar conservative government of Admiral Miklós Horthy. Stalin did not demand, as he did in the other Eastern European countries, that a Communist occupy the important cabinet post of minister of the interior. The only posts held by Communists were the ministries of trade and agriculture.

However, possession of the agriculture ministry permitted the Communist party to build its popularity in Hungary. Under the moderate Communist Imre Nagy, the agriculture ministry expropriated the large Hungarian estates and monastic lands and distributed them among 642,000 formerly landless peasants. Collectivization of the land was not begun immediately in order to gain popular support.

In November 1945, relatively free elections gave the agrarian Smallholders party 60 percent of the parliamentary seats compared to 17 percent for the Communist party. But before the election the head of the Allied Control Commission, Marshal Kliment Voroshilov, had pressured members of the coalition to agree that the Smallholders party could hold no more than half the cabinet posts in a coalition government. Two deputy premiers, one of them the Communist Matyas Rakosi, aided the new Smallholder premier, Zoltan Tildy. When Imre Nagy became minister of the interior in November 1945, as a result of Soviet and Communist party pressure, the Communists gained control over the police. This ministry soon passed to the more ruthless Communist, Láskó Rajk, who intimidated or discredited most of the members of the Smallholders party by 1947. Power soon passed to Rakosi, who was first secretary of the Hungarian Communist party and deputy prime minister and who combined Communists and Socialists into a United Workers' Party in June 1948. The final step was the proclamation of a Hungarian People's Republic in 1949.

Czechoslovakia's Coalition Government

Stalin permitted Czechoslovakia a true coalition government at first, even though Communist-dominated people's committees were in control of the country when it was liberated by Soviet forces in 1945. Because of Stalin's special friendship with prewar Czech President Eduard Beneš, he permitted the exiled Czech government in London to return to Prague in May 1945. Beneš avoided provoking Stalin, unlike the London Poles, by entering into negotiations with him concerning his postwar government in Czechoslovakia and by surrendering the province of Ruthenia to the Soviet

A battle-scarred wall in Budapest, Hungary covered with Communist campaign posters for the 1948 election. A smiling peasant (top) promises more bread and a better life if the Communists are elected. Communist Deputy Premier Matyas Rakosi is pictured at bottom left. The other poster shows the three great national heroes, Rakoczi, Kossuth, and Petofi.

United Press International Photo

Union. Knowing that the Czech Communist party had been popular before the war, Stalin realized that a freely elected government would not necessarily be hostile toward the Soviet Union. It seems unlikely that Stalin had any predetermined plan for the eventual communization of Czechoslovakia.

A free election in May 1946 gave the Communist party 38 percent of the vote, the Socialist party 18 percent, and the Peasant party 16 percent. Communist party leader Clement Gottwald, who became premier of the United Front government, believed that the Czech Communist party could dominate the country without intimidating or persecuting the other parties. Until 1947 the Czech parliament held free and open debate and the press had considerable freedom to criticize the government. But the Communist attitude changed in 1947 when Marshall Plan aid was offered and when decreasing popular support for the Communist party, as revealed in opinion polls and in the rapid growth of other parties, appeared to threaten Communist domination of the government.

Czech acceptance of an invitation to a preliminary conference on the Marshall Plan in July 1947 marked the beginning of the end for the coalition government. Stalin's ultimatum to the Czechs not to attend the conference was reluctantly accepted. Stalin feared that the Czechs would develop a Western-style parliamentary government and be drawn into the U. S. orbit if the country accepted Marshall Plan aid. Such an eventuality obviously would threaten Soviet security. The alignment of Czechoslovakia with the West would divide Soviet Eastern Europe into two parts and give the West a common border with the Soviet Union. The establishment of a Social Democratic government, which Stalin thought would be inevitable, would set a dangerous precedent for other East European countries.

By early 1948 Gottwald, under pressure from Stalin, had established one-party control of Czechoslovakia and silenced all possible opponents. Jan Masaryk, the foreign minister and son of the first president of Czechoslovakia, was killed in a suspicious fall from a government building window. President Beneš resigned in June 1948, since he found it impossible to approve the new Communist-inspired constitution. Once again, as two major powers jockeyed for position, the Czechs had seen their independence snuffed out.

The Revolt of the First Secretaries

By 1947 Stalin was faced with a more direct problem than Western animosity: nationalism, or what the Communists termed national deviation. Immediately after the war all Eastern European Communist parties contained members extremely loyal to Moscow, called Muscovites, who had spent considerable time in the Soviet Union. But the parties' memberships also included Communists whose first loyalty was to their native lands and who were influenced less by the Soviet Union. Thus the parties were split between those who envisioned their parties as part of a monolithic Communist world and those who placed their own countries above any international or ideological considerations. One of the leading nationalists, Wladislaw Gomulka of Poland, sought to enhance his party's following by identifying it with national goals. He avoided terror tactics, refused to alienate the peasantry through premature collectivization, and associated the party with Polish nationalism. Explaining the Polish rejection of collectivization, he said, "Our democracy is not similar to Soviet democracy, just as our society's structure is not the same as the Soviet structure." This stance of nationalist leaders was termed by one expert the "revolt of the first secretaries" of the Eastern European Communist parties.

The most serious first-secretary challenge to Stalin came from Marshal Tito of Yugoslavia, who Stalin feared might set up a Yugoslav-dominated federation of Balkan states that would result in two centers of Communist authority. Tito told Western correspondents in June 1947 that the Balkan states should form a "strong monolithic entity." After several visits with Bulgarian leader Dimitrov, Tito claimed in November 1947 that "the cooperation was so close that the question of federation will be a mere formality." Moreover, because of Tito's support for Communist revolutions throughout the world, Stalin feared that ideological leadership of the Communist world would shift to Tito.

While Stalin had been engaged during and after the war in political horse trading over Eastern Europe, Greece, and Trieste, Tito had been busy promoting the worldwide Communist movement by aiding the leftist forces in Greece. Tito was unwilling to accept the united-front government in Yugoslavia desired by Stalin and the Western Allies. Not only did he establish a one-party dictatorship but by proclaiming Yugoslavia a people's democracy he appeared to place Yugoslavia ahead of the Soviet Union in the transition to a true Communist society. Added to Tito's challenge to Soviet primacy in the Communist world was the distant challenge of Mao Tse-tung's successful Communist movement in China. Stalin had withheld aid from Mao because he was afraid of a strong rival Communist movement.

The People's Democracies

In order to establish Soviet supremacy in the Communist world, Stalin launched a concerted offensive that continued from 1948 until his death in 1953. He first sought to deter the West from any further involvement in Eastern European affairs by making plain the Soviet Union's determination to defend its interests. The Soviet blockade of all land access routes to Berlin on April 7, 1948 (see chapter 1) was the opening salvo in this offensive. To further occupy the West, he ordered Communist parties everywhere to foment unrest and governmental instability. However, the rapid economic recovery of Western Europe as a result of Marshall Plan aid prevented any serious economic–political problems in the West.

It was to Eastern Europe that Stalin directed most of his efforts. He began by setting up so-called people's democracies modeled on the Soviet Union in each country. All coalition governments were to be replaced by one-party dictatorships. All non-Communists, such as Eduard Beneš in Czechoslovakia, were to be excluded from the governments.

The parties were now forced to model their constitutions on that of the Soviet Union and to stress rapid industrialization and the collectivization of agriculture. Countries such as Poland that had spurned collectivization were now compelled to begin it. All Eastern European countries adopted economic planning, usually five-year plans that were coordinated with the Soviet five-year plan.

Although forced industrialization promoted rapid economic growth, it generated enormous problems. As heavy industry and armaments were stressed, the production of agricultural machinery declined. The resultant drop in agricultural output left the countries short of food. As for the cities, the growth of industry brought with it a characteristic shift in population to the urban centers, which resulted in overcrowding, housing shortages, and inadequate services for the population.

Soviet–Yugoslav Split

Central to the effort to reestablish Soviet supremacy in the Communist world was a stepped-up campaign to discredit and bring down Tito's government. When Stalin founded the Cominform in September of 1947, he established its headquarters in Belgrade partly in order to intimidate and spy on Tito and undermine his support within the Yugoslav Communist party.

Tito was accused of being anti-Soviet because of his failure to accept Moscow directives on industrial and agricultural policies. Stalin expected that his campaign would soon bring Tito to his knees, for he told Nikita Khrushchev, "I will shake my little finger — and there will be no more Tito, he will fall." But with Tito, Stalin was to experience a foretaste of that national communism which was to weaken the Soviet empire severely in the 1950s and 1960s. Primarily because of the national issue, Yugoslav Communist party members remained loyal to Tito. Unable to create divisions within the Yugoslav Communist party or to make Tito recant, Stalin had the Cominform expel Yugoslavia in 1948.

Stalin expected that the separation from Eastern European economic affairs would spell disaster for the Yugoslav economy. The Council for Mutual Economic Assistance, or Comecon, had been formed in January 1949, in part to carry out the economic embargo against Tito. When it excluded Yugoslavia from East European trade, Tito again proved his resourcefulness by opening up trade ties with the West and by obtaining an American loan which helped Yugoslavia through a period of acute economic peril.

An important aspect of the split between the Soviet Union and Yugoslavia was the Soviet determination to keep its satellites dependent on it for manufactured goods and to make them serve as reservoirs of raw materials for Soviet factories. Soviet attempts to postpone Yugoslav industrial development exasperated Yugoslav leaders, who felt that they had been extremely cooperative with the Soviet bloc countries. By 1947 Yugoslav trade with the Soviet bloc had increased to 52 percent of imports and 49 percent of exports. However, as the Yugoslavs pointed out, the bulk of the exports were raw materials whereas the imports were primarily higher-priced manufactured goods.

The Yugoslavs had also dutifully adopted the Stalinist economic model of centralization, nationalization of all industry, and emphasis on heavy industry. Soviet leaders, fearing that Yugoslavia might become a better example of a socialist society than the Soviet Union, complained about their uncritical acceptance of the Soviet model.

Expulsion from the Cominform and the trade embargo by all Soviet bloc countries had serious consequences for Yugoslavia. By 1949, a year after the expulsion, Yugoslavia's imports from the Soviet bloc had declined to 3.2 percent and its exports to 7.7 percent of its foreign trade. Since Yugoslavia had been actively anti-Western, supporting the Greek communists and adopting a belligerent attitude toward the United States, ostracism from the Soviet bloc left it balanced precariously between East and West. The Yugoslavs were too Marxist to identify closely with or to depend on the West, yet they could not return to close cooperation with the Soviet bloc. They were therefore forced to alter their practices in order to convince their critics that they were ideologically purer than the Soviet Union.

Attempting to prove that it was not Yugoslavia but the Soviet Union that was following a deviationist course, the Yugoslavs attacked the Soviet bureaucracy as a serious obstacle between the government and the people. To reduce the power of the central bureaucracy, Yugoslavia gave local party officials more authority in 1952. The party, renamed the League of Communists, was no longer the sole authority at the local level. Despite the retention of most decision making in Belgrade, the government increased the authority of local agencies. The alienation of the people was furthered, the Yugoslavs maintained, by Soviet state capitalism that deprived the worker of a share in the management of the Socialist economy. According to Yugoslav propaganda, the Eastern European states had been placed in a position of dependence similar to that of the Soviet people.

To reduce their bureaucracy, the Yugoslavs began a policy of decentralization through workers' councils and communes. Decision making was increasingly assumed by local communes and the workers' councils in industry after 1950. The workers' councils became Tito's primary ideological weapon against the Soviet Union. Even though they did not give workers total control of the factories — power was shared with the Communist party and the local commune — they gave workers a greater voice in the management of their factories than was the case anywhere else in the world. Workers not only helped choose their factory managers but also helped choose and often served on the managing board of their enterprise. Needless to say, the managing board was made up primarily of Communist party members since they were usually the most activist of the workers.

The effectiveness of a factory was no longer to be determined by its achievement of production quotas set by the central government but by capitalistic laws of supply and demand and profit. The Yugoslavs termed it a socialist market economy. Factories now competed against one another for the domestic market as well as for foreign sales. As the communes and workers' councils gained more jurisdiction, the central government would presumably wither away. Although it took years to institute the changes,

Among the stipulations of the United States' agreement to supply Yugoslavia with imports and foreign aid during the Soviet economic blockade was that U.S. observer teams be permitted to verify that food was being equitably distributed. Here, two U.S. army jeeps pass through Yugoslav Customs en route to a food distribution center.

Pictorial Parade

Yugoslavia's impact on the Soviet satellites became damaging to Soviet bloc unity in the 1950s. There were now two roads to socialism.

Placed between two antagonistic powers and in need of development funds, Yugoslavia had no choice but to turn to the West. United States financing helped Yugoslavia through the extremely difficult years from 1949 to 1952 of the economic blockade by the Soviet bloc. Tito then abandoned his stance as an advocate of world revolution and began to advocate peaceful coexistence with the West.

Imports and foreign aid from the United States comprised 34 percent of Yugoslavia's total imports, reflecting the U.S. conviction that this was an excellent opportunity to weaken the Soviet bloc. Thus the collapse that the Soviet Union had expected was averted. Yugoslav leaders had no idea in 1948 that their country would become a model for many developing countries as well as the primary model of national communism in Eastern Europe.

National Deviationism Ends

Although Tito was indomitable, Stalin was able to eliminate national deviationism elsewhere in Eastern Europe. Native Communists were ostracized one after another, and many were executed after being humiliated in show trials: Lucretiu Patrascanu in Romania, Koce Xoxi in Albania, Lásló Rajk in Hungary, Traicho Kostov in Bulgaria, and Vladimir Clementis and Rudolf Slanski in Czechoslovakia were discredited and liquidated. Some of the more powerful leaders, such as Poland's Gomulka, were dismissed from their posts and arrested but never executed.

Even Muscovites who stepped out of line were forced to recant: After proclaiming in 1948 that Communist countries should develop independently, Bulgarian Communist party leader Dimitrov was forced to surrender to Stalinist ideological conformity in 1949. Potential opposition groups such as the Catholic Church suffered severely. Hungarian Cardinal Josef Mindszenty was sentenced to life imprisonment in 1949 after a public show trial. By 1950, the Soviet Union had an iron grasp on the countries of Eastern Europe. In the Soviet Union and outside it, Stalin's opponents were afraid to take a stand against him. Soviet agents made sure that no deviationism occurred. But neither Stalin nor his agents could prevent mass discontent and unrest. Revolts in 1952 in Czechoslovakia and in 1953 in East Germany precipitated by the lowered standard of living and shortage of food brought about by forced collectivization and economic emphasis on heavy industry indicated that discontent may have been suppressed but not eliminated.

The motives behind Soviet policy during this period were a mixture of practical and ideological considerations. The practical necessity, in Soviet eyes, to strengthen Soviet defenses against Western hostility was one such consideration. A second was Stalin's personal desire for total control within an Eastern European sphere of influence and for ideological conformity among Communist parties. For the most part, Soviet moves to increase its authority in Eastern Europe and to enhance the position of the East European Communist parties began before the announcement of the Truman Doctrine and the Marshall Plan. In the case of Yugoslavia, Stalin felt that any surrender to Yugoslav Communist party independence would weaken Soviet authority throughout Eastern Europe. Khrushchev's policy of diversity in Eastern Europe and the resultant revolution in Hungary in 1956 (see chapter 7) were precisely what Stalin thought would happen if Soviet control was relaxed. Only in the case of Czechoslovakia does the Soviet–Western hostility appear to have been the decisive event in the Soviet crackdown.

FURTHER READING

For a more comprehensive description of Soviet policies in Eastern Europe see Zbigniew Brzezinski, *The Soviet Bloc, Unity and Conflict* (1960, rev. ed. 1967). Brzezinski rejects the revisionist argument that the imposition of Stalinist conformity in Eastern Europe came about because of the Cold War. Ghita Ionescu's *The Break-up of the Soviet Empire in Eastern Europe* (1965) is a brief but valuable analysis of the establishment and disintegration of the Soviet bloc. Joseph Rothschild's *Communist Eastern Europe* (1964) reports that the enforcement of Soviet primacy in Eastern Europe was a result, first and foremost, of Stalin's desire to maintain a monolithic Communist bloc subservient to the Soviet Union. Hugh Seton-Watson in *The East European Revolution* (1950, rev. ed. 1957) takes the position that Stalin and the East European Communist parties had a preconceived plan to communize Eastern Europe.

The most comprehensive study of Stalin is Adam B. Ulam, *Stalin: The Man and His Era* (1973). Ulam sees the sovietization of Eastern Europe as a result of Stalin's paranoia and believes that the Cold War had only a limited impact on Soviet policy. Isaac Deutscher's *Stalin* (1961) remains an important study of the Soviet leader. Ronald Hingley's *Joseph Stalin: Man and Legend* (1974) does not measure up to the two earlier works. In the absence of Soviet documentation, Milovan Djilas's *Conversations with Stalin* (1962) is one of the few sources containing statements by Stalin as to his motives and policies. For more works on Soviet foreign policy, see the bibliographies following chapters 1 and 7.

The Soviet–Yugoslav split is described in Robert Bass and Elizabeth Marbury (eds.), *The Soviet–Yugoslav Controversy, 1948–1958: A Documentary Record* (1959). Vladimir Dedijer in *Tito* (1953) and *The Battle Stalin Lost* (1971) provides a personal account of the Soviet Yugoslav confrontation. Dedijer points out Stalin's unwillingness to accept any potential rivals in Eastern Europe. A balanced view of the controversy is presented in Adam Ulam's *Titoism and the Cominform* (1952). Important information on Tito and national communism can be found in Paul Zinner, *National Communism and Popular Revolt in Eastern Europe* (1957).

Coverage of the Communist coup in Czechoslovakia can be found in Josef Korbel, *The Communist Subversion of Czechoslovakia, 1938-1948: The Failure of Coexistence* (1959); Morton Kaplan, *The Communist Coup in Czechoslovakia* (1960); and Paul Zinner, *Communist Strategy and Tactics in Czechoslovakia* (1963). Kaplan's and Zinner's studies are more balanced than Korbel's, which views the coup as a premeditated plan. Kaplan sees the coup as an unplanned and somewhat hasty response to the Marshall Plan and the declining strength of the Czech Communist party.

Polish affairs can be studied in Hans Roos, *A History of Modern Poland* (1966); and Richard Hiscocks, *Poland, Bridge for the Abyss* (1963). For information on Romania see Ghita Ionescu, *Communism in Rumania, 1944-1962* (1964); and Stephen Fischer-Galati, *The New Rumania: From People's Democracy to Socialist Republic* (1967) and *The Socialist Republic of Rumania* (1969). More comprehensive descriptions of the immediate postwar period in Hungary can be found in Bennet Kovrig, *The Hungarian People's Republic* (1970); and Ferenc Nagy, *The Struggle Behind the Iron Curtain* (1948).

3 From Left to Right: European Politics, 1945-1948

There were a few who simply wanted to return to the institutions of the [French] Third Republic. But, to the great majority, this *ancien régime* was doomed.

Charles de Gaulle, in *de Gaulle* by Alexander Werth

When the Second World War drew to a close in Europe in May of 1945, even the victors had little to celebrate. The specter of economic ruin and famine threatened much of the continent. In Great Britain, wartime debts and postwar shortages cut short the victory celebrations. In France, the destruction of large areas of the northeast as well as chaos in internal social and political affairs boded ill for the nation's future. For the defeated, Germany and Italy, the future seemed even bleaker. In Germany the survivors would have to live with widespread destruction, famine, and an economy that had ground to a halt. Countries that had been caught between the major belligerents, such as Belgium and Holland, had also suffered severely from the war.

Before Europe could begin to put the pieces together again, political life had to be restored. In Germany and Italy this meant monumental changes. New constitutions had to be written and new leaders had to be found.

The immediate problem was to find individuals capable of establishing democratic governments who had not been compromised by their associations with previous regimes. Not uncommonly, this search led the occupying powers and European leaders to those who had been on the left of the political spectrum in the prewar years. The popularity of parties on the left, Communists and Socialists, resulted from their wartime opposition to fascism. After the German attack on the Soviet Union in 1941, Communists had played a major role in the various resistance movements.

Parties on the right had little support in the immediate postwar period. The extreme right had been compromised by its prewar association with fascism and the conservative parties by their association with depression and economic want during the years between the two world wars. Few

44

people still favored the conservatives' economic liberalism with its laissez-faire economic philosophy.

Widespread support for economic planning and the nationalization of industry had developed during the war. Only by such measures, many thought, could the economic experiences of the interwar period be avoided. Communist and Socialist parties cooperated in coalition governments throughout Europe in the period immediately after the war. But by 1948 on the Continent and 1951 in England, parties of the center and right — usually Christian Democratic parties — had regained power in most countries, and the left was in retreat. The major reasons for this change were the rapid economic recovery of Europe, the adoption of the welfare state concept even by conservative parties, and the Cold War. The right now seemed more progressive than it had been in the interwar period, and many now associated the left with Soviet expansionism.

Great Britain: The Welfare State Begins

With the only labor party in power among major European countries, Great Britain seemed to be the country in which the most fundamental economic and social reforms would be instituted. Indeed, postwar shortages and wartime promises did compel the government to increase social services and to nationalize certain industries and utilities. During the war the Beveridge Report, introduced in the House of Commons in 1942 to boost morale, had promised all citizens a minimum income and a comprehensive system of social welfare. The report was given wide coverage by the press and accepted by the public, then it was shelved for the duration of the war.

Once the war was over, questions of social welfare became the focus of public attention. An opinion poll taken during the first postwar election campaign showed that the respondents were most concerned about housing, full employment, and social security.

The election campaign reflected the primacy of social issues over foreign policy considerations. When Winston Churchill, the standard-bearer for the Conservative party, warned that a vote for the Labour party was a vote for totalitarianism, Labour countered with a comprehensive program of social welfare. Despite widespread admiration for Churchill, the voters associated the Conservative party with the prewar depression, with its soup lines and widespread unemployment. Labour, on the other hand, by filling the home ministries in the wartime National Government coalition, had gained widespread admiration and support for its mobilization of the home front.

On July 5, 1945, Churchill and the Conservatives were dealt a resounding defeat by the British public. The Labour party, with a majority of 145 votes in the House of Commons, was free to enact its program. The decisive defeat of the Conservatives indicated that during the war large sections of the middle class had become convinced that the government would have to assume responsibility for the less privileged members of society.

Contrary to Churchill's warnings, the Labour party leadership, with its diverse social composition, proved to be reformist rather than revolutionary. Most of the leaders were interested in pragmatic short-term reforms rather than a complete revamping of the society and the economy. Clement Attlee, the new prime minister, had gained valuable experience as deputy prime minister during the war. He was hardly the flamboyant leader one might have expected from a Labour government, but his low-keyed, pragmatic style of leadership was what Britain needed to overcome its serious postwar economic and social problems.

The right wing of the Labour party was represented by the new foreign secretary, Ernest Bevin, who was a part of the trade union faction of the party. The left wing was led by Sir Stafford Cripps, head of the Board of Trade and later chancellor of the exchequer, and by Aneurin Bevan, minister of health. Cripps was an upper-middle-class lawyer, while Bevan had been a miner in his youth.

The economic and social program enacted by the Labour party clearly shows the divisions within the party. Revolutionary minded critics described the Labour measures as the cautious revolution or half-revolution. Certainly the legislation enacted by the Labour government stopped short of being revolutionary in the eyes of the left wing of the party and among most European Socialists as it did not bring about the expected redistribution of wealth. Moreover, while the government reduced the private sector's share in the direction of the economy, it did not go as far as France or Italy in adopting a plan for long-term development (see chapter 4). Government investment and planning tended to be short-term rather than long-term.

But Labour's establishment of the welfare state and its nationalization of major industries and utilities were no small step. The Bank of England and civil aviation were nationalized immediately; the coal and steel industries, public transportation, electricity, and gas followed. Nationalization of only one industry, iron and steel, was strongly contested by the House of Lords and the Conservative party. (The Conservatives denationalized it in 1951, only to have it renationalized in 1967 by Labour.) The Lords' opposition was overcome by the passage of an amendment to the Parliament Act of 1911 reducing the power of the Lords to delay legislation to one session. (The 1911 act had abolished the Lords' right to veto money bills passed by the Commons and permitted the Commons to pass *any* bill if it obtained Commons approval in three successive sessions over a period of at least two years.) Some of the nationalizations, particularly of the Bank of England and of public utilities, were less than revolutionary since the government had already exercised considerable control over their activities. In addition, Labour refused to assume full responsibility for the direction of nationalized industries and instead placed them under the direction of autonomous corporations rather than government agencies, as was done in France and Italy.

The initial legislation providing for the creation of the welfare state consisted of the National Insurance Act and the National Health Service Act, both passed in 1946. The National Insurance Act set up a comprehensive social security program and nationalized medical insurance companies so that the state now subsidized the unemployed, the sick, and the aged. The National Health Service Act instituting socialized medicine faced greater opposition but was also in effect by 1948. Doctors and dentists were forced to work with the state hospitals, where the bulk of the patients were going, but they were permitted to retain a private practice. Although the system was very costly — it was the second highest governmental expenditure — it was so widely accepted by the time the Conservatives came to power in 1951 that more than 90 percent of the medical profession was cooperating with it, and there was no significant effort to repeal it.

No sooner had Labour instituted its program than it began to lose popularity. Many of its problems, especially the economic ones, were beyond its control. Inherited from the interwar years and the war were a huge debt and an outdated industrial plant that made the balance of trade increasingly unfavorable.

Britain's need to import a large percentage of its foodstuffs and raw materials compelled it to export large quantities of processed goods to pay for them. Unfortunately, the loss of markets during the war and the inability to compete with more modernized foreign industries in the postwar period further reduced its exports and inflated its deficits. Britain had had to sell off many foreign investments during the war and no longer had large returns on such investments to offset the huge trade imbalance. Only with the help of loans from the United States could the government be bailed out.

Economic recovery was hampered in the postwar period by the outlay of large sums in support of foreign policy. Until U.S. President Harry Truman's 1947 proclamation of the Truman Doctrine, which provided economic and military aid to Greece and Turkey, Britain bore the brunt of the effort against the leftist forces in the Greek Civil War. At the same time, British troops were caught up in the hostilities between the Jews and the Arabs in Palestine and between the Hindus and the Moslems in India (see chapter 6). To add to these woes, Britain spent $60 million in 1946 and another $60 million in the first quarter of 1947 to feed the Germans in its occupation zone.

To carry out these farflung commitments, Britain still had 1.5 million soldiers in 1947. The decisions to leave India and Palestine in that year and to cut off aid to Greece and Turkey stemmed from economic necessity more than from a genuine desire to retreat from empire. Labour Foreign Secretary Ernest Bevin had in fact long held out against the pressure to withdraw from these areas.

Even the elements seemed to be against Britain during its financial plight. The coldest winter in sixty-six years, with snow piling twenty feet high in

World War II hero General Charles de Gaulle of France being welcomed by an admiring crowd at Chartres.

some areas, brought the nation to a standstill in 1946–1947. The resulting fuel shortages necessitated increased imports of fuel and at the same time cut factory output, which in turn cut exports. The government had no choice; it devalued the pound from $4.03 to $2.80. Although devaluation increased exports and stabilized the value of the pound, the move was unpopular because it increased the price of imported goods and made foreign travel more expensive. Labour's decreasing popularity became apparent when the 1950 elections reduced its lead over the Tories to a mere seventeen seats.

The issue that finally drove the Labour party from power was rearmament. It caused a battle in the party between a right wing that wanted to rearm and cooperate with the United States and a left wing that wanted to follow a neutral course and not rearm. Ernest Bevin, disillusioned by his dealings with Moscow and convinced that Britain had no choice but to cooperate with the United States, led the rearmament forces to victory. In 1951, in response to the financial demands of the Korean War, the majority of the Labour party decided to cut health care, notably dental and optical payments, and to spend more for rearmament. This shuffling of priorities was apparently done to convince the United States of the Labour government's loyalty. In response, Aneurin Bevan, the minister of health, resigned from the cabinet and was followed by a number of others from the left wing of the party. The election of 1951, called by Attlee to increase the Labour majority, instead produced a Conservative victory. Labour would not return to power until 1964.

France: The Fourth Republic

The difficulties facing postwar France were even more complicated than those facing Great Britain. Not only did France have serious financial problems, for which it was dependent on U.S. aid, but it also was faced with more wartime destruction, social dislocation, and political turmoil. For example, the destruction of four-fifths of its railway rolling stock hampered transportation. The political division between supporters of the wartime Vichy government and members of the Resistance had no parallel in Britain. The purge of Vichy collaborators, which took thousands of lives, and the inability of the new provisional government to establish its authority outside Paris until October 1944 brought the country close to anarchy. Some Frenchmen used the occasion to carry out vendettas against personal enemies. Over 5,000 collaborators were killed by partisans before the new provisional government reestablished the legal system.

The leader of the provisional government, General Charles de Gaulle, had not been in France since June 1940, when German troops moved in. A little-known secretary of state for the army at the time of the defeat, de Gaulle was soon to become one of the most influential and controversial leaders in the world. As the organizer of the Free French movement in exile, his leadership was eventually accepted by the underground Resistance movement in occupied France. Embarrassed by the quick defeat of France in 1940, he sought throughout his life to restore French grandeur. The Anglo–American refusal to acknowledge him as leader of the French government in exile, partially due to Roosevelt's and Churchill's personal dislike of his vain and domineering character, was a humiliating experience for him.

But Churchill and Roosevelt had to recognize his leadership after the Free French movement was established in liberated Algiers in 1942 and de Gaulle had the acceptance of the French underground, including the Communists. Three days before the Allied invasion of Normandy on June 6, 1944, a provisional government was set up in Algiers with de Gaulle at the helm. When he returned to Paris on August 25, 1944, at the head of the Allied invasion force, Parisians gave him an enthusiastic welcome. In two weeks he set up the French provisional government, then sent large French forces into the battle against Hitler. But stable political life could not be restored until the provisional government could establish its authority throughout the country.

Political turmoil was avoided during the provisional government period because of the cooperation of the Communists and de Gaulle. The political right was completely discredited because of its collaboration with Germany and its association with the puppet Vichy government.

The postwar cooperation of the left and de Gaulle was an outgrowth of the wartime coordination of military efforts between the Soviet Union and the Western Allies. The leaders of the Communist party, Maurice Thorez and Jacques Duclos, who were responsible for the cooperation, were both Moscow Communists and followed orders from the Kremlin. Whatever their ultimate goals, they chose initially to support a parliamentary government with de Gaulle as its leader. The Communist party cooperated with de Gaulle in disarming the Resistance forces that might have been used by the left to gain power in France. At this point, the Communists apparently hoped to come to power in France as part of a left coalition. Some have suggested that without the Cold War and the subsequent polarization of international politics, the Communists would soon have become a genuine national party with no ties to Moscow. The party's reformist stand and anti-Soviet pronouncements in the 1960s and 1970s tend to support this view.

Equally important in promoting national harmony in the postwar period was a consensus emanating from the war and especially from the Resistance movement. A Resistance Charter, accepted by Resistance leaders in 1942, advocated major economic and social changes when peace was restored. In order to rid the country of "economic and financial feudalism," the charter called for nationalization of key industries and services, economic planning, and the establishment of economic and social democracy. Sharing with the left many Resistance ideas, de Gaulle carried out some nationalization (e.g., the coal mines, the four largest banks, civil aviation, and a few industries) and initiated economic planning.

By October 1945, sufficient order had been established to hold the first postwar election. The three parties representing the major Resistance forces — the Communisits, Socialists, and *Mouvement Republicain Populaire* (MRP) — gained 461 of the 586 assembly seats. At this point the Communists with 26 percent of the vote and the socialists with 24 percent were still cooperating. Both wanted a new constitution that would provide a strong assembly with the power to choose and reject a premier.

De Gaulle, seeing in a strengthened assembly a return to the weak Third Republic form of government, hoped for a constitution with strong powers for the executive. The other major Resistance faction, the Christian Democratic MRP, also wanted a strong executive. Although asked to stay on as premier and president, de Gaulle soon realized that the Communists and Socialists who dominated the new constituent assembly were writing a leftist constitution that would strip him of much of his power. Therefore, on January 20, 1946, de Gaulle retired from active political life for the first of three times.

The search for a new premier revealed the growing divisions in the left-of-center coalition. The Communist party proposed a Communist-Socialist government with the Communist Thorez as premier. The Socialists, fearful of being dominated by the Communists, refused to support any premier who did not have MRP approval. The MRP, distrustful of the Communists, refused to support *any* Communist for premier. To break this deadlock, Pierre Gouin was named premier. Gouin, who was an ineffective leader, was described by a centrist magazine as a "man of goodwill rather than will."

The attempts to formulate a new constitution brought about a clash between those who wanted a strong legislature and those who wanted a powerful executive. Primarily on the basis of MRP opposition, the first constitution was defeated by a national referendum in May 1946 because it did not provide for a strong executive. Another election the following month, necessitated by the defeat of the constitution, made the MRP the largest party in the tripartite coalition, and its leader, Georges Bidault, was chosen premier. When the second constitution, providing for a stronger executive and an upper house in the legislature, was accepted by a national referendum in November 1946, the Fourth French Republic began. In the November elections the popularity of the Communists once again made the French Communist party (PCF) the largest party in the tripartite coalition. (See Table 3–1.)

The selection of a new premier after the November elections and the exclusion of the Communist party from the tripartite coalition in May 1947 revealed how inextricably French domestic affairs were entangled with international affairs. As the largest party, the PCF hoped that its leader, Thorez, would become the new premier, but external events had made even the Socialists extremely wary of the Communists. The absorption of the left wing of the Polish Socialists by the Communist party of Poland and the

Table 3-1　Seats Won in French Elections, 1945-1946

Party	October 21, 1945	June 6, 1946	November 10, 1946
Communist (PCF)	161	153	183
Socialist (SFIO)	150	126	105
Christian Democratic (MRP)	150	169	167
Radical	28	32	43
Conservative	64	67	71
Other	33	36	49

SOURCE: Philip M. Williams, *Crisis and Compromise: Politics in the Fourth Republic,* 3rd ed. (Essex, England: Longman, 1964), p. 532. Copyright © Philip M. Williams, 1958, 1964. Reprinted by permission of Penguin Books Ltd.

return to France of the anti-Communist Socialist leader Léon Blum from Moscow increased the distrust between the two left parties.

Blum's dislike of the Communists grew out of his association with them in the interwar Popular Front government. He felt that any Communist-dominated government would produce a leftist dictatorship and asserted, "Without socialism, democracy is imperfect; without democracy, socialism is helpless." As early as March 1946, the U.S. government exerted considerable pressure on Blum to join an anti-Communist coalition aimed at ousting the Communist-dominated tripartite coalition. U.S. dissatisfaction over Blum's failure to go along with this proposal was made plain when grants of foreign aid were reduced to less than the French requested.

Without Socialist support the Communists had little chance of gaining the premiership, so in January of 1947 they agreed to accept the Socialist Paul Ramadier as the new premier. PCF efforts to keep the tripartite coalition alive were thwarted by three major crises of the Ramadier government: the Indochina War, the Cold War, and a domestic labor dispute.

The Indochina War It was inevitable that France's colonial policy would eventually become an issue in the developing Cold War. Until 1947 the Communist party supported the government's attempt to reimpose its control over Indochina. But only six days after the enunciation of the Truman Doctrine on March 12, 1947, the PCF withdrew its support of France's Indochina policy. Up to this point, Stalin, in keeping with the spirit of Allied wartime cooperation and distrustful of any strong Communist parties outside the Soviet Union, had directed the PCF to cooperate with the other political forces. Now, clearly, the position was reversed. French Communists were told to stop supporting a colonial war.

The Cold War At the heart of the conflict among the coalition parties was the Cold War. Before 1947 the French government had tried to adhere to a neutral position between Moscow and Washington, but the steady deterioration of relations between the two superpowers and the French need of economic aid made this policy impossible.

As late as April 1947 Bidault, now minister of foreign affairs, tried to get Soviet support for the separation of the Ruhr from Germany. However, after being snubbed by Stalin and Molotov at the Moscow conference in March–April 1947, he turned to the United States.

Accepting U.S. help meant giving up plans to strengthen France by incorporating German territory and accepting American and British plans for the economic revival of Germany. Even before this, many French politicians had recognized the advantages of cooperating with the United States. Pierre Mendès-France, later to become premier of France, said, "We must keep up this indispensable Communist scare" since the United States was making a great effort to aid those threatened by Communism.

The End of Tripartism   Ramadier's economic policies precipitated a crisis that resulted in the expulsion of the PCF from the government coalition. The Communist Party had denounced strikes as anarchist even though the largest labor union was under its control. But Ramadier's policy of low wages and high prices to promote business recovery precipitated a massive strike at the government-owned Renault automobile factory in April 1947, forcing the PCF to support the workers against the government. After winning a vote of confidence on his economic policy in the assembly, Ramadier demanded that the Communist deputies resign, and tripartism came to an end.

While Ramadier was receiving U.S. support for his handling of the Communists, a new political party of the right appeared. This party, the Rally of the French People (RPF), led by de Gaulle, also sought U.S. support but failed to get it. De Gaulle's arrogant attempt to make the government call a national referendum on his return to power was decisively beaten back, and for the second time de Gaulle had to retire from the political arena. By the spring of 1948 the government of Robert Schuman, supported by Marshall Plan funds and stabilized by domestic economic recovery, was firmly in control.

Italy: A Policy of Muddling Through

Like France and Great Britain, Italy experienced a wartime and postwar resurgence of the left. Again it was the left's antifascist activities that were responsible for its popularity. The Fascist Grand Council and King Victor Emmanuel III replaced Benito Mussolini with Marshal Pietro Badoglio in July 1943, following the Allied invasion of Italy. However, Badoglio had to flee to liberated southern Italy when German troops took control of northern Italy (including Rome). In the liberated south, a coalition of antifascist parties called the Committee for National Liberation (CLN) challenged Badoglio's claim to the post of head of the Italian state.

The CLN, which wanted a republic, clashed with Badoglio over the fate of the monarchy. King Victor Emmanuel III promised to abdicate immediately in favor of his son, Umberto, who would act as lieutenant governor until a postwar national referendum could decide the fate of the monarchy. Only Communist approval of the king's action, apparently a continuation of Soviet–Allied wartime cooperation, convinced the remaining CLN parties to accept Umberto. With the liberation of Rome in June of 1944, the CLN forced acceptance of Ivanoe Bonomi as head of a new government.

Meanwhile, military and political activities in the north had taken a politically more radical turn because of the German occupation. Resistance fighters formed the Committee of National Liberation for Northern Italy (CLNAI) centered in Milan. The CLNAI, dominated by the left of center —

the Communist, Socialist, and Action parties — desired a far more radical republic than the Bonomi government in the south was willing to institute. The CLNAI opposition to Bonomi was sufficiently strong to have the leader of the Action party, Ferruccio Parri, appointed premier by Lieutenant Governor Umberto.

In May and June of 1945, immediately before Parri came to power, the weakening of the political left set the pattern for the postwar development of Italy. Throughout the north the leftist-dominated CLNAI permitted the participation of workers in the management of industrial enterprises through so-called management councils. The CLNAI also launched attacks on big business to penalize it for cooperating with fascism and to begin the process of destroying what were considered to be the reactionary forces in Italy.

That the left was unable to take full control can be attributed primarily to Allied intervention. The left realized that any outright attempt to seize power would be opposed by American and British forces that were then in the country. As the left attempted to gain Allied acceptance by adopting a moderate reformist position, its basis of strength was systematically destroyed by the Allies. Leftist Resistance groups were compelled to surrender their arms. Workers councils were disbanded, factory managers were urged to reassert their authority, and local committees of liberation, invariably leftist, were replaced by military government.

Parri, convinced of the need for radical reforms in postwar Italy, was thus handicapped from the start. His attempts to institute policies favoring small and medium-size business rather than big business and to redistribute wealth through a more effective income tax were defeated by the Liberals and Christian Democrats in his cabinet, who considered his policies too radical. After only six months in office Parri resigned, blaming the Liberals and Christian Democrats for sabotaging his program. His fall signified the end of radical social and political change in postwar Italy and condemned Italy to a policy of muddling through.

With Parri's fall began the postwar domination of Italian politics by the Christian Democratic party that has lasted to this day. Although the Christian Democrats, led by Alcide de Gasperi, were forced to share power with the Socialists and Communists, they clearly dominated the coalition. It was easy for the coalition to accept an uncontroversial public referendum in June 1946 ending monarchy in Italy but much more difficult for it to reach decisions on complex economic and social problems.

While the Communists and Socialists wanted to nationalize some industry, De Gasperi preferred a laissez-faire policy. De Gasperi and his fellow party members, especially the Catholic clergymen, saw the Communist and Socialist parties as threats to the Church. De Gasperi's attempts to oust the Communists and Socialists from the coalition were helped along by a split in the Socialist party between those who favored cooperation with the Communists and those who did not. The latter, led by

Giuseppe Saragat, broke away from the Socialist party in January 1947 and formed the Social Democratic Party (PSDI).

With his Socialist opposition weakened, De Gasperi used the growing anti-Communist sentiment stemming from the Cold War to break up the coalition. The United States gave De Gasperi considerable support, granting his government political control of the north that had been denied to Parri and increasing its economic aid. During the campaign before the 1948 election, the United States warned that a Communist–Socialist government would not receive any further economic aid. Warning of a Communist dictatorship in Italy, the Christian Democratic party obtained sufficient votes in the 1948 election to govern alone. De Gasperi astutely included representatives of the Social Democratic, Republican, and Liberal parties in his ministry, leaving the Communist and Socialist parties isolated on the left. Since 1948 the Communist party and its working-class supporters have been excluded from governing coalitions in Italy. However, the Communists have managed in the 1960s and 1970s to gain power in many provinces and municipalities. Their popularity in recent elections has won them important positions in the legislature. (This resurgence will be explored in chapter 13.) Because the basis of support for the Christian Democrats has come from the conservative upper and middle classes and

The piazza of Montefiasconi, a village in Italy, during the 1948 election campaign. Almost every available space is covered with election posters and party slogans.
David Seymour—Magnum Photos

the southern peasantry, there has been little support for meaningful economic and social reforms.

Spain: An End to Ostracism

A swing to the left was impossible in Spain and Portugal, where strong dictatorships prevented any normal political activity. General Francisco Franco had clapped a tight police control over his leftist opposition after his victory over the Popular Front government in the Spanish Civil War in 1939. Strong support by Spanish nationalists — and bitter opposition between his opponents, Communists and anti-Communist Republicans — made Franco's task much easier. With a government composed of military men and members of nationalist groups, Franco retained the pragmatic authoritarianism that he had established during the civil war. He feared that the establishment of any clear-cut ideological basis for his regime would alienate some of his nationalist support.

Concerned that the European democracies might turn on Spain for its adherence to the Fascist Anti-Comintern Pact of 1939, Franco declared Spanish neutrality at the outset of World War II. But the swift German victory over France produced a marked pro-German attitude among Spanish leaders. Only economic hardships and the possibility that a close identification with the Fascist powers would bring crippling economic sanctions kept Spain from openly supporting Germany and Italy.

The Nazi attack on the Soviet Union in 1941 caused Franco's vehemently anti-Communist regime to send a force of 20,000 Spanish volunteers to help Germany on the Russian front. But Spain's enthusiasm waned with the Soviet victories at Moscow and Stalingrad and United States entry into the war.

From this point on Franco maintained strict neutrality despite the protestations of the pro-Fascist Falangist party. Spain's neutralism began to bear fruit when the Allies launched their invasion of French North Africa in 1942. At that time President Roosevelt offered assurances that the invasion was not directed at Spanish holdings in Africa and that the Allies would not intervene in Spanish internal affairs.

Franco overcame the immediate postwar problems by again cautiously adapting his policies to satisfy both internal and foreign opponents. At home, he assuaged political opposition from the military, church, and monarchists by reducing the influence of his Falangist party supporters. The Spanish left, still divided and still closely watched, offered little opposition. On the right, no strong conservative alternative existed to challenge Franco, and the military continued to support him. Heated foreign opposition to his regime had little impact since government propagandists portrayed it as an anti-Spanish rather than an anti-Franco campaign. Franco further strengthened his regime in 1947 by declaring

Spain a kingdom with himself as regent and by having it confirmed by a national plebiscite.

Another factor that helped Franco to hold his domestic critics at bay and overcome international ostracism was Spain's growing usefulness to the United States and its allies in the Cold War. In the event of war with the Soviet Union, the United States began to see, that the value of military bases in Spain would be immeasurable. By 1948, most of the anti-Communist West had reopened diplomatic contracts with Spain and the United States had begun to provide Spain with financial aid to overcome the serious economic problems. No longer ostracized internationally, and beginning to recover economically, Franco did not have to alter his internal policies to please republican opponents.

Portugal: Uninterrupted Peace

Before the outbreak of World War II Portugal had a dictatorship that was long established and ideologically more consistent than that of Spain. A professor of political economy at the University of Coimbra, Antonio de Oliveira Salazar, had been brought into the military government in 1928 to resolve the acute financial difficulties, and by 1933 Salazar had become dictator of the military regime. The Portuguese accepted his strong, authoritative leadership primarily because of a yearning for peace and security after suffering through twenty-three antigovernment revolts between 1910 and 1928.

Salazar overcame the Portuguese Fascists, called National Syndicalists, by offering his own brand of Catholic corporatism and by concentrating political power in a single government Party of National Union. To provide order and stability he set up a consultative corporate chamber in place of a senate and brought labor under the jurisdiction of government syndicates.

By providing transportation and communication facilities to Franco, Salazar's regime proved to be a valuable aid to the nationalist forces in the Spanish Civil War. But he refused to aid Franco directly and adhered to the international nonintervention agreement. During World War II, Salazar initially adopted a policy of strict neutrality. Fearing that the war might bring about a polarization of forces within Portugal, he carried out a comprehensive program of civic nationalism. A youth organization, an auxiliary militia system, political purges of suspected opponents, and a government loyalty oath were among the tools used to stamp out all opposition to the regime.

Owing to Portugal's longtime friendship and treaty of alliance with Britain, Salazar was never as pressured as Spain was to enter the war on the side of Germany and Italy. This friendship led Salazar to change his policy of neutrality and to grant the United States and Britain use of military bases in the Azores in 1943 and to stop the shipment of strategic materiel to Germany in 1944.

After the war, Portugal escaped much of the international anti-Fascist campaign because of its wartime cooperation with Western allies and because it retained a parliamentary form of government. Moreover, Salazar instituted a liberalization program to satisfy both foreign and domestic opponents. The program included the restoration of freedom of the press, amnesty for political opponents of the regime, and new parliamentary elections. However, a reduction in the number of persons eligible to vote and a boycott by the opposition made a sham of the elections.

Although some political unrest was evident in the late 1940s, Salazar was able to maintain his authoritarian rule. Serious economic problems were avoided when his regime received economic aid from the Marshall Plan. Membership in NATO gained Portugal international support. By 1950 Salazar's opposition was limited to a few students and intellectuals, a small group of military men, and some members of the middle class.

The Small Nations: Restoring Order

With the exception of Greece the smaller European countries concentrated on domestic affairs in the postwar period. Many had suffered extensively from the war and were faced with considerable reconstruction problems. Large sections of Holland, especially Rotterdam, had been destroyed by German bombs. Although Belgium had suffered less war damage, it was in the throes of internecine political–cultural conflict between the politically radical, anticlerical, French-speaking Walloons and the politically conservative, Catholic Flemish.

Among the Scandinavian countries, only Norway and Finland experienced serious wartime losses. Norway lost one half of its merchant fleet. Finland suffered through a wartime Soviet invasion, the loss of some territory to the Soviet Union, and the burden of heavy reparations in the postwar period. Nevertheless, the Finns managed to retain their political democracy and won admiration throughout the world for their stout resistance to Soviet domination. The Socialist and the Agrarian parties successfully resisted Communist attempts to gain control of the country.

In Norway and Denmark, thousands of German collaborators were arrested at war's end. As in Finland, the Socialist and Agrarian parties dominated the governments as Communist strength waned following the war.

Forced to cooperate with Germany under threat of invasion, Sweden did not have to face the problems of economic reconstruction and political restoration confronting most European countries. The Swedish Socialist party continued to dominate domestic politics as it had done before the war.

Austria, particularly Vienna, had suffered extensively from Allied bombing. Not only did Austria have to recover from serious economic destruction and dislocation but it also had to endure a four-power occupation until 1955, when it became an independent, neutral state.

The city of Rotterdam in the Netherlands, which was almost leveled by German bombs during World War II.

Greece: From Occupation to Civil War

Greece suffered through four years of German occupation (1941–1944) and a destructive civil war before political peace was obtained. A Communist-led National Liberation Front (EAM), with its People's Army (ELAS), challenged the exiled Government of National Unity for leadership when Greece was liberated. The ELAS force could have seized power when the Germans withdrew in October 1944, but it refrained because the Churchill–Stalin agreements, signed two months earlier, assigned Greece to Western jurisdiction and because Stalin issued direct orders not to overthrow the British-backed Government of National Unity.

But in December 1944, encouraged by Tito against Stalin's wishes, ELAS seized power when the government threatened a reorganization that would equalize the Communist and non-Communist military forces in a new national army. British troops compelled the EAM–ELAS to capitulate in February 1945. In the anti-Communist reaction that followed, government security agents and vigilante groups hunted down Communists. Again in March 1946 the Communists tried to seize power. Despite guerrilla activity, parliamentary elections were held in March as scheduled. As the Communists had feared, the proroyalist parties won 206 of the 354 seats in the legislature. This trend continued in the September referendum, when 70 percent of the voters cast their ballots in favor of a restoration of the monarchy.

The Communist guerrillas, with support from Yugoslavia, Albania, and Bulgaria, could not be dislodged from their mountain retreats until funds provided under the Truman Doctrine, totaling $250 million, permitted the buildup of the Greek army in 1948. When the Communist forces shifted from guerrilla warfare to conventional warfare in 1949 they were wiped out by the Greek army.

After nine years of warfare, large sections of Greece were devastated. With support from the Marshall Plan Greece was able to begin a modest recovery from economic misery. But internal political troubles and the lack of economic resources kept it a poor and troubled country.

Stalin had ordered Tito to stop his support of the Greek guerrillas, and Tito's failure to comply was one of the major reasons for the Stalin–Tito rift in 1948. Yugoslav support for the guerrillas ended in July 1949, when Tito had to concentrate his efforts on resisting Soviet pressures. In any case, Tito could ill afford to support a guerrilla war that might well spill over into Yugoslavia. He was also desperately in need of economic aid himself, as a consequence of the economic embargo of Comecon.

Popularity of the Left

With the exception of Spain and Portugal, the political left was popular everywhere among the smaller European states. As in France and Italy, leftist parties had led the resistance in the occupied territory or had been popular in the interwar period. The postwar governments of both Belgium and Denmark contained Communists. Without Allied intervention, a left coalition would undoubtedly have come to power in 1944 in Greece. In Belgium, a Communist attempt to gain power in 1944 was beaten back by Allied troops. However, the popularity of the far left waned quickly because of its identification with the Soviet Union.

The more successful moderate left embodied in the Socialist and Social Democratic parties that came to power jointly or separately in Austria, Switzerland, Denmark, Norway, Sweden, and in Belgium, the Netherlands, and Luxembourg (the Benelux countries) never suffered the political decline experienced by Social Democratic parties in Germany, Italy, and France after 1946. The resilience of the Social Democrats in Northern Europe resulted both from their interwar popularity and from the absence of strong Communist scares in the postwar period; in the 1950s Social Democrats were in power, as in Scandinavia, or shared power, as in the Netherlands, Belgium, and Austria.

In retrospect, the year 1948 seems to mark a breaking point in the postwar history of Europe. By this time, left-of-center parties were out of power in the major continental European countries. Only the more reform-minded Labour party in Britain managed to cling to power until 1951. It was also 1948 when foreign funds, primarily through Marshall Plan aid, started the economic recovery of Europe.

Moreover, 1948 and 1949 were the years of the division of Europe into two hostile camps. Beginning with the formation of NATO in 1949, for a decade European countries had to follow the dictates of either the United States or the Soviet Union in foreign affairs.

But 1948 was also a hopeful beginning for Western Europe. It was in that year that economic recovery began. And that year also marked the inception of long-term plans for economic cooperation that eventually developed into the European Common Market.

FURTHER READING

For sympathetic treatments of the British Labour government see Keith Hutchison, *The Decline and Fall of British Capitalism* (1951); C. R. Attlee, *As It Happened* (1954); Maurice Bruce, *The Coming of the Welfare State* (1961); and Emanuel Shinwell, *The Labour Story* (1963). Details on British industry under the Labour government can be found in Arnold A. Rogow, *The Labour Government and British Industry* (1955); W. A. Robson, *Nationalised Industry and Public Ownership* (1960); and Andrew Shonfield, *British Economic Policy Since the War* (1958). For more critical accounts see Ernest Watkins, *The Cautious Revolution* (1950); R. H. S. Crossman, *New Fabian Essays* (1952); and Richard Titmuss, *Income Distribution and Social Change* (1962). An important source for the nature of British politics is Samuel Beer, *British Politics in the Collectivist Age* (1965).

For standard thorough accounts of the first years of the French Fourth Republic see Philip M. Williams, *Crisis and Compromise: Politics in the Fourth Republic* (1964); Alexander Werth, *France, 1940–1955* (1956); François Goguel, *France Under the Fourth Republic* (1952); Dorothy Pickles, *French Politics: the First Years of the Fourth Republic* (1953); and Gordon Wright. *The Reshaping of French Democracy* (1948). A highly critical account of the first postwar leaders can be found in Ronald Matthews, *Death of the Fourth Republic* (1954). A study by Catherine Gavin, *Liberated France* (1955), heaps most of the blame for the failures of the Fourth Republic on de Gaulle.

Thorough accounts of postwar Italian politics include M. Grindrod, *The Rebuilding of Italy: Politics and Economics, 1945–55* (1955); Norman Kogan, *A Political History of Postwar Italy* (1966); and Giuseppe Mammarella, *Italy After Fascism: A Political History, 1943–1963* (1964).

For the smaller European countries see W. B. Bader, *Austria Between East and West, 1945–55* (1966); and Erika Weinzierl and Kurt Skalnik,

Osterreich: *Die Zweite Republik,* 2 vols. (1972). The Scandinavian countries are treated in Ander O. Fritof, *The Building of Modern Sweden: The Reign of Gustav V, 1907–1950* (1958); D. A. Rustow, *The Politics of Compromise: A Study of Parties and Cabinet Government in Sweden* (1955); Alice Bourneuf, *Norway: The Planned Revival* (1958); and Harry Eckstein, *Division and Cohesion in Democracy: A Study of Norway* (1966). Postwar Spain is given a balanced treatment in Stanley G. Payne, *Franco's Spain* (1967). Portugal is treated in Hugh Kay, *Salazar and Modern Portugal* (1970); and Charles E. Nowell, *Portugal* (1973). The Greek Civil War is competently covered in E. O'Ballance, *The Greek Civil War, 1944–49* (1966); and W. H. McNeill, *The Greek Dilemma: War and Aftermath* (1947). John O. Iatrides treats the first stages of the civil war in *Revolt in Athens: The Greek Communist "Second Round," 1944–1945* (1972).

4 Economic Recovery in Western Europe

> To present the postwar growth as one of history's unpremeditated happenings would be most unhistorical. For what distinguishes the postwar era from most other periods of economic history is not only its growth but the extent to which this growth was "contrived": generated and sustained by governments and the public.
>
> M. M. Postan, *An Economic History of Western Europe,*
> *1945–1964*

In the decade following 1948, revolutionary economic changes laid the groundwork for what many observers termed the New Europe. By 1960 Europe had regained its place as the leading trading area in the world, with nearly one quarter of the world's industrial output and 40 percent of the world's trade.

Few expected the economic recovery to proceed as rapidly as it did. When the United States was financing the initial stages of European recovery through Marshall Plan aid, no one expected that a decade later we would be studying the rapid European growth rates in order to find some means to stimulate the U. S. economy.

Equally unexpected was the integration of much of Europe, including some former enemies, in one large economic entity known as the European Economic Community or, more familiarly, the Common Market. Although the Common Market failed to achieve all that was expected of it and European economic growth rates slowed appreciably in the late 1960s, by the 1970s some of the highly developed European countries began to approach the wealth and affluence of the United States.

Characteristics of European Economic Recovery

Amid the rubble that covered large areas of Europe at the end of World War II were numerous factories that needed only minor repairs before they could resume operations. Only about 20 percent of Europe's factories were demolished or seriously damaged.

In some cases the destruction wrought by bombing provided the impetus for long-term economic growth. The systematic bombing of residential areas necessitated the reconstruction of entire cities, which served as a stimulus to the building trades. Moreover, the productive resources of the World War II belligerents had increased immensely during the war. A team of German researchers estimated that after damages and dismantling, fixed assets in German industry increased by 7 billion German marks from 1936 to 1945. With this increased productive capacity and the shortage of consumer goods throughout Europe, an absence of financial resources remained the only serious obstacle to rapid economic growth.

Wartime destruction of plants, equipment, and capital goods proved to be an added benefit; it permitted a modernization that made European industry highly competitive. The destruction of a portion of Europe's transportation network prompted the complete modernization of a number of national railway systems. France closed down unnecessary lines, eliminated prewar bottlenecks, and electrified one-fifth of its rail network. Now French trains are considerably longer and faster than British trains and can thus ship goods at lower cost.

Marshall Plan Stimulus to Recovery

The capital necessary to finance the initial reconstruction and modernization of European industry was provided by the United States. The desperate need for funds prompted Western Europe to take sides in the developing Cold War. Disagreements with the Soviet Union over Eastern Europe, the Greek Civil War, and the loss of China to the Communists convinced American congressmen to give Europe financial support.

There was a considerable amount of self-interest in the decision since a financially sound Europe would provide a large market for U. S. products. But there was also considerable compassion for those suffering from wartime losses as well as the realization that the European countries would have to be helped more than they had been after World War I. By 1947 the United States had already provided $15.5 billion in aid to Europe, $6.8 billion of that being outright gifts. But the bulk of American aid, $23 billion, was provided by the Marshall Plan from 1947 to 1952.

By the early 1950s, when economic recovery had been attained, Europe was able to finance its own industrialization. Contributing to this economic recovery was the rapid growth of exports. In 1949 German exports doubled over the previous year, and the following year they increased another 75 percent.

Few expected the rapid economic growth stimulated by the Marshall Plan to be more than a short-term phenomenon. But as Table 4–1 indicates, growth rates through the early 1960s were not significantly lower than those of 1948 to 1954. The cyclical fluctuations of boom and bust typical of prewar economic growth were not characteristic of postwar Europe. It was this long-term sustained growth that was closely studied in the United States with the objective of raising its own growth rates above the 3 to 4 percent

Table 4-1   Compound Rate of Growth of Gross Domestic
Product in Selected Countries, 1949-1963
(percentages)

	1949-1954	1954-1959	1960-1963
West Germany	8.4	6.6	7.6
Austria	5.7	5.7	5.8
Italy	4.8	5.6	6.0
Spain	6.4	5.7	—
Switzerland	5.7	4.6	5.1
Netherlands	4.9	4.1	4.7
France	4.8	4.1	4.6
Portugal	4.2	4.0	—
Norway	4.2	2.7	3.5
Sweden	3.5	3.2	3.4
Denmark	3.7	3.4	3.6
Belgium	3.7	2.5	3.2
United Kingdom	2.7	2.3	2.5
United States	3.6	3.3	—
Canada	4.2	4.4	—

SOURCE: David S. Landes, *The Unbound Prometheus: Technological Change and
Industrial Development in Western Europe from 1750 to the Present*
(Cambridge: Cambridge University Press, 1970), p. 497. Reprinted by
permission of Cambridge University Press.

annual rate of the 1960s. Although some economists have sought to single
out one or two primary causes of the high growth rates, there appear to
have been a multitude of reasons.

Trade Stimulus to Recovery

In addition to Marshall Plan aid, the ever increasing foreign trade provided
a continuing stimulus to economic growth by raising foreign sales, personal
income, and domestic demand. In the 1950s the exports of Germany, Italy,
and the Netherlands rose more than 10 percent annually compared to a 6.4
percent growth rate for world exports. Much of the increase resulted from
the worldwide relaxation of trade restrictions.

Most important for Europeans was the easing of trade restrictions under
the auspices of the newly formed Common Market. However, Common
Market membership was not indispensable for rapid economic growth. One
country outside the Common Market, Austria, experienced a growth of
industrial output second only to that of West Germany. Even if there had
not been a Common Market, the worldwide increase in trade would

probably have been sufficient to stimulate European industrial recovery. But the Common Market did provide a number of advantages. It gave European agriculture a much larger internal market and protected it with uniformly high tariffs against foreign, especially U. S., imports. French agricultural exports to Common Market countries increased during the 1950s from about 15 to 41 percent of the country's total agricultural exports.

Demographic Stimulus to Recovery

Demographic changes have provided much of the impetus for the rapid economic growth following the war. A rising birthrate coupled with the influx of refugees and foreign workers swelled the population of Western Europe from 264 million in 1940 to about 320 million in 1970. In the immediate postwar years, refugees from Eastern Europe provided much of the labor for West German industry. More jobs were available than there were people to fill them after 1948, and each additional laborer added to European output and demand. The refugees constituted a large supply of cheap labor, encouraging investment in industry since it assured industrialists that manufacturing costs would remain low and Europe's exports would remain highly competitive in the world market. When the flow of refugees stopped, foreign workers came from southern Europe and then from southeastern Europe, north Africa, the Iberian Peninsula, and Turkey to man the Western European factories.

Refugees had increased the West German population by 4 million and foreign workers had added another 3.6 million by 1962. But it was in France that the demographic change was most marked. After more than a century of remaining steady, the French population increased from 42 million in 1950 to about 50 million in 1966, and de Gaulle foresaw a France of 100 million people by the year 2000. Although some of this increase was the result of immigration, most of it was brought about by a rise in the birthrate.

Beginning in the interwar period, French leaders tried to encourage population growth by raising family allowances. In the postwar period France increased family allowances and added rent subsidies because the French leaders saw population growth as a way to revitalize the country. Foreign workers came to France primarily from Algeria, Spain, Portugal, and Italy. In Switzerland and Luxembourg, one-third of the labor force came from the less industrialized areas of Europe.

A growing population with the wherewithal to buy new housing and a severe shortage of housing units provided a long-term impetus to industrial expansion. Especially in Germany and Holland, entire cities had to be rebuilt. From 1953 to 1964 Germany had the highest per capita housing construction in the West: half a million units a year. Some economists see

An automobile factory in Turin, Italy which helped to meet the growing consumer demand for passenger cars in postwar Europe.

Karl Gullers—Camera Press London

housing construction as the major reason that Europe did not experience a business recession for so long after the war. These economists are still predicting an end to the building boom and considerably lower growth rates. Such a view does not take into consideration the role of government. Massive government support for the building trades has prevented a slump in construction on several occasions since World War II and is being used again during the 1970s to lessen the impact of Europe's worst postwar recession.

At the center of European economic resurgence is the automobile. As one of the leading economic sectors, it has promoted growth in the steel industry, road building, service stations, and countless associated industries. From a production of about 500,000 vehicles in the late 1940s, European vehicle output now tops 9 million units a year. The age when the theft of a bicycle was a tragedy for the European family has passed. Europeans' love for their cars and for driving speeds rival those of American adolescents. The automobile was as much a status symbol in Europe in the 1960s as it was in the United States a decade earlier, and Europeans now buy new cars before they improve their housing. Such status seeking has also led to a decline in the European's love affair with the

Volkswagen "beetle" and a growing desire for larger, faster cars. Only the rise in gasoline prices brought about by the increased price of Middle East oil has dampened the enthusiasm for larger, more prestigious cars.

The New Capitalism

The fact that European economic growth was not seriously affected by economic slumps in the 1950s as it was in the prewar period results from the retreat of laissez-faire economics and the growth of government intervention in the economy. Postwar economic problems were of such magnitude that governments had to intervene to provide basic foodstuffs and raw materials and to prevent unemployment. Reconstruction tasks could often be carried out only by the government. In some cases, governments decided to nationalize industries that were considered indispensable: railroads, airlines, public utilities, and some heavy industry. Called modern capitalism or neocapitalism, it has been characterized by a mixture of private and government initiative in what is essentially a free enterprise system. Government control of banks and budgetary policies had permitted governments to determine the rate of growth of their economies. Now, when European economies seem headed for recession or inflation, governments step in to regulate the economy by manipulating the monetary system as well as supply and demand.

Despite some variations, the new capitalism entailed government acceptance of Keynesian economics and economic planning. Keynes's *The General Theory of Employment, Interest and Money,* written in 1936, provided the theoretical groundwork for neocapitalism. In addition to his rejection of the traditional free enterprise system, Keynes contended that full employment led to high consumption and increased productivity. Full employment could be attained, he said, through governmental manipulation of taxation and expenditure that would sustain the demand for goods and services at a high level. He rejected the generally accepted theory that governmental stimulation of the economy would lead to inflation and rising prices, which would in turn lead to economic chaos. Keynesian economists take the position that if workers are provided with high wages, they will consume more and industry will prosper. If labor and management accept such policies, class conflict should diminish as the two sides decide on appropriate wages to maintain economic expansion.

In practice, some countries have implemented full employment policies and have established wage guidelines and incomes policies that have met most labor demands. The implementation of Keynesian economics has helped governments to avoid fluctuations in the business cycle that brought unemployment and recession. By stimulating demand during periods of recession, governments have been able to prevent serious depressions. On the other hand, inflation has been kept in check by restricting credit and raising taxes.

The policy of full employment was soon supplemented by a policy of economic growth. In order to meet the steadily growing expenditures for social services and armaments, as well as the public demand for improvements in the standard of living, governments adopted a policy of rapid economic growth. And, now that economic progress was being equated with high annual growth rates, various forms of economic planning had to be adopted in order to direct investment to those economic sectors that would maximize growth.

To achieve maximum economic growth, most countries drew up long-term plans and centralized planning in government agencies. By 1960 France, Belgium, Austria, Italy, Sweden, Norway, and the Netherlands had instituted some form of long-range economic planning. Western planning did not specify production quotas or allocate all raw materials and investment funds, as was done in Eastern Europe and the Soviet Union, but set general guidelines for future economic development and provided financial aid to sectors that would stimulate growth.

The amount of interference in the economies varied considerably in Western Europe. In France the precedents for planning were set under the Popular Front government in the decade before World War II. After the war the new planning agency, the *Commissariat du Plan,* became another arm of the government. Great Britain, because of its historic dedication to laissez-faire principles, was slow to institute economic planning. Only after serious economic difficulties compelled repeated government intervention did British leaders become convinced in 1961 that long-term planning was necessary. Soon after the war, Sweden set up a Labor Market Board in which employers and labor plan construction and investment in order to sustain full employment. The one partial exception in this era of planning is Germany. As a reaction to Nazi intervention in the economy, and at the urging of the Allies, postwar West German leaders sought initially to divest the government of control over industry. Yet the government did intervene in the economy every time it granted subsidies, low-cost loans, or tax breaks to favored enterprises.

One economist has described West German industry as "organized private enterprise." Huge industrial corporations commanding enormous sources of capital remain highly competitive in the international market. Instead of government planning, the Federation of German Industry engages in investment planning and long-term forecasting of supply and demand. The federation is dominated by three large banks that obtain agreements among industrial enterprises to avoid competition. Bankers hold important seats on the supervisory boards, or *Aufsichtsräte,* of the major West German corporations, the big three banks holding more than half the seats.

Industrial Concentration and Nationalization

Planning was made easier throughout Europe by the concentration of industry and by government nationalization of important industries. Once a government nationalized the large enterprises in an industry, smaller competitors were forced to cooperate. Compliance with government planning usually brought with it tax relief, state contracts, and loans. These advantages and nationalization have promoted the development of huge industrial corporations.

One such corporation, the *Société Générale* of Belgium, dominates the Belgian economy. As one of its directors put it, "The *Société* is not too large; it's just that Belgium is too small." By 1960 it had under its control 40 percent of the iron and steel industry, 30 percent of coal, 25 percent of electrical energy, and 70 percent of the insurance companies.

Four huge corporations — Royal Dutch Shell, Unilever, Philips, and AKU — dominate the Dutch economy. The annual income of only one, Royal Dutch Shell, is larger than that of Switzerland.

In Italy monopolization and state control have permitted the government to participate extensively in long-range industrial planning. Some of the firms that were nationalized during the Fascist period are now enormous industrial conglomerates. By 1963, the government-owned IRI *(Istituto per la Ricostruzione Industriale)* consisted of 120 companies with 280,000 employees. Financial resources are firmly under the control of the government; the major commercial bank is nationalized, and the IRI controls over four-fifths of the capital of the next three largest banks. The IRI and the other great public corporation, ENI *(Ente Nazionale Idrocarburi),* were responsible for more than one-fifth of all capital investment in manufacturing, transportation, and communications in the early 1960s.

In Austria the nationalized industries account for 24 percent of industrial production and 27 percent of exports. Government control extends also to finance.

In France, jurisdiction over the most important French banks, the *Caisse des Depôts* and the *Crédit National,* gives the French government control over credit.

A noneconomic factor that has contributed mightily to postwar recovery is the belief among industrialists and civil servants alike that economic expansion is not only desirable but attainable. Despite the tendency of some French and English to avoid rapid economic growth lest they be forced to take unnecessary risks to sustain the growth rates, most European industrialists and civil servants have become supporters of what M. M. Postan calls growthmanship. For example, the director of ENI in Italy, Enrico Mattei, while successfully developing Italy's natural gas deposits, pushed production to the point of exhausting Italian resources. As important as the attitude of the managers is the attitude of the general public that economic growth is necessary and achievable. Europeans are now willing to make long-term investments in their economies instead of hoarding their money or sending it abroad in search of profits.

Agricultural Developments

Changes in agriculture have rivaled the revolutionary transformation of industry. Many European countries have made the transition from small-scale subsistence agriculture before 1945 to agricultural production aimed primarily at the much larger urban market. Despite the rapidly growing demand in Europe, a technological revolution in agriculture has produced massive surpluses in the 1970s.

In 1974, 40 percent of the bumper 1973 wine crop had to be distilled into alcohol. And the EEC was also compelled to either buy up or dispose of especially large surpluses of dairy products and meat.

Increased mechanization, greater use of fertilizers and insecticides, improved seed, and modern equipment have produced the surpluses; the number of tractors in the EEC rose sixfold from 370,000 in 1950 to 2,330,000 in 1962. The number of farm animals has been increased through artificial insemination, while their size and quality have improved by better feed and selective breeding.

The development of larger, more efficient agricultural units has not kept pace with technological changes primarily because of government policies. Lest they antagonize agricultural voters, governments have subsidized agriculture and have thus preserved many small high-cost farms. In France, Germany, and the Benelux countries, strong organizations of farmers mobilize their members to prevent any change in this policy. Armed with pitchforks, farmers have opposed all EEC attempts to alter their privileged status.

The Common Market perpetuated the system of government protection and high agricultural prices. High tariffs were set against foreign products as tariffs between the EEC members were slowly reduced. To offset lower international prices, an EEC agricultural fund subsidized members' exports. Until the mid-1970s such protection placed a disproportionate burden on the mass of consumers, who had to pay considerably more for their food than consumers in the rest of the world. Third-world countries have accused the EEC of being a rich man's club because of its exclusion of foreign agricultural products.

One of the major obstacles to British entry into the EEC was Britain's agricultural sector, which is on a larger scale and more productive than those on the Continent. British farms average 200 acres each, compared to a continental average of about 40 acres. But the small total acreage in Britain, necessitating large imports of food, was a sufficient enticement to EEC members once Britain promised it would slowly stop purchasing lower-priced products from its Commonwealth partners.

Membership in the EEC has brought about a major transformation in Italian agriculture. Many peasants who farmed marginal land in the south and central part of Italy were drawn to the industries in northern Italy, Switzerland, Germany, and France. This migration put an end to the tillage of marginal land and thus reduced Italian agricultural output. Italy must now import more food from its EEC partners — at the much higher supported prices — than is produced by the remaining peasant population. While this rationalization of industrial and agricultural production is one of the EEC goals, it has placed a special burden on Italy's balance of payments. In 1974 France felt it necessary to subsidize its exports to Italy when Italy had to reduce food imports to overcome a severe financial crisis.

France: Economic Development

Beneath the surface similarity of postwar economic development there are many national differences. Even within each state there are considerable regional differences and conflicts over the rapid growth of industry. Nowhere is this more apparent than in France. The French economy was encumbered with small businesses and their centuries-old attitude, "What I have may be small but it is mine." Small-business opposition to the concentration of French industry was centered in the PME (Unions of Small and Medium-size Business) and the Poujadist movement. Before the PME accepted the so-called new France in 1958 it constantly opposed the concentration of business and industry and upheld the small family enterprise as typically French.

More violent in its support of a static France and in its opposition to the modernization of French industry was the Poujadist movement. Led by a small grocer, Pierre Poujade, the movement opposed the Common Market, fought higher wages for labor, and sought government support for small businesses. Although Poujadism itself faded, the movement lived on. In the early 1970s Jean Royer, who is both the mayor of Tours and France's minister of commerce and small business, became the new champion of the small businessman. A bill he proposed gives small businessmen who sit on municipal councils the power to veto the building of huge chain stores or supermarkets in their areas. In 1974, serious clashes occurred in France between the local municipal councils and employees of supermarkets that were prevented from expanding.

But there is the other France, dominated by the new citizenry bent on economic modernization. This is the France of the Caravelle, Concorde, Renault, and the Plan. It is also the France of Robert Schuman and Jean Monnet, the architects of French entry into the European Economic Community. It is the France of those teams of industrialists, the *missions de productivité,* who studied in the United States after the war to prepare themselves to put France on a modern economic footing. Although Schuman supported French entry into the EEC primarily to rid Europe of its internecine wars, he was also aware of its great economic potential. Jean Monnet's first economic plan concentrated on the long-term reconstruction of basic industries rather than the alleviation of the housing shortage.

This is also the France that has been renowned for its technical creativity since the nineteenth century. A prime example of this creativity was the conception and production of an excellent jet passenger plane, the Caravelle, long before a similar plane flew in the United States. This creativity also characterized the building of the first supersonic passenger plane, Concorde, in the 1970s. This is of course the France that is responsible for the dramatic social and cultural changes that threaten the individualism and uniqueness of the old France. Laurence Wylie's study of change in the small French village of Roussillon, *Village in the Vaucluse,* indicates that this new France has won out over the France of the PME and Poujade. In the 1950s peasants refused to plant orchards lest they be destroyed in World War III. In the 1960s the peasants were going into debt to plant olive trees that would not mature for twenty years.

Before Charles de Gaulle returned to power in 1958, the French economic miracle was well under way. As Table 4-1 shows, the French gross domestic product had been increasing at over 4 percent a year for a decade. Nevertheless, the stability provided by the de Gaulle regime and the propitious timing of the devaluation of the franc in 1958, immediately before a rapid expansion of world trade, increased the nation's exports dramatically. Gold and foreign exchange reserves jumped from a mere 10 million francs in 1959 to 28.6 billion by late 1966.

West Germany: Economic Development

A superficial view of the West German economy might leave one with the incorrect impression that postwar German economic growth is the result of laissez-faire economics. While it is true that the German government does not engage in long-term planning as the French government does, other institutions in Germany do engage in short-term planning.

As we have seen, the Federation of German Industry, in concert with the banks, manipulates investment in order to regulate industrial output and control prices, and the German government constantly intervenes in the economy by means of taxation and subsidies. One example of this tactic is the 1951 Investment Aid Act, which taxed German business a billion marks in order to finance reconstruction in heavy industry and to develop energy sources. Another measure, the Housing Act of 1950, provided public subsidized housing projects for low-income families and housing projects with tax preferences for the builders. As a result, before 1961 the government financed more than half the housing construction by direct capital investments and tax reductions granted to builders.

The role of German banks in German industry has grown immensely since 1945. Immediately after the war the Allies divided Germany into eleven states, each with its own budget and taxing power. To prevent the concentration of banking typical of the Nazi period, ties between the banking services of the various states were prohibited. However, the Allied decision to fortify West Germany so as to counter the presumed threat from the Soviet Union led directly to the removal of economic barriers between the German states and the reconcentration of German banking. By 1950 the Deutsche and Dresdener banks were again in control of all their branch banks, and the remaining member of the big three, the Commerz Bank, regained control of its branch banks in 1958. Two years later these three banks controlled about 56 percent of German industrial shares. The Deutsche Bank, according to a London banker, is equivalent in size to the English Midland, Barclay's, Hambro's, Baring's, Rothschild's, and Cazenove's all rolled into one.

The banks and industry cooperate extensively to regulate output and avoid destructive competition. By occupying almost one-fourth of all seats on corporate boards of directors, eleven German banks discourage investments that they consider unproductive or that they think will increase competition among firms associated with them. They have been able to convince companies to produce products cooperatively and have prevented the overproduction of goods. While such regulation by banks, firms, and trade associations is never as comprehensive as the national planning in France, it does permit a division of production that is not typical of a true laissez-faire state.

The postwar concentration of industry has permitted closer control. By 1960, the 100 largest firms accounted for 40 percent of industrial production. Seven West German firms were among the twenty largest European enterprises in the 1960s: Volkswagen, Siemens, Thyssen–Hutte, Daimler–Benz, Farbwerke–Hoechst, Farbenfabriken Bayer, and Krupp.

Nationalized until 1961, Volkswagen has epitomized the resurgence of German industry. The car that the British considered too ugly and noisy to achieve mass acceptance has been one of the major factors in West Germany's favorable balance of trade since the early 1950s. In 1967 Volkswagen sold more cars in the United States than in Germany. Cleverly merchandised — "Your second car, even if you haven't got a first" — Volkswagen faced little serious competition from European car manufacturers until the 1960s. Then it was challenged by producers of larger family cars, primarily Fiat, and its European sales slipped below those of Fiat.

Volkswagen was also falling victim to the status consciousness of Europeans, who no longer thought the beetle an appropriate status symbol. In the United States it was challenged by smaller American cars that offered similar economy. Although Volkswagen's sales remain high because of the production of new models and continued high foreign sales, it has been unable to raise its sales in the past four years. In 1974 VW was offering 7,000 marks to any worker who would quit.

Britain: Economic Decline

Compared to the high economic growth rates on the Continent, the British economy has experienced a relative decline since 1945. As Table 41 indicates, the growth of gross national product from 1949 to 1963 was three times as high in West Germany as it was in Great Britain. French, Italian, and Austrian growth rates have been about twice as high. This situation has led one British critic to castigate his country as "the stagnant society."

Another indication of the relative economic decline has been a reduction in the British share of world trade from 21.3 percent in 1951 to 19 percent in 1956. However, when British growth rates are compared to those of the United States and Belgium, which suffered less war damage, the differences in growth rates are considerably less. Unquestionably, there has been a relative decline, but it should be pointed out that Great Britain has sometimes been unfairly compared to countries that were much less developed and in need of massive postwar reconstruction — Germany, Italy, and Japan.

A large share of the responsibility for Great Britain's discouraging economic performance rests with the government. Both the postwar Labour and Conservative governments were reluctant to interfere in industry. Nationalization was viewed not as a means to enhance efficiency but as a last-ditch effort to save stagnant industries. The vast majority of British firms received little support or direction from the government. Lurking in the back of every Labour and Conservative minister's mind was the conviction that the free enterprise system, which had served Britain so well in the past, would be sufficient for the future. Therefore, contrary to the continental experience, long-term planning was rejected in favor of haphazard short-term intervention in the economy.

One example is a Labour decision to reduce industrial investment in the belief that it would ease the pressure on the external balance of payments. The expectation was that industrial imports would be reduced and more capital equipment would be exported. But instead, output went down and more consumer goods had to be imported.

In some cases, large British firms prevented government intervention in the economy. Development councils, proposed by the Labour government to aid research and promote exports, were rejected by large enterprises on the assumption that small firms would dominate the councils and that the councils were a step toward nationalization.

Industrial management hindered economic growth in other ways. Managers failed to modernize their factories and make their products internationally competitive. One study has shown that American-controlled firms in Great Britain have yielded 50 percent higher returns than the British-managed firms because of lower administrative costs, better salesmanship, higher productivity, and greater concentration of capital investment.

The British automobile industry represents a clear example of Britain's inability to capitalize on its postwar potential. With the continental car companies unable to meet European demand, the British had an excellent opportunity to break into the European market. But English car manufacturers resisted mergers and continued to produce a huge variety of automobiles, none of which could capture a large share of the continental market. Even after two companies merged in 1951 to form the British Motors Corporation, the new firm continued to produce the same old cars. Eventually it did turn out the Mini, thereby breaking the tradition of heavy, rugged cars typical of British automakers. But by this time, other European car manufacturers were meeting the European demand.

A 1968 merger of BMC and Leyland Motors into one huge enterprise called British Leyland Motors, coupled with Britain's entry into the Common Market, may eventually raise the sales of British automobiles. But thus far, foreign sales of British cars are restricted to a few Europeans and Americans who consider ownership of a Rolls Royce or a Rover a status symbol.

Italy: Economic Development

Despite a slow beginning, since 1954 the Italian economic growth rate has exceeded those of all other EEC states except West Germany. However, this growth was restricted to the north, where Italians enjoy a standard of living similar to northern Europeans. Except for small pockets of industrialization, southern Italy has remained an underdeveloped area.

In the early 1970s a large portion of EEC development money was still going to southern Italy. Italian politicians and industrialists were at first more intent on developing their markets within the EEC than on developing the south. Fiat, the largest automobile manufacturer in Europe, refused to open plants in the south on the ground that industry had to be concentrated in order to meet modern competition.

To be sure, the concentration of industry and banking has been a major reason for Italy's rapid industrial expansion. The fact that IRI controls a number of banks and 120 companies makes possible a concentration of capital for investment purposes, a reduction of domestic competition, and a focus on the European market. The concentration of oil and gas resources permits ENI to compete with the large American petroleum companies for foreign markets and petroleum resources. Plentiful supplies of labor have kept wages low and Italian products highly competitive in Europe and the international market. In 1966 Italian wages were only about half those in West Germany and Great Britain. Serious labor unrest was avoided through the employment of thousands of southern Italian laborers in Germany, Switzerland, and France.

A rapidly growing domestic and foreign demand and an internal concentration of industry have created a number of mammoth firms. In the

1960s Italy was producing most of the refrigerators used in the Common Market, and Fiat had become the largest automobile manufacturer in Europe. Within Italy the demand for cars continually outstripped the supply. In 1960 one out of every twenty-one Italians owned a car; in 1968, one out of seven. And Olivetti has become one of the world's largest producers of office machines.

Postwar Development Patterns

By the end of the 1960s Europe was divided among a variety of economic organizations and exhibited a multitude of economic faces. Wide differences existed between the advanced industrialized west and north and the predominantly agrarian underdeveloped south. Economic change was beginning to transform Spain, but Portugal, Greece, and Turkey had undergone little economic modernization.

Emigration to the labor-hungry factories of the north provided a measure of relief for a small segment of the population, and worker remittances to their families provided some stimulus to the south, but this could not be a long-term substitute for economic modernization at home. In some cases emigration tended to thwart modernization by siphoning off skilled professionals and laborers. In agriculture emigration often brought improvement by removing surplus population from the land, but sometimes large areas were virtually depopulated, agricultural output dropped, and costs rose as food had to be imported. The short-term benefits of emigration became apparent in the 1970s when a Western European economic recession forced many migrant workers to return to their native countries.

Western Europe itself was shocked by the high inflation rates and reduced growth rates of the early 1970s, as detailed in chapter 13. The Keynesian manipulation of the economy no longer produced immediate results, as it had done in the 1950s and early 1960s. European optimism flagged as growth rates dipped and unemployment figures climbed. Countless economic conferences were held to ascertain the problems and provide the remedies for economic stagnation.

But the slump was probably unavoidable. The growth rates had been extremely high for nearly two decades but could not be sustained indefinitely. With consumption levels approaching those of the United States, Western Europe began to experience similar economic difficulties. There were limits to the demand that could be stimulated in order to perpetuate high rates of growth. Europe was more dependent on exports than the United States, but was now facing competition from areas of high output and low labor cost such as Japan. Rising unemployment held down domestic demand. The advanced states of Europe will undoubtedly be hard put to attain the economic growth rates of the past and will have little choice but to endure a certain amount of unemployment. As John Kenneth

Galbraith pointed out, demand can be artificially stimulated by convincing people that they must buy unnecessary commodities, but there is a point beyond which the market becomes satiated.

FURTHER READING

An excellent survey of European industrialization with coverage of the postwar period can be found in David Landes, *The Unbound Prometheus* (1970). Indispensable examinations of the postwar period are Andrew Shonfield, *Modern Capitalism: The Changing Balance of Public and Private Power* (1969); M. M. Postan, *An Economic History of Western Europe, 1945–1964* (1967); and A. Maddison, *Economic Growth in the West* (1964). A stimulating analysis of the role of labor in promoting postwar growth can be found in Charles P. Kindleberger, *Europe's Postwar Growth: The Role of Labor Supply* (1967).

For details of French planning see J. and A. M. Hackett, *Economic Planning in France* (1961); and Pierre Massé, *Histoire, Methode et Doctrine de la Planification Française* (1962). The British economy is treated in J. C. R. Dow, *The Management of the British Economy, 1945–1960* (1964); and Andrew Shonfield, *British Economic Policy Since the War* (1958). For Germany see Henry C. Wallich, *Mainsprings of German Revival* (1955); and Frederick G. Reuss, *Fiscal Policy for Growth Without Inflation: The German Experiment* (1963). Austrian economic development is covered in K. W. Rothschild, *Osterreichs Wirtschaftsstruktur* (1962). For Sweden see Holger Heide, *Die Langfristige Wirtschaftsplannung in Schweden* (1965). For Italy see Vera Lutz, *Italy: A Study in Economic Development* (1962); and George H. Hildebrand, *Growth and Structure in the Economy of Modern Italy* (1965).

Among the many publications of economic statistics are the Organization for Economic Cooperation and Development annual surveys of all member states, OECD *Observer,* United Nations Statistical Yearbooks, and the United Nations annual economic surveys of Europe.

5 Western European Politics, 1948-1965

France intends to once again exercise sovereignty over her own
territory, at present infringed upon by the permanent presence of
Allied military forces and by the use which is being made of her air-
space, to end her participation in the integrated command, and to no
longer place her forces at the disposition of NATO.

Guy de Carmoy, *Les Politiques Etrangères de la France, 1944–1966*

The rapid economic growth in Western Europe and improved East–West
relations determined the course of political development from 1948 to 1965.
Spared serious economic crisis after 1948, the politically moderate and
right-of-center forces in the major Western European countries were not
challenged seriously by the left. Growing economic affluence, combined
with government extension of social welfare services and full employment
policies, stilled demands for truly revolutionary political change. Parties on
the left, kept from office by the improving economic conditions and their
own revolutionary rhetoric, began to adopt reformist rather than
revolutionary policies. Moderate reformers, such as Willy Brandt in West
Germany, emerged as the new leaders of Socialist parties.

Only the Communist parties of France and Italy, which attracted
primarily working-class support, continued to pay lip service to
revolutionary objectives. But even their revolutionary zeal was dampened
by the Soviet Union's suppression of the Hungarian Revolution in 1956.
Social Democratic parties gained or shared government office in the 1960s
in Italy and Germany only by compromising their former ideals or by
breaking away from their revolutionary associates and becoming reformist
parties similar to the British Labor party and the Scandinavian Social
Democratic parties. In foreign affairs, Europe's economic resurgence and a
reduction of Cold War tensions led to a gradual restoration of European
self-confidence and the reduction of United States influence in Europe,
especially in de Gaulle's France.

Italian Political Affairs

The impact of economic improvement and the Cold War is clearly discernible in Italy during this period. As described in chapter 3, the Cold War and United States pressure had led the Christian Democratic party (DC) to drive the Communist party from the government in 1947. That same year the reformist issue split the Socialist party into a reformist Social Democratic wing under Guiseppe Saragat and the still revolutionary Socialists (PSI) under Pietro Nenni and Lelio Basso. In a quadripartite government coalition held together only by the parties' shared hostility toward communism, Saragat found that there was considerable opposition to his reformist ideas, especially since the dominant Christian Democratic party based its strength on the Catholic Church, big business, big landowners, the lower-middle class, and the peasantry.

Eventually, with the aid of the left wing of the DC led by Alcide de Gasperi, some of the Saragat-backed reforms were begun. In 1949 and 1950 a few large estates totaling 20 million acres were expropriated in the south and sold to the peasants. But after the initial redistribution, the DC failed to push further agrarian reform. Only mass emigration to the industrial areas in the north temporarily relieved the situation. As a result, in the 1953 elections the Communist party gained a million votes in the south.

Meanwhile, Nenni had led the Socialist party into close cooperation with the Communist party. But Nenni, never comfortable with this alliance, offered to break with the Communists in 1953 and enter a coalition government with the DC if his PSI were given important cabinet positions. Rejecting this offer, de Gasperi and then a succession of premiers put together bare majorities that reduced the government to immobility for the next five years. Only domestic prosperity and decreasing international tension made such government inaction tolerable.

A leftward trend in successive elections in 1953, 1958, and 1963 resulted from decreasing Cold War tensions, rapid economic growth, and the moderating position taken by Palmiro Togliatti, leader of the Communist party. The Communists were responding to a growing sense of economic well-being which was reflected in labor's selection of more moderate factory and labor union officials. Shocked by the Soviet Union's crushing of the Hungarian Revolution in 1956, Togliatti became convinced that his rightward shift was the proper course.

When Nenni's PSI decided in 1957 to break with the Communist party and seek a coalition with the DC, Togliatti led the PCI even further to the right in order to restore the left coalition. Despite this, Nenni continued to seek a role for the PSI in a coalition with the DC. The attempt to gain PSI approval for the coalition failed in 1957 when the left wing of the party gained a majority against Nenni. When he finally gained a majority for his position, his left-wing opponents within the PSI broke away and formed the Socialist Party of Proletarian Unity, or PSIUP.

Nenni's efforts finally succeeded in 1962 when DC leaders agreed to a center–left coalition with the PSI. The left wing of the DC, led by Aldo Moro and Amintore Fanfani, had been trying to arrange an "opening to the left" since 1958. Although there was considerable opposition within the DC to a coalition with the PSI, public support for it was growing. A strong trend to the left in the 1958 parliamentary elections indicated that Italians were finding the parties on the left more acceptable and that they were becoming discontented with the government's immobility.

Adding immensely to the public's acceptance of the Socialists and their desire for social reform was the papacy's acceptance of the welfare state in the 1960s. This momentous change in papal policy was a direct result of the election of Angelo Roncalli as Pope John XXIII in 1958. A product of humble beginnings himself, Cardinal Roncalli had gained further knowledge of the world's ills on diplomatic missions to the Balkans and as papal nuncio to France. When he became pope he was determined to bring the church into line with modern political and social change. This meant a reversal of the papacy's century-old opposition to all forms of socialism and, in the 1960s, adjusting to the institution of the welfare state throughout Europe. In the 1961 Papal Bull *Mater et Magistra* (Mother and Teacher) Pope John expressed the papacy's approval of the mixed economy, economic planning, and social justice. A second major papal encyclical, *Pacem in Terris* (Peace on Earth), confirmed this new papal attitude only a few weeks before the 1963 elections.

Within the DC Moro maneuvered his party closer to the PSI by encouraging DC–PSI coalitions at the local level. With the support gained from forty such coalitions, Moro and Fanfani convinced the majority of the party to accept the PSI in 1962. The PSI had to accept a pro-Western position, including continued membership in NATO and the EEC, and the DC accepted the PSI plan for the nationalization of electric power and the establishment of more regional governments. The DC had originally opposed the regional governments, fearing the left would control most of them. When the left made further gains in the 1963 elections, indicating an increased desire for reforms, Moro was able to convince the recalcitrant DC deputies that his course was necessary in order to keep the DC in power. After some initial difficulties, Moro put together a left–center cabinet with Nenni as vice-premier. This leftward trend continued into the 1970s as Cold War tensions declined and the Communist party became even more reformist.

West German Political Affairs

More than any other European country, West Germany reflects the impact of economic prosperity on government and politics. In what is often described as the German economic miracle, the Federal Republic had once again become a major economic power by mid-century. German exports rose from 8.4 billion to 52.3 billion marks between 1950 and 1963 and comprised 11 percent of world exports. During the same period, industrial production nearly tripled. (See chapter 4 for comparative growth rates and reasons for the economic recovery.) This rapid recovery permitted Christian Democratic (CDU) Chancellor Konrad Adenauer to rule in an authoritarian manner. Convinced that the failure of the Weimar Republic in the 1920s resulted from a weak executive and internecine warfare among the many political parties, Adenauer believed with de Gaulle that too much democracy would lead to political failure and economic chaos. Supported by widespread voter approval for his policies of stability and anticommunism, Adenauer instituted a policy of chancellor democracy that circumvented the authority of parliament whenever possible. Few voices were raised in opposition to his extensive use of executive authority lest economic growth be slowed or the delicate position of Germany in international affairs be destroyed.

The government placed increased industrial production above social equalization. But because of the booming economy, industrial workers could boast of higher salaries than those paid in other major continental countries. Sharing in the prosperity, the trade unions dropped all references to Marxism and initiated a form of unionism similar to that of North America (see chapter 9). Members of the Confederation of German Trade Unions (DGB) take a major part in developing social legislation within the federal parliament, and workers are included on the governing boards of industrial enterprises.

In some respects the Adenauer government provided West Germans with the stability and self-confidence to recover from wartime defeat and destruction and to be accepted by other European states. His staunch anti-Nazism, which led to his imprisonment during World War II, and his efficient and honest government restored German pride and European trust in a reconstituted German state. His friendship for France permitted the restoration of the French-occupied Saar region to Germany in 1957 and led to extensive cooperation between France and Germany. His foreign policy had a strong pro-Western orientation, and the West needed allies in the Cold War and the Korean War. Together, these led first to German rearmament within NATO, including French acceptance of rearmament when Britain promised to keep troops in West Germany; and ultimately they led to German independence in 1955. Adenauer also guided West Germany into membership in the Council of Europe, the European Coal and Steel Community, and eventually the EEC.

One unfortunate outcome of Adenauer's aggressively pro-Western policy was his rejection of a Soviet offer in 1954 of German unification in exchange for neutrality. Adenauer also feared that his party would lose office in a reunited Germany since most East Germans, being Protestant, would not vote for the Catholic-based CDU.

Actually, the Soviet Union attached so many conditions to the unification proposal, especially the withdrawal of all Allied troops before elections could be held, that the Allies would never have accepted them. Moreover, both the Soviet Union and the West wanted a Germany created in their own image. Khrushchev wanted a reunited Germany only if it retained the "political and social achievements" of East Germany. Of course, the Allies and Adenauer were unwilling to accept the extensive social changes already instituted in East Germany. Finally, neither France nor the Soviet Union was happy at the prospect of a new German state of nearly 70 million people.

Perhaps the greatest change brought about by the sustained prosperity in Germany was the transformation of the German Social Democratic Party (SPD). Until the mid-1950s the SPD was led by prewar Socialists who had suffered severely under the Nazi regime. Their first postwar leader, Kurt Schumacher, had spent ten years in Nazi concentration camps. Under his leadership the SPD favored reunification, opposed close association with the capitalist West, and strenuously opposed NATO, German rearmament, and European integration. However, when the party failed to gain major national office or influence political and economic affairs, some of the younger members began to challenge the SPD's orthodox Marxist program and agitate for a reformist course within a laissez-faire state. At the local level, reformers slowly replaced those desiring more revolutionary change.

The most dramatic change was the election of the reformer Willy Brandt to head the SPD in Berlin in 1958. Large election gains for the CDU in the 1957 parliamentary elections provided the reformers with a major argument for adapting the SPD program to what they saw as the economic and political realities of the day. At the Bad Godesberg party conference in 1959, communism was condemned by a reformist majority who declared, "The dictatorship of the proletariat is no longer a reality in our time."

By a vote of 324 to 16, the conference reversed party policy on almost every important issue. It dropped Marxist terminology, rejected nationalization of industry, approved private property, and accepted the Western alliance and rearmament. The economic success of the German socialmarket economy had overwhelmed those who still favored a Marxist approach.

The selection of Willy Brandt to head the party sealed the victory of the reformers. In their eyes, their choice of course was proved right in the 1961 parliamentary elections when SPD seats in the *Bundestag* increased from 169 to 190 and CDU seats dropped from 270 to 242.

The 1961 elections indicated further that the CDU was beginning to lose its hold on the German electorate. A measure of the disenchantment could be attributed to the slowing of economic growth and the onset of a mild recession. But other factors were political infighting in the CDU and Adenauer's increasingly authoritarian behavior. In 1959 Adenauer had agreed to take the post of president and give up the chancellorship to Ludwig Erhard. When he realized that Erhard, whom he personally disliked, would be the real ruler in Germany and the presidency would be only a titular post, Adenauer went back on his word. This type of behavior was tolerated when economic growth was rapid and Germany's future was in doubt; now it became intolerable.

After the election losses in 1961 Adenauer managed to gain support for his plan to form a new cabinet only by promising to retire before the 1965 elections. But before he retired he became involved in another incident that was to blemish his own reputation and that of the CDU. Adenauer's defense minister, Franz Josef Strauss, irritated when the magazine *Der Spiegel* published what he considered to be secret military information, arrested five members of the editorial staff. When both Strauss and Adenauer refused to take responsibility for the affair, the Free Democratic party members of the cabinet threatened to resign and thus bring down the government. Strauss was eventually forced to resign, and Adenauer promised to resign in the fall of 1963.

This incident brought into question Adenauer's, and indirectly the CDU's, commitment to democratic government. It tarnished Adenauer's reputation and made the ministry of his successor, Erhard, much more difficult. Throughout West Germany it unleashed a spate of criticism of many CDU programs. Critics contended that Germans had not received the proper education in the principles of democracy because of Adenauer's authoritarian government. The criticism further indicated that the German public did not want a return to arbitrary government.

When Erhard failed to stem the economic recession and the Free Democrats quit the coalition government in 1966, the way was paved for the SPD to share power with the CDU in 1966 and gain power in a coalition with the Free Democrats in 1969.

French Political Affairs

The changes in French socialism and politics have been as dramatic as those in West Germany. As early as 1948 the Socialist party (SFIO) accepted the Western orientation of French foreign policy and coalition with the Christian Democrats (MRP). Socialist leader Ramadier refused to support the candidacy of Communist leader Thorez for French premier. The exclusion of both Communists and Gaullists from the government after 1947 produced an extremely fragile centerleft coalition of the SFIO, MRP, Radicals, and Moderates. This quadripartist coalition, held together primarily by a shared dislike for the left and right, could not agree on a unified economic or colonial policy.

Governments fell rapidly as colonial problems multiplied, but even successes in colonial policy were not always sufficient to insure government stability. Premier Pierre Mendès-France had ended French involvement in the Indochina war and granted autonomy to Tunisia in 1954, but he fell from office the following year when he was unable to change his Radical party's economic policies from laissez-faire to economic planning.

France's Communist party had also changed considerably since the war. By the 1960s it had become cautious and bureaucratic, offering little that was different from the government and spawning a multiplicity of new left groups that were highly critical of the Communists. A group of French left-wing intellectuals at the Club Jean Moulin declared that "Nobody knows any more what socialism is. . ." and asserted that European neocapitalism had raised living standards in Western Europe more than socialism had in Eastern Europe.

Economic recovery had other important political ramifications. When Charles de Gaulle returned to power in 1958, it enabled him to institute many of the policies he had favored for a decade or more and provided the wherewithal for France to play the leading role in Europe.

However, it was a colonial issue, Algeria, that had the greatest impact on French domestic policy in the 1950s. The Algerian rebellion brought down the Fourth Republic, returned de Gaulle to power, and enabled him to change dramatically the French tradition of a dominant legislature. It also thrust de Gaulle and France into a position of European dominance that prompted some observers to dub European history from 1958 to 1968 "the de Gaulle era." For Europe as a whole, de Gaulle's resolution of the Algerian problem instilled a new confidence and respect that enabled Europe to chart a more independent course.

The Fourth Republic was split over Algeria. The right, including the Gaullists, strenuously opposed any concessions to the Algerian rebels. Support for the right came from more than a million French settlers (*colons*), four-fifths of them born in Algeria, and from a large segment of the French army. The loss of Indochina in 1954, the failure of the Anglo–French force against Egypt's Nasser in 1956, and the granting of independence to Tunisia and Morocco in 1956 (see chapter 6) made French rightists and the army determined to keep Algeria. The army, numbering nearly half a million in Algeria by 1957, had concluded that the French government could not be trusted to "save" Algeria for France. Attacks from the right diminished the stability of the Fourth Republic and led to a steady decline in its control over the army.

Ironically, a decisive attempt to resolve the Algerian issue by the normally indecisive Fourth Republic brought about its downfall. On the last day of January in 1956 an Algerian reform bill, providing for regional autonomy and equality of voting for Muslims and Europeans in Algeria, was rendered unworkable by French military action against the Algerian rebels, who now refused to accept the bill. The Fourth Republic selected a new ministry headed by Pierre Pflimlin, a man the army and the *colons* expected would offer concessions to the Algerian rebels. But army units with *colon* support occupied the palace of the governor–general in Algiers and set up a

Committee of Public Safety with General Jacques Massu at its head. The rightists and certain army officers then planned a paratroop attack on Paris.

This anarchic situation enabled the Gaullists to demand the return of de Gaulle to prevent a civil war in France. After a round of negotiations with President René Coty, the national assembly approved de Gaulle as the new premier on June 1, 1958. When de Gaulle told the French Assembly that he had formed a government to preserve the republic, one skeptical deputy warned, "Today, chamber music. Tomorrow, a brass band."

The crisis atmosphere gave de Gaulle the opportunity to institute the kind of government that would provide the strong executive authority he desired. Never wavering from his conviction that the French government should not be dominated by the legislature, de Gaulle pushed through a constitution that increased the power of the executive and reduced the authority of the assembly. The constitution that set up the Fifth Republic, approved by eighty percent of the voters on September 28, 1958, permitted the president to appoint the premier and to dissolve parliament, but it required an absolute majority in the assembly to dissolve parliament. Although the premier and the cabinet theoretically shared executive authority with the president, de Gaulle now wielded power comparable to that of the American president.

Elections in November further solidified de Gaulle's position by giving the Gaullist UNR (Union for the New Republic) 189 of the 576 seats in the National Assembly. A new electoral system required a runoff election in districts where no candidate received a majority. In the runoff election, voters who had originally voted for non-Communist candidates now gave their votes to the remaining non-Communists and reduced the representation of the Communists and their allies from 150 deputies to only 10. De Gaulle was selected as president by an overwhelming 78.5 percent of the votes from an electoral college of over 80,000 voters.

In 1958 de Gaulle's objectives were not yet clear even in his own mind. He was influenced by foreign criticism and the possibility that a United Nations vote of condemnation might thwart his objective of restoring French prestige in the world. Now, armed with the new powers given him by the new constitution, he could tackle the Algerian problem with increased confidence and bring the army back under the control of the government.

To gain military support, de Gaulle at first kept his aims vague, thus leading the army to believe that he would keep Algeria French. Although he wanted to retain Algeria, he realized by 1959 that the Algerian rebels, led by the FLN (National Liberation Front), would not accept continued French suzerainty. His offer of Algerian self-determination in September 1959 was refused by an ever more confident FLN leadership and violently opposed by the French army leaders in Algeria, who now felt betrayed. In January 1960 a mass uprising against de Gaulle's policies, the Barricades Revolt, failed when metropolitan France rallied to his side.

Algerians celebrating their hard-won independence in the Place du Gouvernement.

When de Gaulle began to speak about a possible Algerian Republic after November 1960, the French army and *colons* in Algeria adopted yet more violent tactics. A Secret Army Organization (OAS) was set up in Algeria to intimidate those who would support a free Algeria and to bring down de Gaulle's government by means of terrorism and assassination. In April 1961 the army generals in Algeria rebelled, took over the government of Algeria, and threatened military action against metropolitan France. Only de Gaulle's immense prestige made defeat of the generals possible. Supported overwhelmingly in France, he appealed directly to military units not to support the generals. When the air force and the navy chose to follow him, the army generals had to surrender.

De Gaulle was now determined to resolve the Algerian problem and end military disobedience by granting independence and bringing the army home. On March 18, 1962, negotiators for the FLN and the French government met at Evian-les-Bains and decided to grant Algeria its full independence on July 3, 1962. These Evian Accords granted the *colons* equal rights and provided compensation for the property of those who wished to leave Algeria. Despite widespread OAS terrorism to keep the French settlers in Algeria, within a year only 100,000 remained. With the Algerian problem resolved and the French army firmly under his control, de Gaulle could now turn to his goal of making France the leader of Europe.

To increase French prestige and strength, de Gaulle believed, the authority of the president had to be increased further and the power of the political parties had to be reduced. He viewed political parties as divisive forces and therefore tried to circumvent them by appealing to the populace through national referendums. To strengthen the office of the president he held a referendum in 1962 on the direct election of the president. Despite the opposition of the National Assembly, which had not approved the referendum, it won the support of 67.7 percent of the voters.

Now de Gaulle no longer had to please the electors, who were associated with political parties, in order to stay in power. When the assembly censured his ministry, with Georges Pompidou as premier, de Gaulle dissolved the assembly and called new elections. Often he threatened to resign, and often he warned of the weaknesses of parliamentary government. These ploys helped the Gaullists to gain 250 of the 480 seats and an absolute majority in the assembly.

Despite the election success, de Gaulle's popularity soon began to decline. Many resented his blocking of British entry into the EEC in 1963. Others shifted their support away from de Gaulle when it became apparent that he wished to reduce French democracy to a façade. A growing number felt that France should not try to develop an independent French military deterrent — as we shall see — but should concentrate on domestic problems. The vote in the 1965 presidential elections reflected a shift toward the left. In the first popular election of a president since 1848, de Gaulle captured only 44 percent of the votes; François Mitterand, candidate of the newly formed Left–Federation (Socialists, Communists, and Radicals) carried 32 percent; and the other major candidate, Jean Lecanuet, representing a Centrist coalition, received 16 percent. France was not yet ready for a Socialist president. In the runoff election against Mitterand, de Gaulle gained 54.5 percent of the vote. Despite this victory, popular resentment against de Gaulle would soon reduce Gaullist support and steadily increase the strength of the left in French politics.

Even before de Gaulle had resolved the Algerian problem he began to implement another of his major goals, the reduction of United States influence in Europe. Since de Gaulle was little influenced by ideologies, except for his dislike of the French left, he did not believe in a struggle between communism and capitalism for world dominance. He viewed Soviet actions in terms of old-fashioned balance-of-power considerations rather than from the American perspective. In other words, he felt that Soviet expansionism was limited to Eastern Europe and therefore posed no threat to Western Europe. What is more, he believed a reduction of American influence in Western Europe would not lead to a sovietization of Western Europe but would enhance French power in Europe.

In March 1959 de Gaulle began to withdraw French naval units from the NATO Mediterranean Command as the first step in the French withdrawal from NATO. The United States defeat of the Soviet Union in the Cuban missile crisis in 1962 and subsequent United States/Soviet steps toward détente convinced de Gaulle that his perception of the Soviet "threat" was accurate.

In order to establish France as an independent third force between the two superpowers, de Gaulle undertook the development of an independent French nuclear force. In 1964 he refused to sign the nuclear test ban treaty sponsored by the United States and the Soviet Union since it would prevent France from developing its own nuclear force. In 1965, France pulled out of the South-East Asia Treaty Organization (SEATO) and refused to participate in NATO military maneuvers. In 1966 French forces were withdrawn from NATO, and its headquarters was transferred from Paris to Brussels. Contributing to this show of independence was an economic upsurge that brought France a $6 billion gold reserve by 1965.

Despite these actions, de Gaulle was unable to resolve European–Soviet differences unilaterally. By this time, Soviet leaders were more interested in dealing directly with the United States to resolve world and European problems. Still, de Gaulle had begun the gradual loosening of United States/European ties, and other countries followed suit in the late 1960s and 1970s as the United States became mired in the Vietnam War.

British Political Affairs

After defeating a divided, ideologically confused Labour party in 1951, Great Britain's Conservative party retained office until 1964 through the acceptance of the welfare state, the impact of several periods of rapid economic growth, and the continued division in the Labour party. Returning to power at the age of 77, Winston Churchill changed little of the previous Labour governnent's programs. Improving economic conditions permitted Churchill to end food rationing, an issue that had contributed to Labour's defeat, and to carry out the Conservative campaign promise to build more than 300,000 houses a year to relieve Britain's housing shortage and stimulate the economy.

Now convinced that the British wanted the welfare state, Churchill did no more than increase medical fees slightly. Labour's nationalization program was reversed only in the iron and steel industry and in road transport. The Conservatives did, however, change Labour's policy of raising income taxes to achieve a more equitable distribution of wealth. The Conservatives hoped that the reduction of income taxes would also stimulate the economy.

When a heart attack forced Churchill to retire in 1955, Anthony Eden became prime minister. A business boom in 1954 and 1955 and another reduction in income taxes put an even larger Conservative majority into the House of Commons in the 1955 elections.

Within a year after Eden assumed power he was called upon to deal with Egyptian leader Gamal Abdel Nasser's nationalization of the Suez Canal (see chapter 6). Backed by the majority of the Conservative party and by France, Eden tried to force a reversal of Nasser's policy. In the face of stiff United States and United Nations opposition, Britain was forced to back down. Before the crisis had passed, Eden suffered a breakdown and was replaced by Harold Macmillan.

"Supermac" proved to be a more capable leader than Eden. Supported by improving economic conditions, Macmillan spent little time on domestic affairs. He travelled more than 80,000 miles in eighteen months in an attempt to ease Cold War tensions and restore British respectability after the humiliation of Suez. At home, his government slowed investment in the economy and restricted credit in order to avert another devaluation of the pound. Although these measures eventually put the brakes on economic growth and added to the unemployment rolls, a renewed business boom in 1958 and 1959 gave the Conservatives an even larger majority in the House of Commons in the 1959 elections. Labour's support for an expansion of welfare programs apparently contributed to its resounding defeat.

The Labour party was plagued by divisions over social welfare and rearmament throughout the decade. Led by Aneurin Bevan, the left continued to demand more attention to social welfare. The right, under the leadership of Hugh Gaitskell, a former Oxford University economics don, and Clement Attlee, opposed an extension of welfare and the growth of the bureaucracy it would bring about. After the 1959 elections, the right wing convinced the party to jettison nationalization in favor of expanding economic growth through full employment and periodic stimulation of the economy.

Leftist intellectuals writing for the *New Left Review,* shocked by the Soviet suppression of the Hungarian Revolution, began to emphasize democratic socialism in place of class conflict and economic controls. Labour support for British development of the hydrogen bomb in 1957 produced a new left movement, the Campaign for Nuclear Disarmament (CND). The CND and the left wing of the party finally got Labour to reverse its stand on nuclear weapons but not its drift toward a more moderate political and social program.

An economic downturn after 1959, reflected in a growing inflation rate and an unfavorable balance of trade, undermined Conservative support. Although Macmillan resorted to a wage freeze, increased indirect taxes, and initiated some very unconservative economic devices to overcome the economic downturn — even including a modified form of economic planning — he was unable to turn the economy around.

The economic malaise stemmed from a variety of shortcomings in the British economy described earlier (see chapter 4), as well as from growing competition from the continental European countries and Japan. Adding to Conservative woes in 1963 was de Gaulle's veto of British entry into the Common Market. Although British entry would certainly not have brought immediate relief to the British economy because of the dislocations accompanying entry, it was a severe blow to Macmillan's much-publicized plans for British entry.

Then Macmillan's secretary of state for war, John Profumo, became the subject of a scandal. As banner headlines reported day after day, he was involved with a call girl, and she had been asked by a naval attaché of the Soviet Embassy to get all the information she could from Profumo on Britain's nuclear arsenal. Although Macmillan demanded and got Profumo's resignation, he was himself compelled to take some of the responsibility, and he tendered his resignation.

Macmillan was replaced by Sir Alec Douglas-Home. Even though Douglas-Home lacked the charisma of Macmillan and of the Labour candidate, Harold Wilson, he won the election by a slim four-seat margin. Despite all the Conservatives' problems, there was still considerable anxiety about a Labour government.

Scandinavian Political Affairs

There was little anxiety about left-of-center governments in Scandinavia. With the exception of Finland, where the Agrarian and Socialist parties shared power, the Scandinavian countries had Socialist-dominated governments from the end of the war until the mid-1960s. Only Denmark had a brief interruption, from 1950 to 1953, of Social Democratic or Labor party leadership. The Social Democrats might have gained power in Finland were it not for the Soviet Union's preponderant influence and its distrust of the Social Democrats. As the conservative parties in Western Europe had profited from the postwar economic resurgence, so did the Socialist parties in Scandinavia.

Economically, Europe had been divided into two blocs, the European Economic Community (France, Italy, West Germany, and the Benelux countries) and the European Free Trade Area, or EFTA (Austria, Denmark, Great Britain, Norway, Portugal, Sweden, and Switzerland). This caused some economic dislocations, but in general the Scandinavian countries profited from the expansion of both. In 1960 about one-third of Swedish exports were going to partners in EFTA and another one-third to the EEC. Denmark, always a major exporter of farm products, managed to bring its industrial exports abreast of its agricultural exports by means of a concerted industrialization program coupled with tariff reductions among EFTA countries.

The Norwegian Labor party and the Swedish and Danish Social Democrats, which had been in power since the interwar years, increased their popularity during the rapid economic expansion by extending social welfare services. Sweden adopted compulsory health insurance and pension plans, family allowances, and other social measures that cost the country $3 billion a year (see chapter 9). By 1965, Denmark and Norway had similarly become social welfare states.

The economic resurgence had contributed to Socialist success in the 1950s, and the economic downturns in the 1960s undermined their leadership. An economic slowdown in Denmark in the mid-1960s, caused by the high tariff walls erected by the EEC, resulted in a devaluation of the kroner. Adding to the Socialist woes were exceedingly high direct and indirect taxes, needed to support the welfare state, that were increasingly resented by the population. When both the Social Democrats and their coalition partner, the Socialist People's party, lost votes in the 1968 elections, a group of center parties formed a governing coalition.

Labor's thirty-year rule in Norway, weakened also by the EFTA–EEC split, ended when the Conservative, Liberal, and Center parties formed a coalition cabinet. However, these changes had little effect on domestic policies since all Scandinavian parties accepted the welfare state.

Benelux Political Affairs

Politics in the Benelux countries are incredibly complex because of the plethora of parties — ten parties won parliamentary seats in the 1963 elections in the Netherlands — and because ethnic and religious differences intrude into the political arena.

In Belgium the division between Flemish-speaking Belgians and French-speaking Belgians (Walloons) often cuts across party lines. In general the Flemish support the Catholic party — the Social Christians — whereas the Walloons favor the Socialists and the Liberals. State support for Catholic schools became a major issue in the 1950s and was resolved only through a compromise that permitted the state to supplement the salaries of teachers in church-sponsored schools. Controversy over Louvain University (the Flemish wanted it to be exclusively Flemish) was resolved only by a division of the university into separate Flemish and Walloonian institutions.

Relatively slow economic growth — the gross national product, or GNP, grew at a rate of only 2.7 percent in the 1950s — exacerbated the ethnic–linguistic division. The Walloons, who had dominated the country in the interwar period, suffered most from the economic stagnation. Most new industry was built in the Flemish region because of its superior transportation facilities, and the southern Walloon area bore the brunt of the economic decline because the coal resources in that area had been exhausted. When the government tried to revitalize industry in 1960 by applying austerity measures, including reductions in welfare benefits and public works as well as various aids to industry, a twenty-seven-day general strike brought down the government.

In the 1960s the Flemish–Walloonian division continued to inhibit government attempts to resolve the nation's economic problems. Ministries fell in 1965 and 1968 primarily over the language issue. There was some relaxation of tension late in the decade as EEC aid ended the economic stagnation and encouraged a greater sense of community. Moreover, the economic impact of losing the Belgian Congo and Ruanda-Urundi was offset by the improving economic conditions. The creation of dual ministers for education, culture, economy, and community problems further reduced the Flemish-Walloon acrimony.

Despite the multiplicity of parties in the Netherlands and the division of most institutions along religious lines, rapid economic growth has tended to keep the turmoil down to manageable proportions. Although the Netherlands had suffered severely from German bombardment during the war, its geographic location at the mouth of the Rhine and its traditional focus on commerce contributed to its rapid recovery as world trade picked up and German industry expanded. Rotterdam has become the leading seaport in Europe and the Dutch, the major EEC shipping nation. The loss of Indonesia in 1949 had little effect on the Dutch economy, as evidenced by the doubling of industrial output from 1954 to 1964 and by the growth of commercial activities.

The Catholic People's party and the Labor party dominated the political scene throughout the 1950s and 1960s. A Labor and Catholic People's party coalition ruled the country until 1958, when Labor lost support by its unorthodox policy of wage-fixing. After 1958, the Catholic People's party in coalition with two Calvinist parties took over the premiership. Both major parties lost votes and suffered internal splits in the mid-1960s, but they continued to dominate the coalition governments or renew their association, as they did in a ministry in 1965 and 1966.

Austrian Political Affairs

The easing of Cold War tensions, coupled with rapid economic growth, had a singular impact on Austrian political affairs. Occupied by the wartime Allies since World War II, Austria had had no chance to regain its national sovereignty during the Stalin era because Stalin considered Austria to be of strategic importance in central Europe. But in 1955, Khrushchev, in a move to reduce Cold War tensions, agreed to end the occupation of Austria in return for an Austrian pledge of permanent neutrality.

At first, Austrian politics was changed little by the sudden end of occupation. The Social Democrats and Christian Socialists, which had shared political office and civil service jobs in direct proportion to their votes since the occupation began, continued their coalition for eleven years after the occupation ended. Both parties were cautious about resuming normal political activities lest there be a dangerous polarization of the kind that had erupted in civil war during the 1930s. However, rapid economic growth and the Social Democrats' adoption of a reformist rather than revolutionary course soon stilled fears of political chaos. With the restoration of political confidence, the coalition was ended in 1966 when the Christian Socialists gained sufficient votes to rule independently.

Iberian Political Affairs

In southern Europe, where economic transformation was minimal, political affairs remained authoritarian. Spain and Portugal, under the dictatorships of Francisco Franco and Antonio Salazar, stoutly resisted political and social change into the 1960s. Opposition political parties continued to be banned in Spain but Franco was unable to prevent them from forming or put a stop to their clandestine activities. Despite opposition to his regime among the citizenry, Franco continued to receive support from the Catholic Church, the army, and the Falange (the official party of the regime).

When opposition developed within the church and the army, Franco was obliged to permit limited reforms. Liberals among the Catholic clergy grew more outspoken in their opposition to Franco's authoritarianism; and young army officers, eager for faster promotions and economic modernization, agitated for change. A group of Catholics in the so-called Opus Dei movement, including some government ministers, urged both economic modernization and closer association with the EEC.

Franco's strongest opposition came from separatists in the northern Catalan and Basque regions, who increasingly resorted to violence to achieve more autonomy. But the opposition groups, including the political parties, were unwilling to undertake a cooperative challenge of the regime. In the 1960s Franco weakened some of his opposition when he granted limited reforms. He relaxed press censorship, abolished military courts, gave the minorities greater rights, divided the executive powers between himself and parliament, and permitted the free election of 100 members of the 600-member parliament.

The regime was further strengthened when the long period of economic stagnation was brought to an end. Increased investments by the United States, Germany, and France provided the necessary industrial capital. In return for permitting American bases in Spain, Franco received both economic and military aid. And as an added fillip, the Spanish economy got a boost from the flood of tourists who came to savor the sunny Mediterranean beaches and low prices.

The Economy in Political Affairs

As the Cold War's significance in domestic politics dwindled, economic factors predominated as determinants of political success or failure. While rapid economic growth in the 1950s had kept the right in the ascendant in the major European countries and had sustained social democracy in the Scandinavian countries, economic downturns in the mid-1960s generated strong and sometimes successful challenges from political adversaries. Labour replaced the conservatives in Great Britain and the German Social Democrats gained a share of the Christian Democrats' political power.

One of many travel posters encouraging tourism in Spain.

Although the Italian Christian Democrats remained the dominant political party, they faced a growing challenge from parties to their left. Since the French economy did not begin a serious downturn until the late 1960s, and since de Gaulle's diplomatic successes were still fresh in the minds of the French up to that time, the Gaullist-led UNR remained strong until then. But center and left coalitions formed, and de Gaulle's margin in 1965 was much narrower than expected, heralding the beginning of the challenge to Gaullist political dominance. In Scandinavia, only the Swedish Social Democrats managed to stay in power in the 1960s. The ruling Norwegian Labor party and the Social Democrats in Denmark fell from power primarily as a result of economic issues.

A particularly significant factor in the changing political fortunes of Europe's ruling parties was social welfare. In many of the major states the electorate was demanding extended welfare programs and reforms, whereas in Scandinavia the electorate was demanding a halt to the extension of even more elaborate welfare programs. In countries where social welfare and an economic downturn were combined issues, the parties in power were seriously weakened or were supplanted as the dominant parties.

FURTHER READING

Important studies of British politics are Samuel H. Beer, *British Politics in the Collectivist Age* (1965); R. Rose, *Politics in England* (1964); and R. M. Punnett, *British Government and Politics* (1968). Valuable analyses of the relationship between politics and the social structure of Britain are provided in H. Thomas, *The Establishment* (1950); Kingsley Martin, *The Crown and the Establishment* (1963); D. V. Glass, *The British Political Elite* (1963); and Anthony Sampson, *Anatomy of Britain Today* (1965). British elections are treated in the studies of David E. Butler, *The British General Election of 1951* (1952) and *The British General Election of 1955* (1956); David E. Butler and Richard Rose, *The British General Election of 1959* (1960); and David E. Butler and Anthony King, *The British General Election of 1964* (1965). A standard work on political parties is R. T. McKenzie, *British Political Parties* (2d rev. ed., 1964).

Valuable background studies of the development of French political ideologies and alignments and the relationship between society and politics can be found in D. W. Brogan, *Development of Modern France* (1940); and David Thompson, *Democracy in France* (1958). Postwar French politics is analyzed in Philip Williams, *Crisis and Compromise: Politics in the Fourth Republic* (1964); Philip Williams and Martin Harrison, *Politics and Society in de Gaulle's Republic* (1971); Lowell G. Noonan, *France: The Politics of Continuity in Change* (1970); Stanley Hoffman (ed.), *France: Change and Tradition* (1963); Raymond Aron, *France: Steadfast and Changing* (1960); Jacques Chapsal, *La Vie Politique en France depuis 1940* (1966); and François Goguel and Alfred Grosser, *La Politique en France* (1964).

Valuable studies of de Gaulle are Alexander Werth, *De Gaulle: A Political Biography* (1966); and J. M. Tournoux, *La Tragédie du Général* (1967). French communism is treated in Charles A. Micaud, *Communism and the French Left* (1963); George Lichtheim, *Marxism in Modern France* (1966); and J. Fauvet, *Histoire du Parti Communiste Français* (1965). For further information on Christian Democracy see Mario Einaudi and François Goguel, *Christian Democracy in Italy and France* (1952); and M. P. Fogarty, *Christian Democracy in Western Europe* (1957).

The best studies of Italian politics are Giuseppe Mammarella, *Italy After Fascism: A Political History, 1943-63* (1964); Norman Kogan, *A Political History of Post-war Italy* (1966); and Joseph LaPalombara, *Interest Groups in Italian Politics* (1963). The Italian Communist party is competently treated in Donald Blackmer, *Unity in Diversity: Italian Communism and the Communist World* (1968). The Christian Democratic party is covered in Mario Einaudi and François Goguel, *Christian*

Democracy in Italy and France (1952); and M. P. Fogarty, *Christian Democracy in Western Europe* (1957).

For further information on the nature of West German politics see Lewis J. Edinger, *Politics in Germany* (1968); Theodor Eschenburg, *Zur politischen Praxis in der Bundesrepublik* (1966); Edward Pinney, *Federalism, Bureaucracy and Party Politics in Western Germany* (1963); and Uwe W. Kitzinger, *German Electoral Politics* (1960). For a comparison of East and West German politics see Arnold J. Heidenheimer, *The Governments of Germany* (3d ed., 1971).

The workings of the West German parliament are treated in Gerhard Loewenberg, *Parliament in the German Political System* (1967). The transformation of the Social Democratic Party is analyzed in Douglas A. Chalmers, *The Social Democratic Party of Germany: From Working Class Movement to Modern Political Party* (1964). Two important studies of Adenauer are Arnold J. Heidenheimer, *Adenauer and the CDU: The Rise of the Leader and the Integration of the Party* (1960); and Richard Hiscocks, *The Adenauer Era* (1966). A more critical and controversial treatment of Adenauer and German politics is presented in Ralf Dahrendorf, *Society and Democracy in Germany* (1969).

For the smaller states of Western Europe see D. A. Rustow, *The Politics of Compromise: A Study of Parties and Cabinet Government in Sweden* (1955). Norway is treated in Harry Eckstein, *Division and Cohesion in Democracy: A Study of Norway* (1966). For the Netherlands see Arend Lijphart, *The Politics of Accommodation: Pluralism and Democracy in the Netherlands* (1968). Iberian affairs are studied in Stanley G. Payne, *Franco's Spain* (1967); Hugh Kay, *Salazar and Modern Portugal* (1970); and Charles E. Newell, *Portugal* (1973). For Austria see Erika Weinzierl and Kurt Skalnik, *Die Zweite Republik*, 2 vols. (1972).

6 The End of European Empire

We prefer self-government with danger to servitude in tranquillity.

Kwame Nkrumah, *Autobiography*

During the two decades following World War II, Europe lost its Asian and its African empires. The Asian empire was the first to go because of national liberation movements that began before World War I. By 1965, most of Africa had followed the Asian countries to independence. Over forty countries with one-quarter of the world's population had overthrown colonialism in this brief span of time.

Although World War II had provided a powerful stimulus to the independence movements, many of the liberation struggles, especially those in Asia and the Middle East, were well under way before the war. Japan's successful challenge of Russian imperialism in the 1905 Russo–Japanese War provided an early impetus to nationalist groups throughout Asia by convincing them that the European powers were not invincible.

During World War I the European powers weakened themselves by promoting nationalist movements against each other: Germany encouraged Arab nationalism against the French in the Maghreb; and the British and French promoted nationalism in the Middle East against Germany's ally, Turkey. Wartime promises of concessions in return for aid against their enemies further loosened the grasp of Europe's nations on their colonies. As World War I drew to a close, the anti-imperialist propaganda campaign launched by Lenin after the Bolshevik Revolution in November of 1917 instigated a countermovement in the West.

U.S. President Woodrow Wilson's support for self-determination in his Fourteen Points was followed by Briton David Lloyd George's pledge in 1918 that self-determination was applicable to the colonies as much as it was elsewhere. During the interwar years, Europe's dominance in Asia weakened to the point that only the final push of World War II was needed to end it.

Stages on the Road to Independence

National independence movements commonly passed through three stages before independence was achieved. During the first stage, traditional elites tried to stave off westernization and preserve the native culture and institutions. Tribal chieftains in Africa, for example, engaged in ineffective protests against the vastly superior military might of the colonial powers. Only in Ethiopia and Morocco did leaders of this first, so-called protonationalist stage manage to retain power after independence.

The second, or bourgeois, stage was a direct result of Western modernization of native economies and societies. Except where it was deliberately held back, as in Vietnam, a Western-educated middle class emerged to challenge and in time replace the traditional native elites. In order to destroy the old social order, the colonial powers usually encouraged these middle-class groups, in the expectation that they would remain loyal because of their acceptance of Western ideas, techniques, and institutions. World War I led to a rapid expansion of this Westernized elite.

When the colonial powers concentrated all their efforts on World War I in Europe, a native industrial class grew rapidly. This new elite occupied an ambivalent position in the colonial countries. Despite superior training, the members of the group were allowed to fill only the subordinate positions in the colonial administrations. Denied equal status with the European administrators on the one hand and separated from the traditional society on the other, they were often frustrated in their attempts to bring about the changes they desired or find positions that fit their training. India's Jawaharlal Nehru, who later adopted a more revolutionary posture, aptly described their ambivalent feelings: "Indeed, I often wonder if I represent anyone at all, and I am inclined to think that I do not, though many have kindly and friendly feelings toward me. I have become a queer mixture of the East and West, out of place everywhere, at home nowhere."

Although the members of this group eventually demanded independence for their countries, their social base remained narrowly middle class. They refused to appeal to the masses of workers and peasants for support, thus generally permitting leadership of the independence movements to pass to more revolutionary countrymen. Independence came during this second phase of the liberation struggle only when the colonial powers withdrew because of financial and international pressures, as in Nigeria and Tanganyika.

For the most part, national liberation movements succeeded during the third, or mass revolutionary, stage. Nationalist leaders such as Mahatma Gandhi and Jawaharlal Nehru in India, Mao Tse-tung in China, Ho Chi Minh in Vietnam, Kwame Nkrumah in Ghana, and Achmed Sukarno in Indonesia mobilized the masses of peasants and workers to overthrow their colonial overlords. Gandhi's policy of massive civil disobedience, adopted in the 1920s, presented the colonial powers with an insurmountable obstacle to their continued rule and provided subsequent nationalists with techniques that were invaluable in their own liberation struggles. Both Gandhi and Mao established elaborate ties between the masses and revolutionary leaders that were adopted by nationalists elsewhere. While this three-stage struggle went on for more than a half-century in India, it was telescoped into less than fifteen years in Africa due primarily to the debilitating impact of World War II on the colonial powers.

India's Independence Movement

The parent of all independence movements was clearly that of India. Beginning in 1885 with the Congress party movement, India provides one of the best examples of the three-stage division of nationalist movements. The first leader of the Congress party, G. K. Gokhale, accepted British rule and asked only for greater integration of educated Indians in the colonial administration. After 1905 a Western-educated elite led by B. G. Tilak rose to leadership in the party. This is the group that ultimately rejected piecemeal reforms and British suzerainty and demanded independence. However, the group's failure to appeal to the Indian masses left the independence movement in the hands of students and a few middle-class leaders. Britain had, in fact, promoted the buildup of a Western-educated elite to support it against the traditional nationalists.

World War I and its aftermath irretrievably weakened the British hold on India. From this point on the British could only engage in delaying tactics as they watched the nationalist movement gather momentum and pass into the third stage. To maintain their influence, in 1917 the British promised the gradual development of self-governing institutions and in 1919 they committed themselves to internal self-government by installments. But by this time the Congress party was demanding independence on its own terms.

When Gandhi organized the party on a mass basis with the Nagpur Constitution of 1920, it had a chain of command stretching to the district and village level. His policy of massive civil disobedience stymied the British despite their superior resources. Gandhi's top aide, Nehru, overcame rightist opposition within the party and pushed through a social reform program that tied the masses to the new leadership. Winston Churchill seriously misread the Congress party's new revolutionary program and its impact on the masses when he said in 1931: "They merely represent those Indians who have acquired a veneer of Western civilization, and have read all those books about democracy which Europe is now beginning increasingly to disregard."

Other British leaders had by 1935 become sufficiently convinced of the strength of the Congress party to pass the Government of India Act, which provided for the election of provincial legislatures and the establishment of provincial cabinets. By granting local rights and maintaining control over foreign affairs and other national issues, Britain hoped to stop the independence movement. But the Congress party would now be content with nothing less than complete independence.

Efforts to secure Indian cooperation against Germany during World War II finally convinced British leaders that they had no choice but to grant India its independence. When Britain requested Indian aid in 1939, the Congress party not only refused but also withdrew its representatives from the provincial parliaments. Britain responded by jailing many of the Congress leaders. However, the Japanese march through Indochina and Burma forced the British to seek an accord in 1942.

For its cooperation the British representative, Sir Stafford Cripps, offered India full dominion status within the British Commonwealth after the war. Gandhi, mindful of earlier promises that went unfulfilled as well as of Britain's predicament in the war against Germany, would not compromise. Instead, the party passed a Quit India Resolution that promised cooperation if independence was granted or massive resistance if it was refused. Again Congress leaders were put in jail, where they remained until the end of the war.

The absence of the major leaders of the Congress party permitted the Moslem League, led by Mohammed Ali Jinnah, to build up its strength. Street clashes between Moslems and Hindus increased in number and intensity as the Moslem League pushed for its own separate state once independence was achieved.

With the Labour party victory in the 1945 British elections, independence for India awaited only the resolution of the Moslem–Hindu dispute. In the elections for a central legislative assembly set up by a sympathetic Labour party the Moslem League and the Congress party captured most of the seats. But the Moslem League refused to take part in a cabinet headed by Nehru.

While the British engaged in fruitless attempts to bring the two sides together, continued street clashes divided the two sides even further. Convinced by February 1947 that a unitary Indian state could be achieved only if the two factions were compelled to resolve their differences, Britain announced that it was pulling out of India by June 1948. Realizing that no compromise was possible, in July 1947 Britain passed the India Independence Bill that set up two independent states: India and Pakistan.

After a massive migration of Moslems and Hindus and considerable bloodshed, India and Pakistan became independent states in August 1947. Both were given the option to turn their backs on the British Commonwealth; both decided to remain within it. Despite the partition, India became a powerful symbol for countries still under colonial domination. After studying Gandhi's policies, Nkrumah said it "could be the solution to the colonial problem." In fact, many nationalist leaders adopted the same policy of passive resistance and appeal to the masses.

Shortly after India gained its independence, nationalist pressures in Ceylon and Burma, in combination with financial problems at home, led Britain to relinquish its jurisdiction over these two countries.

China's Independence Movement

Although China remained independent during the imperialist period, it was unable to prevent the European powers and Japan from establishing hegemony over most of its colonial areas and major cities. The three-stage nationalist pattern is associated in China with three people: Kang Yu-wei, Sun Yat-sen, and Mao Tse-tung.

In Kang's time (the late 1800s) China was ruled by the Manchus, a Mongoloid people who had invaded in 1643 and had stayed on to found the Manchu dynasty. As if that weren't enough of foreigners, in the Sino–Japanese War of 1894–1895 China had suffered defeat at the hands of Japanese forces. Furthermore, before the turn of the century Western powers were clamoring for economic concessions.

Kang stirred up popular sentiment against aliens, and promoted enthusiastic but ill-planned and ill-directed attacks on foreigners. Most notable of these was the Boxer Rebellion in 1900, which the Western powers crushed with singular brutality.

Mao Tse-tung (dark clothing) chatting with peasants in Yenan, China in the late 1930s. Peasant support was crucial in the later success of Mao's forces.
Eastfoto

Realizing the futility of such tactics, a new reform group sought to rid China of the Manchus. This is the group, led by Dr. Sun Yat-sen, which later came to be called the Kuomintang. In 1911 Sun succeeded in overthrowing the Manchus and establishing the Republic of China. Before World War I, Sun had been convinced that a Western-style democracy could modernize China and eliminate foreign influence. He won the support of the growing Chinese business class, which wanted a stronger government to protect it against foreign competition.

By 1919 Sun no longer believed that a narrowly based liberal government could counter Western influence. Adopting passive resistance and the boycott of foreign goods, Sun began the transition to the third stage of nationalism. This transition was completed when he reorganized the Kuomintang as a mass party with an army aimed at revolution and aligned the Kuomintang with the Communist party led by Mao Tse-tung.

When Sun died in 1925 the nationalist movement split between the followers of Mao and the more conservative followers of Sun's successor, Chiang Kai-shek. Chiang rejected social reform, whereas Mao proclaimed an agrarian revolution in 1927. Now Chiang, leading the Kuomintang forces and supported by businessmen, financiers, and landlords, attacked Mao's Communist forces, pushing them back into the far north of China. While Mao built up Communist strength in Shensi province in the 1930s the corruption-riddled Kuomintang split into factions as the Japanese took over control of most of the heavily populated areas of China.

During World War II a shaky truce existed between Mao and the Kuomintang in the face of the Japanese threat. When the Japanese empire collapsed in 1945, the United States tried to arrange a coalition between the Communists and the Kuomintang. Neither side was willing to cooperate, and civil war broke out again in 1946. Although Chiang's forces controlled most of the cities, they could not subdue the countryside. Despite more than $2 billion in American aid, Mao's forces gradually pushed southward, gaining the support of China's peasants with their policy of land reform.

Mao said, "Whoever wins the support of the peasants will win China; whoever solves the land question will win the peasants." Now his prophecy was borne out. Winning the support of the peasantry as they advanced, the Communists took control of Peking in January 1949 and proclaimed the Chinese People's Republic in October. By 1950 the Kuomintang was driven off the Chinese mainland onto the island of Formosa, now called Taiwan. Mao's organization of the peasantry and guerrilla warfare tactics were to provide the theories and techniques for the conquest of power in other underdeveloped countries.

Indochina's Independence Movement

The lesson of China was not lost on Ho Chi Minh, the Indochinese nationalist. As early as 1925 he formed the Revolutionary League of the

Youth of Vietnam to exploit popular discontent over French colonialism and to organize the peasantry and workers. Groups representing the first two nationalist stages existed in Indochina but were never strong enough to challenge the revolutionaries. A protonationalist Constitutional party, formed early in the century, opposed both social revolution and demands for independence, and it refused to support nationalistic uprisings in Tonkin and Annam in 1930 and 1931. No democratic–liberal group could gain major support. French colonial policy restricted business activity to French and Chinese entrepreneurs, thus thwarting the development of an indigenous middle class that might have favored a moderate nationalist course.

The Vietnamese National Party (VNQDD), a liberal nationalist group formed in 1927, gained the support of only a small group of intellectuals. Denied legal existence by the French and ideologically incapable of appealing to the peasantry or workers, it joined Ho Chi Minh's Communists in the abortive revolts in Tonkin and Annam. Remnants of the VNQDD fled to the Kuomintang in China and did not return to Indochina until World War II.

The Communist party, which Ho had formed in 1930, also suffered severely when the French crushed the Communist-led Annam revolt in 1930 and 1931. French Governor General Pasquier declared, "As a force capable of acting against public order, Communism has disappeared." Ho Chi Minh fled to Moscow, where he remained until 1941. The Indochinese Communists were permitted a legal existence between 1933 and 1939, but a three-way division into Trotskyites, Stalinists, and followers of Ho, together with close French scrutiny, prevented a serious challenge to French rule.

The Communists were forced into hiding again in 1939 after the signing of the Stalin–Hitler pact led to the outlawing of the Communist party in France. But, as in China, the outbreak of World War II was to have a major impact on the liberation struggle. After an initial abortive Nationalist–Communist attempt to overthrow the French, the Communists and many VNQDD supporters united under the banner of the League for the Independence of Vietnam, or Vietminh, to resist the Japanese invaders. Hitler's invasion of the Soviet Union and Japan's attack on Pearl Harbor propelled the Vietminh into a new role as opponents of fascism.

During the war the Japanese permitted France's Vichy government to continue the administration of Indochina. Ho and the Vietminh, supported by Chiang Kai-shek after 1942, refused to make an all-out effort against the Japanese because they feared that Japan might destroy them; they chose instead to wait for the expected defeat of the Japanese, which would give them the opportunity to assume power. The Japanese paved the way for the Vietminh by disarming and imprisoning the French, who were supplied by the Free French Forces of Charles de Gaulle and were planning an attack on the Japanese. When Japan capitulated on August 14, 1945, the Vietminh assumed power under the banner of the hastily organized National Liberation Committee of Vietnam. Ho Chi Minh proclaimed the independence of the Democratic Republic of Vietnam in September 1945. Ho's leadership was acknowledged by Bao Dai, the former emperor of Annam under the French.

Distrusting Ho Chi Minh, the Western Allies had other plans. They assigned administration of the area north of the sixteenth parallel to the Chinese Nationalists and the area south of the sixteenth parallel to the British. The British immediately released the French soldiers and administrators from prison and helped them reestablish their control over the Saigon area. Fearing Chiang Kai-shek, the Vietminh wanted a close association with the French. The left-dominated government in Paris reached an agreement with Ho Chi Minh in March 1946 that recognized his government as a free state within a French federation in Indochina.

But the French administrators and military in Saigon sabotaged the agreement by setting up the free state of Cochin-China in the south. In response the Vietminh established a dictatorship in the north. In December 1946 war broke out, and the French drove the Vietminh back to their guerrilla bases in the mountains. The military justified the attack by reporting that the Vietminh had tried to kill all the Europeans in Hanoi. What Paris was not told was that the Vietminh action followed on the heels of a French naval attack on the Vietminh quarter of Hanoi that killed 6,000 Vietnamese. The French now set up Bao Dai as the puppet ruler of all Vietnam and granted Cambodia and Laos independence in internal affairs. France hoped it would later be able to set up a federation of states under French hegemony in Indochina.

French attempts to wipe out the Vietminh were frustrated by Vo Nguyen Giap, who had mastered guerrilla warfare tactics while fighting with Mao's Communist forces in China. Guerrilla warfare continued until 1949, when Mao's victory in China permitted him to start supplying the Vietminh. As the fighting shifted to more conventional warfare after 1950, the United States began to supply the French. Viewed as a part of the worldwide Communist expansion, the Truman administration considered Ho Chi Minh a puppet of the Chinese and the Soviet Union.

American financial aid increased from $150 million in 1950 to $1.3 billion by 1953. In spite of this aid, the French attempt to challenge the Vietminh in their mountain strongholds failed in 1954. At the battle of Dien Bien Phu a French force of 16,000 had to capitulate to the Vietminh after an eight-week siege. The United States provided no military aid at this time because it had just negotiated an end to the war in Korea and President Eisenhower was opposed to another land war in Asia.

The Geneva Conference, called before the battle of Dien Bien Phu, was meeting to bring the war in Indochina to an end when news of the French defeat came. The announcement put France in a very weak negotiating position. The French agreed to withdraw from north of the seventeenth parallel, and the Vietminh agreed to pull their troops out of the south. Elections were to be held in 1956 to decide on a government for all of Vietnam. The United States representative at Geneva, John Foster Dulles, refused to take part in the agreement. In 1956, when South Vietnam refused to hold elections, the move had United States support.

The second stage of the struggle to liberate all of Vietnam began after 1956, with the United States protecting South Vietnam against the Vietcong nationalists in the south and against North Vietnam. Another long war ensued. The Vietcong and North Vietnamese resorted to guerrilla warfare against vastly superior American military power. And, despite U.S. efforts to set up a stable government in South Vietnam, a succession of incompetent, corrupt administrations could not win the support of the South Vietnamese. Eventually, international and domestic criticism of the American role in Vietnam forced the United States to withdraw in 1974.

Indonesia's Independence Movement

The impact of World War II was even more decisive in Indonesia, where the nationalist movement never completely reached the third stage. Neither the Sarekat Islam movement led by Tjokro Aminoto nor the Partai Nasional Indonesia (PNI) formed by Achmed Sukarno in 1927 made a successful appeal to the peasantry. Led by students and members of the professions, the PNI could not withstand Dutch military attacks.

But the power of the Dutch was broken by the German conquest of the Netherlands during World War II and the Japanese occupation of Dutch territories. When Japan was defeated and World War II came to a close, before the Japanese pulled out of Indonesia they encouraged Sukarno, who had cooperated with them, to set up an independent state. The Dutch, weakened by war, had no choice but to acquiesce when Sukarno proclaimed Indonesia a republic in August 1945. When the Dutch regained their strength, they tried to divide the nationalists and destroy the independence movement by occupying the cities and imposing an economic blockade. Although they managed to capture Sukarno and other nationalist leaders in 1948, the United States exerted overwhelming diplomatic and economic pressures on the Dutch to relinquish their Far Eastern empire. Since Sukarno and other nationalists had crushed a Communist regime set up in Madium in September 1948, the United States evidently hoped it would obtain a strong anticommunist ally by supporting an independent Indonesia under Sukarno.

In August 1949 the Dutch, realizing that they lacked the military strength to defeat the rebels, agreed to the establishment of the United States of Indonesia within a larger Netherlands–Indonesian Union. However,

North Vietnamese President Ho Chi Minh (front) leading a tour of inspection of a North Vietnamese army unit in the 1960s.

Camera Press London

Sukarno was unhappy with this federalized solution and the continuing ties to the Netherlands, and in 1950 he set up the unitary Republic of Indonesia. Since the nationalists were divided when independence came and the masses had not been included in the nationalist movements, a long struggle then ensued to destroy regional loyalties and weld Indonesia's masses into a modern nation-state.

Arab Independence Movements

Most of the Arab states in the Middle East and north Africa had gained a measure of independence long before nationalism had developed into a third stage. As a result of the collapse of the Ottoman Empire during World War I and the increased influence of Great Britain and France throughout the Arab world, these new states emerged under native dynasties or aristocratic oligarchies but with special ties to the British or French. Iraq, Palestine, and Transjordan were under a British mandate and Syria and Lebanon under a French mandate from the League of Nations. Morocco and Tunisia were French protectorates. The other areas were directly controlled (French Algeria and Italian Libya), dominated (British Egypt), or independent (Saudi Arabia and Yemen).

During the interwar years Britain and France employed several methods to head off middle-class nationalism: propping up existing dynasties, granting quasi-independence, or creating territorial divisions. Britain preferred to support existing dynasties or grant quasi-independence. Immediately after World War I it supported Reza Khan in Iran and King Farouk in Egypt, and it installed Feisal as king in Iraq. France used the territorial division method in Syria when it destroyed the unity the Syrians had achieved under the Ottoman Empire by dividing the country into six administrative zones. One of these areas later became the present state of Lebanon. These divisions created a heated Syrian nationalism that was suppressed only through large-scale imprisonment and exile of Syrian leaders. To this day Syria remains a principal center of Arab nationalism and opponent of Western imperialism.

Three Syrian political groups — the Muslim Brotherhood, the League of National Action, and the Baath Party — led the struggle for a united Arab Islamic Empire and emancipation from colonial rule. However, by remaining narrowly intellectual and pan-Arab these parties were unable to tap the energies of the masses. As a result France had little difficulty in overcoming the nationalistic movement in the interwar years.

Despite British and French opposition, middle-class nationalism grew. In Tunisia, Habib Bourguiba's middle-class, nationalist Neo-Destour party replaced the Islamic-inspired Destour party that desired reforms within a French-dominated Tunisia. By 1943 the nationalist Moroccan Istiqlal party based on the middle class rose to prominence. In Iraq and Egypt, middle-class opposition came primarily from the military; many educated Arabs joined the military because they found little opportunity to use their talents elsewhere in their underdeveloped traditional societies. Reforms in Iraq, Egypt, and Syria were begun by military leaders after successful revolts against traditional rulers.

The First Arab–Israeli War   Immediately after World War II, British and French influence began to crumble in the Arab world. With de Gaulle cynically remarking that their actions "stank of oil," Britain and the United States forced the French out of Syria in 1946. But the event that led to a general attack on Western colonialism by shocking much of the Arab world into the third stage of nationalism was the Arab–Israeli War in 1948-1949.

The war was partially a result of British policies that stretched back to World War I. In order to obtain Jewish and Arab support against the Central Powers, Britain had made promises to both. The Balfour Declaration of 1917 promised the Jews a national homeland in Palestine, yet the Arabs believed all of Palestine had been promised to them by Sir Henry McMahon, British high commissioner for Egypt during World War I. The British mandate over Palestine, granted by the League of Nations in 1923, instructed the British to establish a Jewish national home in Palestine and facilitate immigration. The mandate promised a home, not a state. The Arabs began to protest the influx of thousands of Jews into their midst.

As anti-Semitic policies in Europe increased the flow of Jewish immigrants in the interwar period, Britain reacted to the Arab opposition by trying periodically to curtail Jewish settlement. Despite British actions, the Jewish population of Palestine increased by about 350,000 during the interwar period. When Britain put limits on the number of immigrants permitted during World War II, Jewish terrorist groups resorted to violence in order to force the British to accept more of the Jewish refugees fleeing persecution in Europe. Caught between Arab demands to limit Jewish immigration to Palestine and Jewish violence to prevent any such limitation, in 1947 Britain asked the United Nations to resolve the dilemma.

The United Nations decided to partition Palestine into a Jewish state and an Arab state and to internationalize Jerusalem. In May 1948, when Britain pulled out its troops, war broke out between the new state of Israel and the neighboring Arab states. Although vastly outnumbered, Israel relied on superior organization to achieve victory in February 1949. Now Israel encompassed not only the area assigned to it by the United Nations but the new city of Jerusalem, a corridor to the coast, and the remainder of Galilee as well. Nearly a million Arabs fled Israel in the wake of rumors of impending massacres and orders by their leaders to leave. The Palestinians established no permanent settlements elsewhere; to this day they remain refugees, symbols of Arab humiliation and a permanent irredentist force that has never accepted the new Israeli state.

The Arab defeat, blamed on the traditionalist regimes in the Arab world, generated military revolts in Syria, Jordan, and Egypt. The Syrian and Jordanian revolts failed initially to replace the existing regimes with a modernizing leadership. But in Egypt the corrupt British-supported regime of King Farouk was overthrown by General Mohammed Naguib and Colonel Gamal Abdel Nasser, an act which was to have a far-reaching impact in the Arab world. Naguib abolished the monarchy and began the modernization of Egypt by replacing the old elite with fellow officers. He was supplanted by the more energetic Nasser, whose interests focused on more revolutionary changes in society and the ouster of the British from the Suez Canal.

Nasser eliminated all opponents, put an end to parliamentary government, and adopted a single mass organization to arouse and channel political consciousness. With these measures he set a pattern for many of the one-party governments that followed political liberation throughout Africa. Nasser's ultranationalist dictatorship and those that followed were grounded on the premise that political democracy without social democracy is meaningless.

The Suez Crisis One of Nasser's ways of providing more social democracy was to improve the lot of the peasantry by building the Aswan High Dam, which regulated the flow of the Nile River. This led him into conflict with Britain and France over the Suez Canal.

Nasser expected aid from Britain and the United States for building the

Aswan Dam. When aid was refused, Nasser responded by nationalizing the Suez Canal on July 26, 1956. Nasser had purchased arms from Czechoslovakia because the West would not provide him with the type or quantity of weapons he wanted. Also, he had recognized Communist China in 1955. Now the United States denied him aid because of what it considered to be his anti-Western attitude. In the Cold War milieu of the 1950s, the United States equated neutralism with opposition and viewed Nasser's actions as setting a dangerous precedent of playing off West against East.

England and France decided on joint action to capture the Canal Zone, coordinated with an Israeli attack ostensibly to destroy guerrilla bases in the Sinai Peninsula. The effort was a dismal failure. Israel captured a large part of the Sinai and Anglo–French forces captured Port Said, but United States and international pressure forced a halt to the attempted seizure of the Canal Zone. (The United States feared that the Anglo–French invasion would have a deleterious effect on Western popularity and influence in the Middle East. Further, because the United States was leading the attack in the U.N. against the Soviet Union's invasion of Hungary, it could not at the same time approve the invasion of Egypt.)

The subsequent withdrawal of Anglo–French forces rid Egypt of all foreign influence, left it in control of the canal, and greatly enhanced Nasser's reputation, especially among third-world countries. It now seemed possible to oppose the militarily superior colonial powers by appealing to the United Nations and world opinion. The Suez fiasco provided a major impetus to national liberation movements in sub-Saharan Africa. In the Middle East, Nasser's military junta served as a model for similar governments in Syria and Iraq.

Africa's Independence Movements

The weakened international position of Britain and France after 1956 accelerated the process of national liberation in Africa. Indochinese and Algerian pressures on France and a national resistance movement centering around the traditional sultan brought independence to Morocco before the three stages of nationalism had fully developed. The middle-class Istiqlal party had led a national resistance movement against the French since 1943. But it was the exile of the sultan in 1953, inspired by French *colons,* that promoted mass resistance of the kind usually associated only with ultranationalists, in support of the sultan's traditional regime. The sultan, Mohammed V, had the support of his people not only because of his reform program but also because the sultan was by tradition the country's Islamic leader. The French *colons* set up a puppet government, but the populace demanded the return of the legitimate ruler. When the traditionally antisultan Berber tribes transferred their support from the puppet government to the exiled sultan and began to attack European settlers, France reinstated the sultan in November 1955 to end the growing anarchy. In March 1956 France granted Morocco full independence. Faced with a *fait accompli,* the other protecting power, Spain, was forced to acquiesce.

During the next five years Mohammed V tried to change Morocco to a modern constitutional monarchy. But the challenge of the ultranationalist Neo-Istiqlal party headed by Ben Barka led Mohammed and his son, Hassan II, to depose the left-leaning government of Premier Abdallah Ibrahim and slow Morocco's progress toward genuine constitutional government. A struggle ensued in the 1960s between the more conservative middle-class Istiqlal party and the social revolutionary Neo-Istiqlal party under the watchful eye of the kings.

Again, in Tunisia, independence came before the nationalist movement reached the ultranationalist stage. The bourgeois Destour party had led a movement for greater independence from France since 1919. Although led by the middle class, it differed from the bourgeois second stage in that it was willing to accept administrative reforms and greater middle-class participation under French auspices and Islamic influences. The secular Neo-Destour party, formed in 1934 under Habib Bourguiba's leadership, adopted a mixture of bourgeois and ultrarevolutionary aims. Bourguiba's party appealed to the masses through a revolutionary reform program but stopped short of the ultranationalist, anti-Western aspects of the typical third-stage nationalists. This pattern also characterized the independence movements in Liberia, Nigeria, and Tanganyika.

Bourguiba was often hard-pressed by more radical Arab and African nationalists, especially in neighboring Algeria, to justify his pro-Western stance. Nevertheless, his program led to national independence in 1956 because the masses identified with his leadership and because France's position weakened after 1956. The French settlers feared they would lose their privileged economic status if Tunisia gained independence. The punitive actions they instituted, which included the exile and imprisonment of Bourguiba, instigated a mass reaction among the Tunisian populace in 1954. Alarmed by the outbreak of partisan warfare, Premier Mendès-France promised Tunisia internal autonomy only one week after he negotiated an end to French involvement in Indochina. Bourguiba was returned to Tunisia and independence was proclaimed on March 20, 1956. Because Tunisia achieved its independence under what was essentially second-stage leadership, it has retained a parliamentary, democratic form of government and a pro-Western political orientation. Revolutionary neutralist groups have not been able to change Tunisia's moderate pro-Western policies.

The stampede to independence of sub-Saharan African states after 1956 was the result of many factors that instilled a new confidence in African nationalists. Independence for Morocco and Tunisia in 1956, the successes

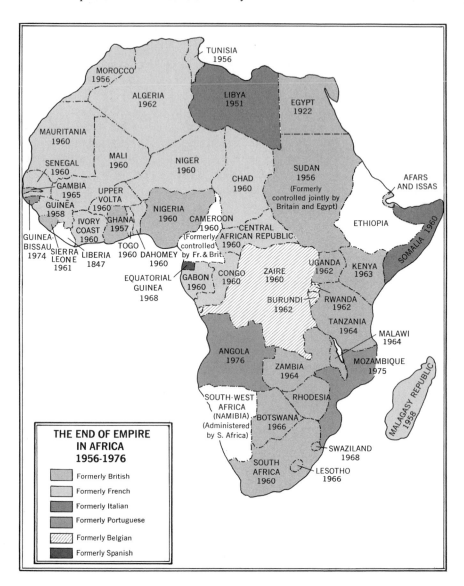

THE END OF EMPIRE
IN AFRICA
1956-1976

- Formerly British
- Formerly French
- Formerly Italian
- Formerly Portuguese
- Formerly Belgian
- Formerly Spanish

of the Algerian rebels, and the Suez debacle were obvious immediate factors. While these events speeded up the liberation process, the independence movements had already reached the ultranationalist stage in Ghana and the bourgeois stage in several colonial areas.

World War II had already seriously weakened the control of Europeans over their colonies. Africans came into contact with nationalists in India and with African nationalists serving in the British and French military during the war. The defeat and occupation of France convinced many Africans that their European overlords were not invincible.

At home, increased economic activity in support of the Western war effort increased the size of the native lower-middle class — nurses, teachers, mechanics, artisans, and so on. After the war, these people were frustrated by their inability to find jobs and by the Europeans' monopoly on the top administrative positions. In addition, the Cold War led the United States and the Soviet Union to seek support among third world countries by encouraging independence movements.

The events of 1956 were instrumental in ending France's dream of assimilating French colonial areas within a greater France and in convincing the British that granting independence was the only alternative. Before the war, assimilation into a greater French Union had been accepted by many African nationalists. In 1936 an Algerian nationalist, Ferhat Abbas, asserted,

> Six million Moslems live on this soil which has been French for a hundred years; they live in hovels, go barefoot, without clothing and often without bread. Out of this hungry mass we shall make a modern society . . . elevate them to human dignity so that they may be worthy of the name of Frenchmen.

By the time Ferhat Abbas became premier of the provisional government of the Algerian Republic in 1958 he had become a staunch advocate of Algerian independence.

Britain's system of local administration permitted its colonies to make a smoother transition to independence. Having been brought into colonial administrations in the nineteenth century, many Africans had become capable administrators. When Britain's Asian empire was lost in the late 1940s, most British leaders recognized that African independence was inevitable. As British administrators gradually relinquished their control, well-trained Africans easily picked up the reins of government.

In late 1956, most French colonies demanded and received the *loi-cadre* (semiautonomy) from a weakened France. Because of the weakness of the European powers, independence often came to sub-Saharan Africa when the ultranationalist groups were just forming. In cases where the nationalist movement had reached the third ultranationalist stage, the transition from the second to third stage may have taken only a few years. The Belgian Congo provides a perfect example of this telescoping of the nationalist movements. In 1956 Patrice Lumumba's demands were for more liberal measures for the educated Congolese; two years later he formed the *Mouvement National Congolais,* a mass ultranationalist party.

Unfortunately, the independence movements often were splintered by regional and tribal differences that were overcome only through civil war. These divisions encouraged and in some cases forced the new states to set up one-party governments or military regimes in order to overcome the opposition.

In Ghana (Gold Coast) ultranationalists had gained control of the independence movement before independence came in 1957. Ghana provides the best example of the three-stage nationalist transition, with the Aborigines' Rights Protection Society, the Gold Coast Convention (GCC), and the Convention People's party (CPP) representing the three stages. Typically, the CPP, headed by Kwame Nkrumah, became dissatisfied with the moderate leadership of the GCC and formed its own mass-based political party. Nkrumah claimed that "a middle-class elite, without the battering-ram of the illiterate masses" would never be able to "smash the forces of colonialism." His "positive action" campaign of strikes and boycotts was deeply influenced by his training in Marxian economics in the West and by Gandhi's tactics in India.

Finding Nkrumah's policies too revolutionary, Britain imprisoned him in 1950. A British Commission Report in 1948 said, "We have no reason to suppose that power in the hands of a small literate minority would not tend to be used to exploit the illiterate majority." It recommended that Britain retain control over Ghana until literacy and political experience had reached a stage whereby the masses could not be exploited. However, when the CPP won an overwhelming victory in the 1951 elections, Britain decided that it was politically expedient to release Nkrumah from prison and include him in the government.

Granted self-government in 1951, Ghana's leaders had considerable experience when full independence came in 1957. Despite this advantage, Ghana has suffered from regional and tribal opposition to the central government since independence. Nkrumah's attempt to build up support among his countrymen, including assuming adulatory titles such as savior, increased middle-class opposition to his government. In order to curb the opposition, he became president in 1960 under a new CPP constitution that permitted him to rule without parliament. Several years after he forbade the existence of other political parties, Nkrumah was overthrown by a military coup that was supported by his middle-class opponents and the powerful Ashanti tribe. The Ashantis had gained important positions in the military and among Nkrumah's political opponents.

The Nigerian nationalist movement, split along strong tribal lines, was a more complicated but perhaps more typical example than Ghana of the African independence struggles. Not one but two protonationalist groups emerged, the Nigerian National Democratic party led by Herbert Macauly and the traditionalist Muslim Northern People's Congress (NPC) based on the Fulani–Hausa tribe in the predominantly Muslim north. At first the NPC opposed independence since the powerful Muslim leaders did not desire integration with the more Westernized non-Muslim south and west.

Among the Ibo tribe in the east a Westernized group, the National Council of Nigeria and the Cameroons (NCNC), was set up by a newspaper publisher, Dr. Nnamdi Azikiwe, in 1944. Azikiwe had gained popularity before the war when he spoke out against British control and for independence.

In the more urban west, dominated by the Yoruba tribe, Chief Obafemi Awolowo put together the Action party. Basically a middle-class-led group, the Action party at first followed a pro-Western moderate course toward independence. After gaining independence, Awolowo switched to a neutralist and more radical program of Nigerianization. But he stopped short of any Nkrumah-style ultra-Africanism with its strong appeal to the urban and peasant masses.

Independence necessitated bringing these disparate groups together by satisfying regional and tribal differences. Britain, fearful that it might alienate the Muslim north by granting autonomy prematurely, encountered increasing resistance from Azikiwe and Awolowo. NPC resistance was overcome when younger NPC members persuaded their colleagues to form an NCNC–NPC coalition, which chose NPC leader Abubaker Tafawa Balewa to be the first prime minister of Nigeria. The organization of Nigeria on a federal basis permits considerable local autonomy; for example, the Muslim leader in the Northern Province, Sir Ahmadu Bello, was able to retain much of his local authority. Azikiwe, who at first favored a coalition with the Action party, accepted the NPC coalition because of pressure from within his own group. This compromise permitted Azikiwe to become governor-general of independent Nigeria in 1960. Awolowo, as a member of the opposition in the new government, resorted to more radical policies and was imprisoned in 1963. After independence a genuine ultranationalist Nigerian Socialist party formed.

Nigeria is one of the few African states to retain a Western-style parliamentary system that permits political opposition. Most African leaders believe that political power has to be centered in one group or party that can bring about the needed modernization without having to deal with crippling parliamentary opposition.

In British East Africa, Tanganyika obtained independence in 1961 under the leadership of the Tanganyika African National Union (TANU) headed by Julius Nyerere. When independence came, TANU stood somewhere between the bourgeois and ultranationalist stages of nationalism. It was organized on a mass basis but it lacked the social revolutionary and anti-Western aspects of a genuine ultranationalist program.

Not until 1966, after Tanganyika had merged with Zanzibar to form the new state of Tanzania, did Nyerere adopt a revolutionary program that included nationalization of banks and industry and a cooperative agricultural program. Tanganyika was spared the divisive tribal rivalries characteristic of most African states because none of its 120 tribes were large enough to challenge the government.

Nyerere's government was similar to many others in Africa in that no organized opposition was permitted. However, considerable differences were to be found within TANU. Before 1966 a strong left wing, composed of the trade union and cooperative movements, was critical of Nyerere's moderate social policies. This group was instrumental in swinging Nyerere's policies to the left in 1966. Differences such as this, which exist in many one-party governments in Africa, have led political observers to conclude that the decision-making process is often as democratic in these states as it is in some multiparty systems. In foreign affairs, Nyerere chose to keep his country in the British Commonwealth along with the other seven former British colonies and protectorates in East and West Africa.

With the exception of Guinea, the French territories in Africa followed a similar path to independence. All had experienced the French policy of assimilation to 1956 that reduced tribal authority and administered the eight colonies of French West Africa and the four in Equatorial Africa and Madagascar from the administrative centers at Dakar and Brazzaville.

The events of the mid–1950s crushed French hopes that these territories could ultimately be incorporated into a greater France as Guadeloupe, Martinique, French Guiana, and Réunion already were. With the granting of the *loi-cadre* in 1956, the colonies were given the right to exercise full executive power through their local assemblies and cabinets. In 1958, de Gaulle gave the colonies a choice: autonomy within a community of French nations, complete independence, a continuation of their present status, or incorporation within France as a department. Twelve of the colonies chose autonomy within the French community and Guinea opted for complete independence. Beginning in 1960 the twelve colonies that had chosen autonomy were granted their independence as de Gaulle recognized the futility of trying to keep them in a larger French community. Nevertheless, most of them retained close economic and cultural ties with France after independence.

Only Guinea, under the ultra-African leadership of Sékou Touré, deviated from an essentially moderate Westernized leadership common to all the French territories. Most leaders in French Africa had acquired their political education in the *Rassemblement Democratique Africain* (RDA), the strongest of the African political parties represented in the Chamber of Deputies in Paris. Except for a period of Communist influence from 1948 to 1954, the RDA remained in the hands of moderate Francophile leaders such as Félix Houphouët-Boigny from the Ivory Coast. Houphouët-Boigny, a member of the Mollet cabinet and leader of the RDA, was the main author of the *loi-cadre*. Once the colonies received autonomy, the RDA often became the leading party in the individual states.

Only in Guinea and Senegal did the RDA lose out to more Socialist,

Africanist parties. After independence, power fell to a Westernized elite that normally set up the one-party state dominated by a strong personality, such as Houphouet-Boigny in the Ivory Coast or Leopold Sedar-Senghor in Senegal.

The Pattern of Nationalism

What we have seen in Asia, the Middle East, and Africa is a three-stage pattern of nationalism that emerged as a result of Western modernization and domination along with traditional feelings of uniqueness and pride. The occasional failure of the third ultranationalist stage to develop before independence can be attributed to the weakness of the colonial powers and their realization that continued domination might drive their colonies into savage resistance. With Portugal's loss of its colonial empire in the 1970s, only two states that have large white populations — South Africa and Rhodesia — have managed to suppress their nationalist movements. But the events of 1976 indicate that black majority rule will prevail in Rhodesia within the next two years, either through a compromise between whites and more moderate blacks, or through violence from revolutionary guerrilla forces.

FURTHER READING

For an outstanding concise interpretation of the politics of national liberation see the chapter on decolonization in Geoffrey Barraclough, *An Introduction to Contemporary History* (1967). For a more detailed description see F. Mansur, *Process of Independence* (1962).

The decline of the British Empire is described in Rupert Emerson, *From Empire to Nation* (1960); Eric Estoric, *Changing Empire: Churchill to Nehru* (1950); and John Strachey, *The End of Empire* (1960). French colonialism and its decline is described in Guy De Carmoy, *The Foreign Policies of France 1944-1968* (1970). The role of the French army in the colonial territories is covered in John Ambler, *The French Army in Politics, 1945-1962* (1966).

For the collapse of colonialism in Asia see K. M. Pannikar, *Asia and Western Dominance* (1953); J. Romein, *The Asian Century: A History of Modern Nationalism in Asia* (1962); Truong Buu Lam, *Patterns of Vietnamese Response to Foreign Intervention; 1858-1900* (1967); P. Spear, *India, Pakistan and the West* (1961); Ellen Hammer, *The Struggle for Indochina, 1940-54* (1955); and G. M. Ziadeh, *Nationalism and Revolution in Indonesia* (1952).

The course of national liberation in the Middle East is described in M. Rowlatt, *Founders of Modern Egypt* (1962); Philip K. Hitti, *Islam and the West* (1962); and John Campbell, *Defense of the Middle East* (1960).

Nationalism and the stages of the independence movements in Africa are analyzed in Immanuel Wallerstein, *Africa: The Politics of Independence* (1961); George W. Shepherd, *The Politics of African Independence* (1962); and Thomas Hodgkin, *Nationalism in Colonial Africa* (sixth impression, 1968). For a comparative study of European rule in Africa see A. J. Hanna, *European Rule in Africa* (1961). Two studies that describe the three-stage pattern of nationalism in Africa are D. E. Apter, *The Gold Coast in Transition* (1955); and J. S. Coleman, *Nigeria: Background to Nationalism* (1958).

7 From Stalin to Khrushchev: The New Course and Polycentrism

> The heart of Lenin's comrade-in-arms and the inspired continuer of Lenin's cause, the wise teacher and leader of the party and the people, has stopped beating. Stalin's name is boundlessly dear to our party, to the Soviet people, to the working people of the world.
>
> *Pravda,* March 5, 1953

The above announcement signaled the end of an era, but several years were to elapse before the nature of the new era became clear. Between Stalin's death and the denunciation of his so-called cult of personality that Nikita Khrushchev made at the Twentieth Party Congress in 1956, a struggle for power raged between the Stalinists and the proponents of a new course.

The Stalinists continued to support heavy industry, the collectivization of agriculture, the extreme centralization of economic planning, and, in foreign policy, continued hostility toward the West. The followers of the so-called new course stressed increased production of consumer goods, light industry, decentralization of economic decision making, relaxation of internal political controls, and the achievement of a *modus vivendi* with the West.

This internal Soviet division, combined with national communist movements and what the Soviet Union classified as revisionism, was to lead to a progressive disintegration of Soviet hegemony in Eastern Europe. Although the Soviet Union still had military control over most of Eastern Europe in the 1960s, the Soviet satellites had gained a large measure of independence. Furthermore, where only one leader of world communism had been acknowledged before 1948, at least three centers existed in the 1960s: the Soviet Union, Communist China, and Yugoslavia.

Postwar Society under Stalin

During World War II Stalin had liberalized his regime in order to rally popular support for the war. After the massive purges of the 1930s when almost all the old Bolshevik leaders had been wiped out, the war years brought a welcome reprieve from fear and insecurity. Loyalty to the state rather than loyalty to Stalin became the major criterion for social acceptance. Emphasis was placed on the fatherland and past Soviet heroes. The Russian Orthodox Church escaped persecution for the duration of the war. When the Communist party relaxed its admittance requirements in 1943, party membership swelled from 3.4 to 6 million. The army experienced a similar relaxation when the Communist party commissars who had formerly shared command with the army officers were limited to an advisory role.

Such relative freedom led many Soviet citizens to expect that the quality of life would improve in the postwar period. They were in for a rude shock.

Soviet society grew more repressive after the war. Instead of liberalization, citizens were faced with a conservative restoration, a return to total orthodoxy. The immediate postwar period has become known as the Zhdanov era, after anti-intellectual party bureaucrat Andrei Zhdanov, who reimposed the ideological uniformity that had existed before the war. The secret police (NKVD), headed by Lavrenti Beria, rounded up all people classified as enemies of the state and exiled them to Siberian labor camps run by the NKVD. War heroes such as Kliment Voroshilov and Georgi Zhukov were demoted to minor posts, and party control over the military was reestablished.

These acts reflect Stalin's apparent fear that a complex society with many centers of authority would threaten his authoritarian control. He considered himself responsible for the Soviet victory over Germany and particularly resented the praise heaped upon the Soviet generals. By humbling these generals — he made Voroshilov ask permission to come to each Politburo meeting — he could enhance his own feeling of importance.

In the arts, the postwar period was marked by a return to social realism. Creativity was sacrificed to a pervasive uniformity. Writing had to sing the praises of Soviet society and the Communist party. Writers, social scientists, even natural scientists had to follow the party line. One of the greatest sins was cosmopolitanism; composers Dimitri Shostakovich and Sergei Prokofiev and film director Sergei Eisenstein were adjudged guilty of this sin. In all fields, particular emphasis was placed on Stalin's role as the savior of the Soviet Union. It was this Caesarian worship that Khrushchev denounced as the cult of personality.

When Stalin died in 1953 he apparently had been planning another major purge. The arrest of some prominent doctors, most of them Jewish, for plotting to kill government officials seems to have been the opening move in a much broader purge. Stalin is reported to have told Minister of State Security E. Ignatiev, "If you do not obtain confessions from the victims, we will shorten you by a head." Khrushchev charged that among the intended victims were some of the top members of the party: Anastas Mikoyan, Voroshilov, and Vyacheslav Molotov.

The Postwar Economy under Stalin

The Soviet Union experienced a postwar economic restoration of Stalinism similar to the social one. As in the 1930s, supply, demand, and investment were directed by an extensive bureaucracy with headquarters in Moscow. Stalin again stressed heavy industry at the expense of agriculture and consumer goods. Agriculture was to provide the necessary capital for industry; it contributed one-third of the gross national product but received only 15 percent of total investments.

Soviet production figures, which were always inflated until the late 1950s, reported that industrial output had reached the 1940 level by 1953. Despite this growth, the standard of living remained among the lowest in Europe. Real wages rose 83 percent in the Soviet Union (according to inflated Soviet statistics), but doubled in Western Europe between 1950 and 1966. Moreover, the concentration on producer goods caused serious shortages of consumer goods.

Most industrial products were either of poor quality or outdated. In part this was because there was no competition and no need to please the customer. And in part it was because some of the quotas set by the central planners left factory managers no choice but to turn out inferior products. According to Khrushchev, most Soviet leaders were aware of these problems but were afraid to go counter to Stalin's view that only centralized control could make things work. As a result, local factory managers were deprived of all decision-making power.

The Choice of Stalin's Successor

At the time of Stalin's death, no one had sufficient support to fill his dictatorial shoes. When Soviet leaders asked the citizenry not to panic they revealed their own fears. As Nikita Khrushchev was to say, "If you put fifteen of us [in the Presidium] end to end, it would not make a Stalin." It was not clear at this point whether the next leader or leaders would come from the Communist party organization or the state organization, since Stalin's dictatorial regime had severely curtailed the authority of the party.

It soon became apparent that the supporters of the new course were in the majority. The closest followers of Stalin soon lost out in the power struggle. Beria, who was head of the secret police and best qualified to assume Stalin's position, was liquidated on trumped-up charges. But another close follower, Molotov, was to remain as one of the top policy makers until 1955, when his hard-line foreign policy objectives were defeated.

Soviet leaders soon began to stress the collective nature of leadership. Georgi Malenkov succeeded Stalin as both party secretary and chairman of the council of ministers, but he was removed as party secretary after only a few weeks by the Central Committee. This move heralded the greater diffusion of power and the revival of the Communist party's role as the major decision-making body. Stalin had limited the party's power to merely rubber-stamping all his decisions. Now, after Beria was liquidated, it was the power of the secret police that was severely circumscribed.

Until Khrushchev became dominant, the party Presidium made all policy decisions. Throughout the 1950s, party organs made major decisions on leadership and policy changes. Khrushchev realized the importance of the party; in 1957 he defeated his opponents by appealing a Presidium decision against him to a meeting of the party's Central Committee. The decision to remove Khrushchev from power seven years later was made by a majority of the Presidium and the Central Committee. True, some decisions had already been reached before the meetings of the government organs, but they were not always final, as the reversal of the 1957 Presidium decision attests.

Nikita Khrushchev's rise to power corresponded to Georgi Malenkov's fall. The battle was waged over Malenkov's advocacy of the new course and Khrushchev's support of heavy industry and agriculture. In stressing improvement in the standard of living through concentration on light industry, housing, and consumer goods, Malenkov promised "an abundance of food for the people and of raw materials for consumer goods industries in the next two or three years." A struggle then ensued between Khrushchev and Malenkov over the economy and ultimately over party leadership.

Malenkov's program would have required a massive shift in economic priorities, thus reducing investment in heavy industry and armaments. Khrushchev was able to convince most of the party members that such a course would imperil Soviet security since there was not enough money for heavy industry and armaments as well as for agriculture and consumer goods. And, Khrushchev argued, huge investments in machinery were needed so that enormous new territories in Kazakstan and western Siberia (virgin lands) could be opened up to agriculture.

With the majority of the party behind him, Khrushchev became first secretary of the party in September 1953 and finally forced Malenkov to resign as chairman of the council of ministers in February 1955. With the appointment of Nikolai Bulganin as Malenkov's successor, Khrushchev had established his ascendancy.

Khrushchev's Leadership

Once Khrushchev gained the upper hand in the Soviet Union he tried to find a new way to deal with the growing revisionism in the Soviet bloc. It had become clear to Khrushchev that some liberalization was necessary to prevent massive upheaval in Eastern Europe. Therefore, in 1955 and 1956 he launched a campaign to put the Soviet Union in the forefront of this liberalization. As a first step he had to counteract Tito's influence in Eastern Europe, for Yugoslavia had taken the lead by abandoning collectivization in 1953, initiating worker self-management in industry, and turning the Communist party into a broader, more national organization called the League of Communists.

The Khrushchev offensive began with the denunciation of Stalin at the Twentieth Party Congress of the Soviet Union in 1956. By making Stalin the scapegoat for all the evils in Eastern Europe, Khrushchev hoped to take the onus off the present Soviet leadership. This policy was of course dangerous since any criticism of former leaders could reflect on him and on the party as well.

A 20,000-word speech denouncing Stalin's cult of personality was the opening move to reestablish Soviet authority. Dissolving the Cominform in April 1956 confirmed Khrushchev's earlier promise to Tito that ideological uniformity would not be imposed on the East European countries. Finally, his announcement of the doctrine of diversity at a meeting with Tito on June 20 seemed to put the Soviet stamp of approval on different roads to socialism. It was not long before Khrushchev's new policy was to be put to the test.

The Poznan Riots

Only ten days after Khrushchev's meeting with Tito, riots erupted in Poznan, Poland. These riots were not solely the result of Khrushchev's policies; primarily, the workers were protesting their low standard of living, which had its roots in earlier Soviet pressure to concentrate on heavy industry. Malenkov's new course, which was urged on Polish leaders to improve relations with the masses, actually divided the leadership into Stalinists and followers of the new course; and at the same time it accelerated worker demands for economic improvement. Revelations at the Twentieth Party Congress further undermined the credibility of Polish Stalinists: it was reported that Soviet agents had destroyed the Polish Communist party leadership in 1938 and remade the party to conform to Soviet desires.

Even before Khrushchev's 1956 offensive, Polish intellectuals had become increasingly critical of the hard-line Polish leadership. Following the onset of the new course, they had discussed the inappropriateness of agricultural collectivization in Poland and the lack of worker participation in industrial management. Undoubtedly, Yugoslav deviationism in agrarian and industrial policies had a further impact upon the Polish debate.

Among the noteworthy consequences of the Polish revolt were the ending of collectivization in Polish agriculture and the establishment of workers' councils in Polish industry.

The workers' revolt for bread and freedom and the refusal of the police and army to fire on them left the Polish leadership with two options: to comply with the popular demands or depend on Soviet troops to put down the rioters.

The reform movement had had its effect. Polish leaders, in an unprecedented move, apologized to the workers for their poor conditions and promised reforms. At a meeting of the Central Committee between July 18 and 28, attended by Nikolai Bulganin and Georgi Zhukov, Polish leaders tried to pick their way between two equally undesirable extremes: an anti-Communist revolution or Soviet intervention. Bulganin told the Poles, "Every country can go a different way to socialism" — as long as it did not break up the Soviet bloc. This was rejected at the meeting, but it became the basis for the final settlement.

During the next three months the Polish leadership came to the conclusion that only the return of the recently discredited national communist leader, Wladyslaw Gomulka, could resolve the crisis. During these three months Poland had obtained the support of Communist China and Yugoslavia for its national communist course by convincing the Chinese that the Polish national road was not to be similar to the Yugoslav one. Early in October worker intervention helped the Polish leaders survive an attempted coup by Stalinists. With the Polish Stalinists defeated, Soviet leaders decided it was time to come to an understanding with the reformist forces.

On October 19 Nikita Khrushchev, Lazar Kaganovitch, Anastas Mikoyan, and Vyacheslav Molotov flew unannounced to Warsaw. Khrushchev accused the Polish leaders of misleading him about the internal situation, but the recently rehabilitated Gomulka convinced the Soviet leaders that Poland was going to remain within the Soviet bloc and that Poland's anti-Stalinist views were no more radical than those of the Soviet Union. Moreover, he convinced Khrushchev that only a somewhat revisionist course would be acceptable to the Polish masses.

The Soviet visit was not altogether in vain. Since Khrushchev had previously enunciated a policy of diversity and had accepted the Yugoslav revisionists, the Polish promises of support for Soviet foreign policy and continued control of the Communist party in Poland were sufficient to allay Soviet fears.

Despite Soviet acquiescence on the decollectivization of agriculture and a deemphasis of heavy industry, there was little else about the Polish policy that was revisionist. Until Gomulka fell from power in 1966 he followed a basically conservative course, in part because he realized that Poland's geographic position demanded a close working relationship with the Soviet Union and in part because he disliked radical revisionism.

Gomulka continued to oppose Titoism and a liberalization of the press in Poland. Eventually, he stilled most of the voices that had demanded greater liberalization, or the so-called Polish spring in October. His conservatism extended even outside his own country. He joined in the denunciation of the 1956 Hungarian Revolution which followed on the heels of the Polish revolt and ironically was inspired at least to some extent by Poland's defiance of the Soviet Union.

The Hungarian Revolution

The Hungarian Revolution presented a much more serious challenge to the Soviet Union than the Polish uprising had done. While Poland threatened to establish its own brand of national communism, the Hungarian Revolution seemed to many Soviet leaders to threaten the very existence of the Communist party. Poland continued to acknowledge the supremacy of the Soviet Union in Eastern Europe, but Hungary aimed to chart a neutral course by severing its ties with the Soviet Union. If this uprising had been allowed to succeed it might have engendered similar revolutions throughout Eastern Europe.

Hungarian political and economic developments prior to the 1956 revolt mirror those of the Soviet Union. Malenkov's new course was followed in Hungary by Imre Nagy's new course. Appointed premier in July 1953, four months after Stalin's death, Nagy saw as his task the restoration of economic stability and confidence in the Communist regime. His predecessor as premier, Matyas Rakosi, who retained his position as leader of the Communist party, had brought Hungary to the brink of economic catastrophe by his Stalinist emphasis on the buildup of Hungarian heavy industry at the expense of the rest of the economy. Nagy began to divert the country's resources to light industry and stopped the forced collectivization of agriculture.

The economic relaxation led to a corresponding intellectual relaxation. Intellectuals began to discuss not only the nature of the changes in Hungarian communism but also the value of a communist system. A group of intellectuals gathered in the Petöfi Circle — named after a nineteenth-century nationalist poet and established by the Communist party in March 1956 as what the party hoped would be a harmless escape valve — and debated the possibility of achieving democracy in a Communist state. Nagy and the intellectuals appear to have been influenced by the independent course in Yugoslavia, believing it possible for Hungary to achieve the same independent position.

Nagy's plans were cut short by the fall of his Soviet protector, Malenkov, in February 1955. Rakosi now seized the opportunity to regain leadership over both the state and the party, reinstituting a Stalinist hard line. Nagy gave in without a fight, perhaps because he expected Rakosi would fail in his attempt to reimpose ideological conformity.

Yet Nagy could hardly have expected the shakeup in the Soviet bloc that was to result from Khrushchev's denunciation of Stalin at the Twentieth Party Congress in February 1956. While Rakosi tried to reestablish his authority, Khrushchev was exonerating Bela Kun, a discredited former Rakosi rival and a national communist. Buoyed up by Khrushchev's action, Hungarian intellectuals demanded an investigation of Rakosi's past, especially the part he had played in the liquidation of the national communist, Lásló Rajk. Rajk had been accused of Titoist deviationism and executed during the Stalinist purges in 1949. In March 1956 Rakosi conceded Rajk's innocence.

Three months later the Hungarian Writers Union and the Petöfi Circle, inspired by Gomulka's successful stand in Poland, openly opposed Rakosi in the columns of the party newspaper *Szabad Nep*. The Soviet Union opposed Rakosi's plan to silence his opposition by arresting Nagy and 400 intellectuals, both because the plan might fail and because it certainly would not endear the Communist party to the Hungarian population.

Wanting a more popular leader for the Hungarian Communist party (CPH), the Soviet leaders chose Ernö Gerö as Rakosi's successor, but he was not acceptable to the majority of the anti-Stalinist intellectuals. According to Tito, distrust of Nagy led the Soviet leaders to make it "a condition that Rakosi would go only if Gerö remained. And this was a mistake, because Gerö differed in no way from Rakosi." Had the Soviet leaders supported Nagy at this point when he still had a chance to put himself at the head of the reforming forces, they might have prevented the more radical revolution that was to follow.

The first stage of the revolution was touched off when a group demonstrating in support of the Polish insurrection was fired upon by the Hungarian police on October 23, 1956. Several mass demonstrations had already been held by the Petöfi Circle to demand a new party congress and the reinstatement of Nagy. For example, three days earlier, 200,000 people marched in Budapest, chanting the Petöfi verse, "We will never again be slaves."

Gerö made his most serious mistake on that fateful day when he called on the Soviet army to put down the demonstration. In the minds of most Hungarians this act completely discredited the party and increased their desire for a non-Communist Hungary. The use of Soviet troops stimulated a violent reaction. Workers set up anti-Soviet, anti-Communist workers' councils throughout Hungary. In the countryside student parliaments and socialist revolutionary councils arose spontaneously, demanding free elections, the withdrawal of Soviet troops, and the dissolution of the security police.

When segments of the Hungarian army joined the revolt, Soviet leaders decided that only a Communist government headed by Nagy could survive without Soviet support. On October 28 Soviet troops began to withdraw from Budapest, and Nagy set up a new government.

By now, hatred of the Soviet Union and the Hungarian Communist party had reached such intensity that even Nagy would have found it difficult to install a solely Communist government, had he wanted to do so. Nagy not only permitted the reestablishment of opposition parties but also set up a coalition government with Social Democratic, Smallholder, and National Peasant party participation. By October 31, he had withdrawn Hungary from the Soviet bloc and proclaimed Hungarian neutrality.

These acts confirmed Khrushchev's fears about Nagy. Hungary had presented the Soviet Union with a challenge to its authority which it could not ignore. If the Hungarians were permitted to continue, the Soviets faced the prospect of more anti-Communist revolts in Eastern Europe and an end to Soviet hegemony in Eastern Europe. Even Tito approved the crushing of the "fascist counterrevolution" in November. Despite the valiant opposition of most of Hungary's population, the Soviet army soon smashed all resistance.

Because the next Hungarian Communist party and government leader, János Kádár, called on the Soviet Union to put down the revolution, he was

The aftermath of an anti-Soviet demonstration in Budapest, Hungary on October 31, 1956. A huge statue of Soviet Premier Josef Stalin was toppled by demonstrators and dragged two miles to the center of the city, where it was broken apart by souvenir hunters.

Keystone Press Agency, Inc.

termed "a standing affront to national memory and pride." But since the revolution he has led Hungary to its own national communism. Having been imprisoned by Rakosi for his nationalism, Kádár was not unaware of the desires of his countrymen. If we compare conditions in the early 1960s in Hungary and Poland, where Gomulka instituted a more orthodox regime, we might wonder whether it was the Hungarians or the Poles who won in 1956. Kádár removed the Stalinists from the party and concentrated on promoting economic development and raising the standard of living. Yet the Hungarian people never accepted Kádár fully; the memory of 1956 continued to rankle.

The Hungarian Revolution seriously eroded Khrushchev's support in the Soviet Union. The cost of putting down the revolt and financing the recovery of Hungary put the brake on Soviet economic growth. Certain of Khrushchev's enemies, Bulganin among them, used the financial crisis and the Hungarian debacle as grounds for challenging Khrushchev's position. In defense, Khrushchev tried to blame the highly centralized government agencies for the economic failures. His proposal for lodging economic decision making in regional economic commissions, called *Sovnarkhozy,* gained the support of a majority of the Central Committee in May 1957.

Since local party officials then were given more say in local economic affairs, support for Khrushchev increased among party members. But in June 1957, while he was on a trip to Finland, his opponents managed to gain a majority in the Presidium. When he returned he was vigorously attacked by Malenkov, Molotov, and Bulganin for creating economic problems and violating the principle of collective leadership. Undaunted, Khrushchev had the entire Central Committee called together in June 1957 and gained a majority over his opponents. As a result, a so-called anti-party group, including Malenkov, Kaganovich, and Molotov were expelled from the Presidium of the party. Such an exercise of party democracy, not used since Lenin, indicated the changed nature of party leadership.

Polycentrism

Khrushchev faced an equally serious challenge to Soviet leadership of international communism. The revolts in Hungary and Poland as well as Yugoslav deviationism threatened Soviet domination in Eastern Europe. In fact, international communism underwent a three-way division in the 1950s among revisionists, dogmatists, and national communists. The split left the Communist world with several centers of power, a state of affairs known as *polycentrism.*

The *revisionists,* mainly Yugoslavia, rejected the Soviet model in its entirety, contending that it was the Soviet Union — not Yugoslavia — that had strayed from the path of Marxism–Leninism. They began to decentralize economic and political decision making to prove that they were

In 1964, eight years after the Hungarian Revolution, Soviet Premier Khrushchev (left), architect of the Soviet attempt to quash the revolution, is warmly welcomed in Budapest by János Kádár, who became premier of Hungary at the time of the uprisings.

Keystone Press Agency, Inc.

closer to the communist society envisioned by Marx than the highly centralized dictatorial government in the Soviet Union.

The Yugoslav revisionists were labeled deviationists and were vehemently opposed by the *dogmatists,* especially Communist China and Albania. In international affairs the dogmatists supported a continuation of the struggle with capitalism and violently opposed peaceful coexistence. At home they opposed a relaxation of Stalinist principles.

The *national communists,* led by Gomulka, stressed Communist solidarity in foreign affairs but insisted that each state be permitted to achieve communism in its own way. They held that local conditions were sufficiently different to preclude adoption of the Soviet economic and social model without adjusting it as needed. In practice, most of the states led by national communists retained much of the Soviet model.

Revisionism in Yugoslavia   It was the revisionist Yugoslavs who offered the most serious challenge to the Soviet model. There the establishment of the League of Communists reduced the strong centralized control of the party. Communist critics charged that many capitalist practices characterized the economy. Some Communist critics, in fact, have begun to see Titoism as nothing more than Western European social democracy.

Much of Yugoslavia's unorthodox mixture of Communist and capitalist practice has grown out of an ideological need to defend itself against charges of deviationism and a fundamentally pragmatic approach to Communist economic practices.

Khrushchev's denunciation of Stalinism and confirmation of the Yugoslav path to socialism in 1956 seemed to clear the way for a rapprochement between the Soviet Union and Yugoslavia. However, the Soviet's crushing of the Hungarian Revolution and subsequent efforts to achieve greater unity among Communist bloc countries encouraged Tito to maintain more stoutly the principle of national independence. Khrushchev ignored Tito's demand that the Soviet Union act against Stalinist leaders throughout Eastern Europe. In fact, Stalinism became more rigid in Eastern Europe after the Hungarian uprising. Led by Walter Ulbricht in East Germany and Antonin Novotny in Czechoslovakia, Eastern Europe became more dogmatic than the Soviet Union. Attacks on Yugoslavia in the Soviet and East European press and accelerated economic pressures led Tito to take a much more militant ideological position.

The 1958 draft program of the Yugoslav Party Congress asserted that Yugoslavia was closer to Marxism–Leninism than the Soviet Union was. With worker self-management and the diffusion of political power to local communes, the 1958 program stated, the League of Communists "will gradually, in the long run, disappear with the developing and strengthening of ever more inclusive forms of immediate socialist democracy."

Furthermore, the program asserted Communist parties were not the only creators of socialism. This was an apparent attempt to solidify Yugoslavia's position as a bridge between East and West by implying that Western European welfare states were also finding their way toward socialism. Although the program suggested no major change in Yugoslav policy, it was anathema in China and Albania.

Dogmatism in China   What China considered to be Khrushchev's coddling of deviationism became the immediate cause for the division of the Communist world into three major centers — the Soviet Union, China, and Yugoslavia — and many minor centers.

However, the development of the Sino–Soviet–Yugoslav split had long been evident. The Chinese had been disenchanted with Khrushchev's leadership since his denunciation of Stalin in 1956 and had long been opposed to the Soviet Union's territorial acquisitions in Asia, its monopoly of economic power within the Communist bloc, and its policy of peaceful coexistence.

China especially resented the favored economic position of the Soviet Union among the other Communist countries. Stalin had treated China the way he had treated the East European countries: as economic dependencies of the Soviet Union. In his view, China's function was to provide cheap raw materials to the Soviet Union and to serve as a buyer of Soviet manufactured goods. Rejecting that role, China propagandized that the Soviet Union should have raised all other Communist states to the Soviet economic level.

Since Stalin and Khrushchev were more interested in developing the Soviet Union than in fomenting world revolution, they were not interested in building up China. In fact, Stalin and Khrushchev were more afraid of China than of the West. Soviet propaganda against the Chinese smacked of the late nineteenth century, when Westerners were warning of the "yellow peril."

Chinese and Soviet claims to the same territory — Sinkiang, Amur, Sakhalin, Tranbaikalia — were much more immediate than Western threats. The failure of the Soviet Union to back China against India in 1962 was seen by Chinese leaders as further evidence of Soviet revisionism. However, to say, as some have done, that the Sino–Soviet rift is national and not ideological is to overlook a major element in the conflict.

The Chinese tolerated Khrushchev's denunciation of Stalin only because they thought the world Communist movement should be unified around the Soviet Union. From 1956 to 1958, they tolerated Soviet revisionism because they were much more afraid of polycentrism. In 1957 and 1958, as Khrushchev implemented his own pragmatic brand of communism in the Soviet Union, China attempted the Great Leap Forward to collectivize and communize China completely. When this experiment failed, even greater emphasis was placed on Stalinist orthodoxy (except for the Stalinist emphasis on industry at the expense of agriculture) in order to assure unity at home and save face abroad. Khrushchev's unsuccessful attempt to unseat Mao in 1959 by instigating a party revolt exacerbated relations.

At a series of conferences and party congresses from 1960 until Khrushchev's fall from power four years later the Soviet Union tried to discredit China. At the Twenty-second Party Congress in Bucharest during June of 1960, Khrushchev succeeded in obtaining majority support for his condemnation of Chinese factionalism. Unsubdued, the Chinese continued to charge that the world Communist movement was threatened by compromise with the enemy. Khrushchev's attempt to resolve differences with the United States at the summit conferences at Camp David (1959) and Paris (1960) were vehemently denounced in Peking.

The Soviet decisions to remove Stalin's body from the Kremlin, where it had rested in state next to Lenin's body, and to expel the pro-Chinese Albanians from the world Communist movement at the Twenty-second Congress of the CPSU in 1961 were an indirect slap at the Chinese. The gap became virtually unbridgeable with the withdrawal of Soviet forces from Cuba in 1962 and the signing of the Nuclear Test Ban Treaty a year later. The Chinese saw these actions as final proof that the Soviet Union would use nuclear weapons only to further its own interests and not to achieve world revolutionary aims.

National Communism in Romania　The establishment of a form of national communism in Romania in 1963 and 1964, influenced by the previous divisions in world communism, was even more clearly the outcome of Soviet economic policies and Khrushchev's anti-Stalinist offensive. Inspired by Yugoslav disaffection, and opposed to continued Soviet economic exploitation, in 1953 Gheorghe Gheorghiu-Dej set Romania on an increasingly independent course by eliminating the Moscow Communists from Romanian party leadership and abolishing the hated Soviet–Romanian joint companies (sovroms). Inspired by Malenkov's new course in the Soviet Union, Romania also sought to obtain a more diversified economy by increasing expenditures on the production of consumer goods.

Responsibility for Romania's decision to follow an independent course can be laid at the feet of Khrushchev, whose liberalization provided a major impetus to Romanian national communism. Gheorghiu-Dej was opposed to revisionism at home and believed that a liberalization in the Soviet regime would undermine his Stalinist position in the Romanian party.

Throughout the 1950s Romania drew closer to China as both nations resisted Khrushchev's policy of ideological conformism within the Communist world. Gheorghiu-Dej and Mao resented Khrushchev's continuing denunciations of Stalin and his pressure on them to follow suit. The Stalinist line in Romania hardened, and the likelihood of integration within the Soviet bloc dwindled.

When a pro-Khrushchev force in Romania allegedly challenged Gheorghiu-Dej's leadership in 1957, a campaign ensued to remove all revisionists — that is, Khrushchevites — from power. In order to strengthen the regime at home and continue Romania's drive toward economic independence from Moscow, as early as 1954 Gheorghiu-Dej decided to bolster the economy with aid from the West. Trade with the West reached 20 percent of Romania's total foreign trade in the following year, reflecting a distinct improvement in economic conditions. By 1960, Gheorghiu-Dej had strong support from the Romanian masses for his independent course.

Comecon and Economic Nationalism　The final shaping of Romanian national communism stemmed from Khrushchev's attempt to make Comecon a supranational economic agency with jurisdiction over the economies of each member state. Khrushchev saw Comecon as an answer to the growing economic division of labor in the Common Market. Only by achieving a similar division of labor in Comecon could the Communist countries keep pace with economic growth in the West. Romanian fears that the Comecon envisioned by Khrushchev would frustrate its own industrialization were well founded. Khrushchev planned to have Romania continue as a supplier of raw materials, especially oil, to the more developed Comecon countries — Czechoslovakia, East Germany, and the Soviet Union.

Khrushchev's determined drive in 1962 and 1963 to integrate all the East European economies was to founder on the rocks of economic nationalism. In advance of a meeting in July 1963 to determine whether Comecon was to be a supranational body, Romania got the support of both China and Yugoslavia to keep it international — and also received promises of financial support from the West. As an international agency, Comecon can suggest integrative measures but cannot enforce them as a supranational body could do. At the meeting, not only was supranationalism defeated but the right of member states to develop independently was upheld.

Now embroiled in his dispute with China and Albania, Khrushchev could not force the majority of East European states to accept a reinvigorated Comecon. Because of a continued friendship with China as well as with the Soviet Union, in 1963 Romania attempted to mediate the differences between the two.

Strong support of Soviet foreign policy in recent years has taken the sting out of Romania's earlier rejection of economic cooperation: it subscribed to Khrushchev's policy of peaceful coexistence and backed the Nuclear Test Ban Treaty. Coexistence suited Romania's goal of developing trade with the West in order to promote economic independence. Yet the Romanians may in fact have been saved by a more fundamental change — the unexpected fall of Khrushchev in October 1964.

Khrushchev's Fall from Power

Failures in both domestic and foreign policy led to Khrushchev's fall. The slow disintegration of Soviet hegemony in Eastern Europe, the growing disagreement with China, and the Cuban fiasco had undermined Khrushchev's position. His opponents were especially upset by his hasty decision to set up missile sites in Cuba and the humiliation of having to dismantle them.

Added to his foreign policy debacles were a number of economic failures. Especially harmful was the failure of Khrushchev's agricultural Virgin Lands project, which did not provide the promised amount of food. Despite a 17 percent increase in the acreage sown to crops from 1960 to 1963, massive imports of Canadian wheat and rationing of bread were necessary in 1963. Rather than increasing the acreage, Khrushchev should probably have farmed the existing tilled land more intensively, since he could have concentrated machinery and fertilizer on the existing arable land.

The failure of the sixth five-year plan added to Khrushchev's woes. The attempt to match the space program of the United States while investing heavily in new plants and equipment overtaxed Soviet resources. As defense spending rose by one-third between 1959 and 1963, the rate of industrial growth declined. The GNP growth rate declined from 10 percent in 1958 to about 3 percent in 1962 and 1963. Khrushchev also lost the support of the military and the heavy industry advocates in 1964, when he began to emphasize the production of consumer goods.

Despite these setbacks, Khrushchev's opponents had to maneuver his fall while he was vacationing in the Crimea. Called back by the Presidium, he was unable to turn the table on his opponents by appealing to the Central Committee because his supporters were in the minority there.

Two days after his removal from office, *Pravda,* the Soviet newspaper, denounced his "hare-brained scheming, immature conclusions, hasty decisions, and actions divorced from reality."

The new Soviet leaders were presented with an Eastern Europe entirely different from the one that Khrushchev had inherited. The change was in part a consequence of Khrushchev's policies but in greater measure an outgrowth of economic nationalism and the decline in East–West tensions. As the Soviet Union felt less threatened by the West, it was willing to permit considerably more independence in Eastern Europe than it had at the height of the Cold War.

FURTHER READING

Soviet internal affairs are analyzed in Merle Fainsod, *How Russia Is Ruled* (2d ed. 1963); Leonard Schapiro, *The Communist Party of the Soviet Union* (1964); Robert Conquest, *Power and Policy in the U.S.S.R.* (1961); Adam B. Ulam, *The New Face of Soviet Totalitarianism* (1963); and John Reshetar, *The Soviet Polity* (1971).

For the Soviet role in world affairs see Alvin Z. Rubinstein (ed.), *The Foreign Policy of the Soviet Union* (1960); Louis Fischer, *The Soviets in World Affairs* (1960); David Dallin, *Soviet Foreign Policy After Stalin* (1961); and Philip Mosely, *The Kremlin and World Politics* (1960).

The best studies of the changing nature of the Soviet bloc are Zbigniew Brzezinski, *The Soviet Bloc, Unity and Conflict* (rev. ed., 1967); and Ghita Ionescu, *The Break-up of the Soviet Empire in Eastern Europe* (1965). Some preceptive short studies of polycentrism are in Kurt London (ed.), *Eastern Europe in Transition* (1966); Alexander Dallin (ed.), *Diversity in International Communism* (1963); and Paul Zinner (ed.), *National Communism and Popular Revolt in Eastern Europe* (1956).

Scholarly treatments of Khrushchev can be found in Edward Crankshaw, *Khrushchev: A Career* (1966); Carl A. Linden, *Khrushchev and the Soviet Leadership* (1966); and Abraham Blumberg (ed.), *Russia Under Khrushchev* (1962).

Competent studies of the Romanian separate road and Romanian communism are Ghita Ionescu, *Communism in Rumania 1944–1962* (1964); Stephen Fischer-Galati, *The New Rumania: From People's Democracy to Socialist Republic* (1967); Stephen Fischer–Galati, *The Socialist Republic of Rumania* (1969); and David Floyd, *Rumania: Russia's Dissident Ally* (1965).

For Poland see Hansjakob Stehle, *The Independent Satellite: Society and Politics in Poland Since 1945* (1965); James F. Morrison, *The Polish People's Republic* (1969); Richard Hiscocks, *Poland, Bridge for the Abyss* (1963); and Nicholas Bethell, *Gomulka: His Poland, His Communism* (1969).

The Hungarian Revolution is detailed further in Paul Kecskemeti, *The Unexpected Revolution* (1961); Ferenc A. Vali, *Rift and Revolt in Hungary* (1961); Paul E. Zinner, *Revolution in Hungary* (1962); Bennet Kovrig, *The Hungarian People's Republic* (1970); and Tamas Ceczel, *Ten Years After: The Hungarian Revolution in the Perspective of History* (1967).

8 European Unity

> The creation of a large internal market is indispensable to make it possible for Europeans to take their place in the world again.
>
> Jean Monnet, *Les Etats-Unis d'Europe Ont Commencé: Discours et Allocutions, 1952–1954*

> Why should we have recourse to this idea, to this new-fangled supranational institution [European Coal and Steel Community]? To enable Germany to accept restrictions on her own sovereignty which is being gradually and irrevocably restored to her. And if we wish to make Germany accept these restrictions, we must set her an example. . . . It will mean identical renunciation on both sides and in the most delicate matters, such as the army and the production of coal and steel, products essential to the preparation of war and for the formation of policy.
>
> Robert Schuman, *French Policy Towards Germany since the War*

The omnipresent fear and impotence of small nations in a world dominated by superpowers, the desire to incorporate Germany into a federated Europe so as to prevent a recurrence of war and its attendant devastation, the longing for the economic advantages thought to be inherent in a larger economic unit — together, these provided the initial impetus for European integration. The unification movement had slowed by the 1950s, but then the Soviet Union crushed the Hungarian Revolution, the British and French failed at Suez, and Europe lost its colonial empire. All these now convinced a growing number of Europeans who had originally opposed union that closer cooperation might be their only salvation. Externally, the United States pressured Europe to cooperate so that it could pay for more of its own reconstruction, restore its markets for American goods, and prevent calamitous political developments similar to those that followed World War I.

As French author and critic André Malraux noted, Europe was united only under Rome and under Christianity in the medieval period. By the end of World War I the triumph of the national state was complete. Few questioned the right of the national state to command the obedience of the people living within its borders. Nineteenth-century philosophers such as Hegel, as well as countless less romantic nationalists, justified the carving up of Europe into smaller national states that began in earnest with the French Revolution. The French Revolution had shown how brittle empires were and how powerful a political entity could be when supported by its citizenry.

Hegel and the romantics found in the national state the proper vehicle for the full development of a people's genius. In their view the empires and Christian Europe had impeded the full development of this genius. To them, true creativity in literature, music, and the other arts was no more than the ability to express this folk genius embodied in the national state. Nationalism became one of the major forces in the disruption of the Ottoman and Hapsburg empires before and during World War I.

The Beginnings of Unity

Until after World War I, few questioned the legitimacy of the national state. Count Richard Coudenhove-Kalergi, an aristocrat brought up in the Hapsburg monarchy, was the strongest advocate of European unification in the interwar years. Others, such as French Prime Minister Aristide Briand, had prepared a memorandum for a united Europe in 1930, but Europe was already on its way to an unlooked-for union under the jackboots of Adolf Hitler's Third Reich.

From the sufferings of World War II emerged a much more broadly based desire for some form of European union. Countless wartime resistance fighters decided that the Europe of nation states should be replaced by a unified and therefore less warlike Europe. A Dutch resistance publication of 1944, *De Ploeg,* visualizing a divided postwar Europe under the influence of either the United States or the Soviet Union, had this to say: "We Dutch are Europeans and we believe in a future for Europe. We do not belong to the Americans, who see Europe as senile and who from the outset are dividing it up into an Asiatic and an American sphere of interest."

European leaders of the stature of Winston Churchill, Pope Pius XII, Paul-Henri Spaak, Alcide de Gasperi, Robert Schuman, and Konrad Adenauer added their voices to the outpouring of support for a united Europe. Numerous organizations, Britain's United Europe Movement and Coudenhove-Kalergi's European Parliamentary Union among them, sprang up in support of European union.

In addition to the desire of Europeanists to avoid wars, the economic arguments for European union were compelling. Integration of the European economy would promote large-scale, low-cost production that would lead to greater economic output and an improved competitive position in the world market. Moreover, a customs union would enlarge the European market for member countries by bringing down the high tariff walls that ated them. Europeanists were convinced that a primary factor in American productivity and competitiveness was the huge American commn market of 160 million people. Despite these advantages, many Europeans were unwilling to relinquish a measure of national sovereignty in order to attain economic integration. Two outside influences were dominant in breaking down resistance to European economic integration: the Cold War and American pressure in support of European integration to block possible Soviet expansion into Western Europe.

The Organization for European Economic Cooperation

The first major step toward integration was taken in 1947 when the United States asked for the establishment of a common European organization to plan the distribution of American aid under the European Recovery Program, known more familiarly as the Marshall Plan. Presented with the possibility of forestalling a severe postwar economic crisis, seventeen European nations, acting in concert, set up the Organization for European Economic Cooperation (OEEC) to distribute the funds and promote trade among the member nations. Only the East European countries, pressured by Stalin, refused to take part. Since the OEEC was to remain an international rather than a supranational organization — the United States eventually became a full member — there was never any possibility that a participant would have to sacrifice its national sovereignty.

The rapid expansion of trade across European borders — it doubled between 1948 and 1955 — convinced many Europeans of the OEEC's value. But attempts to expand it into a European customs union, with common external tariffs against nonmembers, encountered the resistance of Britain, which did not want to jeopardize its own economic ties with its Commonwealth partners. To those who wanted further European unification it became clear that the OEEC was incapable of achieving this. Still, it had brought Europeans together to discuss their financial needs and had in this way helped break down some opposition to integration.

The Council of Europe

The second major step toward integration was taken with the establishment of the Council of Europe. In May 1948, European federalists convoked a Congress of Europe that was attended by 750 delegates, including some of Europe's leading statesmen: Churchill, Spaak, de Gasperi, Schuman, and Léon Blum. This body's proposal for the political and economic unification of the Continent led a year later to the establishment of the Council of Europe, a permanent European assembly that was to plan some form of European integration.

The council's attempts to put together some form of union encountered serious resistance. Once again, none of the Eastern European states joined in the deliberations. Britain signed the agreement reluctantly because of the governing Labour party's concern for Britain's Commonwealth partners and its disapproval of what it considered to be the anti-Soviet orientation of the council. Beneath the surface was Britain's feeling that it really did not belong to Europe and that its interests would be best served by acting as a middleman between Europe and the United States.

As a result of British opposition, the Consultative Assembly of the Council of Europe was limited to the right of recommendation and had no true deliberative power. A Committee of Ministers, comprising the foreign ministers of the member states, was the sole decision-making body. Obviously, the foreign ministers would act as representatives of their individual states rather than as spokesmen for a new sovereign body. Thus the council was reduced to making recommendations and offering advice rather than moving toward any real supranational integration of the European states.

The first president of the Council of Europe, Paul-Henri Spaak, angrily denounced those who thwarted the establishment of a meaningful supranational body when he resigned his office in 1951. In his words, "If a quarter of the energy spent here in saying no, were used to say yes to something positive, we should not be in the state we are in today."

Had the movement for European integration stopped with only the OEEC and Council of Europe to its credit, there would be little need today to speak of a possible united Europe. However, there were strong pressures for decisive action. Especially instrumental in promoting tighter bonds was the unstable international situation. The 1948 Communist coup in Czechoslovakia convinced many opponents of integration that a larger European community was necessary to forestall Communist thrusts into central and Western Europe. The United States, searching for support in the Cold War with the Soviet Union, encouraged a stronger economic and military organization.

When the Soviet Union exploded its first atomic bomb in 1949, the general sense of insecurity increased. The outbreak of the Korean War lent new urgency to pan-European deliberations because it seemed to some a clear indication of the Communist world's intentions, and to many more it imparted fears for German security. While the United States was tied down in Asia, the reasoning went, American troops would be in short supply in Germany, and that would make Germany a tempting target for Soviet aggression. Europeans were of course aware that the United States wanted to rearm Germany in order to steel her defenses against the Soviet Union. This step the other European countries did not favor unless there was some larger European organization to control a rearmed Germany.

The European Coal and Steel Community

France took the lead in the negotiations for a genuine supranational body. Led by two of its greatest Europeanists, Commissioner of Planning Jean Monnet and Foreign Minister Robert Schuman, France proposed in the Schuman Plan a pooling of Europe's coal and steel resources that would, in the words of Monnet, make war between France and Germany "not only unthinkable but materially impossible."

In the summer of 1952, Schuman's proposal came to fruition when France, Germany, Italy, and the Benelux countries put into force the agreement setting up the European Coal and Steel Community (ECSC). Britain refused to join because of what it considered to be the excessive power given the nine-member High Authority of the ECSC, whose decisions were binding on all members. Britain, with fewer economic problems and with important ties to the United States and to its Commonwealth associates, was not prepared to sacrifice its national sovereignty. Had Britain joined the ECSC, the integration of its coal, steel, and iron industry with the six would have made avoidance of the next step, the Common Market, almost impossible. Many British Labour leaders continued to see such supranational organizations as a conspiracy of big business to circumvent the demands of national labor movements.

The European Defense Community

Strangely enough, attempts to form a common European military force encountered opposition not only from the British but ultimately from the very country that had initially proposed it: France.

In October 1950, French Prime Minister René Pleven proposed, as a military counterpart to the ECSC, a unified European army made up of small national contingents from each member nation. France was aware that the United States wanted to rearm Germany because of U.S. fears that the Soviet Union might put pressure on or even attack in Europe to help North Korea by diverting U.S. troops from Asia. France therefore offered the Pleven Plan to avoid the establishment of an independent German military force. Even in Germany there was support for the proposal, because German leaders hoped a common European military might bring an end to Allied occupation.

Perhaps a new supranational army with recruits from all states could have been realized if the former national contingents had been left intact. Yet it is difficult to see how even that proposal could have succeeded without a supranational political organization, and that was never a possibility.

In any case, the Pleven Plan for a European Defense Community (EDC) became the victim of events. The need for a European army diminished with Stalin's death and the thaw in Soviet–Western foreign relations. Although U.S. Secretary of State John Foster Dulles continued to threaten to cut military aid to Europe if the EDC was not accepted, United States demands for a European force became less insistent with the end of the Korean War. As for the French change of heart, there were several motivations for it. After France's defeat by the Vietminh at Dien Bien Phu in May of 1954, and the subsequent withdrawal of all French forces from Southeast Asia, many French leaders saw surrender of jurisdiction over its army as yet another disgrace. The French premier at this time, Pierre Mendès–France, was not a strong supporter of the EDC. He found it too anti-Soviet and too drastic a move toward supranationality

The English refusal to cooperate in the EDC was the final blow, because France feared an EDC that did not have the participation of British forces to offset those of Germany. On August 30, 1954, the French Assembly rejected the EDC by 319 to 264 votes. With the EDC defeated, the only way to deal with a German military force was to integrate it into the North Atlantic Treaty Organization (NATO) forces. Once French fears of a rearmed Germany were allayed by Britain's promise to keep its forces on German soil indefinitely, German military contingents joined NATO in 1955.

The European Economic Community

Fortunately for the Europeanists, economic integration was not stymied by the failure to reach a military agreement; the apparent success of the Coal and Steel Community in promoting production and trade was a persuasive argument for those advocating further economic integration, even though the ECSC had encouraged overproduction of steel and had thereby lost the support of some industrialists. With production increasing twice as fast among the six as in Great Britain from 1950 to 1955, many former opponents of European economic cooperation became ardent supporters of further economic unification.

Foreign affairs were again significant in marshaling support for closer economic cooperation. The extent of the decline in France's importance was made abundantly clear by Nasser's nationalization of the Suez Canal in 1956. This action triggered speculation as to whether Europe would be cut off from its supplies of fuel. Monnet's new Action Committee for the United States of Europe said that Europe's life might "in the near future, . . . be paralyzed by the cutting-off of its oil imports from the Middle East." British and French attempts to make Nasser return ownership of the canal to the original stockholders met resistance not only from Egypt but also from the United States, which sought to prevent war in Egypt. Even French and British bombardment of Egypt, coordinated with an Israeli attack into the Sinai desert, failed to produce the desired results.

The cutting off of oil imports to France led to a winter of unheated homes and immobilized automobiles and made French leaders starkly aware that France could not act alone and that its alliance with the United States did not guarantee unconditional support for any French action. Britain attempted to obtain U.S. financial support so as to stabilize its finances after its military action had caused a worldwide run on the pound, but it was turned down. That the Soviet Union was unhampered in crushing the Hungarian Revolution was further proof that individually, Europe's nations were helpless in the world of superpowers.

Recognizing the weakness of the individual nations of Europe, the French now threw their support to the negotiations for the European Economic Community (EEC) and a joint atomic development agency (Euratom).

The Council of Ministers of the ECSC had already begun negotiations for a further integration of Europe's economy. Led by Paul-Henri Spaak of Belgium, the Benelux countries took the initiative in these discussions. Belgium, the Netherlands, and Luxembourg had already been brought together in a customs union; now the objective was to establish an area free of internal tariffs similar to that in the Benelux countries and the United States. At a meeting at Messina in 1955 the council decided to discuss the possibility of a common tariff among the ECSC member states. This was the initial step toward economic unity. The organization it led to is the European Economic Community, (EEC), or Common Market. The Rome Treaty of 1957, the founding treaty of the EEC, envisioned the elimination of customs barriers by 1967 and the development of an economic unit that could compete with the United States.

Authority in the EEC was lodged in four bodies — a Council of Ministers representing the interests of each member state, an elected Commission representing the supranational interest, a Court of Justice, and a European Parliament. The founders realized that the members would not be willing initially to sacrifice all their national jurisdiction over their separate economies.

The Council of Ministers, made up of the foreign ministers (or their representatives) from each member state, considered and voted on proposals from the Commission. The size of each member's vote was determined by the size of the state. France, Germany, and Italy had four votes each, Belgium and the Netherlands two, and Luxembourg one.

The Court of Justice was comprised of seven judges appointed by the separate governments for a maximum term of six years. The court settled disputes among the member nations.

The European Parliament, to which delegates from national parliaments are sent, and which Europeanists hoped would soon blossom into a genuine supranational assembly, could question the Commission members and force the resignation of the Commission by a two-thirds vote. Normally, decisions were reached through a rather exhausting process of having the Commission submit and resubmit proposals before they were accepted by the Council. In the 1950s this system provided a good balance between national and supranational interests, but in the 1960s de Gaulle's narrow view of EEC duties and authority severely reduced the power of the Commission and thus the hopes for a united Europe.

In 1960 Europe was far from the unity envisioned by many EEC founders. In fact it was divided into three economic areas: the EEC, the Eastern European Comecon countries, and a new British-led European Free Trade Area (EFTA) consisting of Britain, Sweden, Denmark, Norway, Portugal, Switzerland, and Austria. EFTA's primary aim was to remove trade barriers between member countries. Before the formation of EFTA in 1959, Britain had tried to set up a larger free trade area that included the EEC. But EEC members were fearful that it would keep them from their goal of making the EEC a fully integrated economic area. EFTA did not, for example, include a common external tariff.

In practice, EFTA had a very limited impact on the redirection of trade in Europe. Austria, Sweden, and even Great Britain traded more with EEC members than with members of EFTA. Richard Mayne, an EEC official, correctly sees it as "partly a salvage operation, to secure whatever benefits were possible on a smaller and more scattered basis" than the EEC envisioned. Given Britain's close ties to the United States and the Commonwealth and rather ambivalent feelings about its Europeanness, in 1959 an organization such as EFTA seemed the only possibility.

Only two years later, convinced by the EEC's economic success and discouraged by its own economic problems and declining role in the world, Great Britain decided to seek admittance to the EEC. The British were especially concerned with the news that the EEC had decided to institute political as well as economic cooperation, which would exclude Great Britain from any possibility of future integration with the six. A communiqué from a meeting of the six in July 1961, setting up a committee to draft a political treaty, announced that the EEC sought "to give shape to the will for political union already implicit in the Treaties establishing the European Communities." The British need not have worried. This statement was issued by the Fouchet Committee, which later failed to reach an agreement on political cooperation.

Britain's conception of itself as an intermediary between the United States and Europe was undermined by President John F. Kennedy's grand design to bring Europe and the United States closer together and prevent the imposition of high tariffs between the United States and the EEC. The so-called Kennedy Round of tariff negotiations, which resulted in the U.S. Trade Expansion Act of 1961, did reduce tariffs 30 to 50 percent (depending on the commodity) on trade between Europe and the United States. Included in the trade expansion act was a clause that would have permitted President Kennedy to cut tariffs even further if Great Britain had been an EEC member.

President Kennedy, as well as his predecessors, hoped to see Great Britain join the EEC. In March 1961 George Ball, U.S. under-secretary of state for economic affairs, told Edward Heath, later to be prime minister, "So long as Britain remains outside the European Community, she is a force for division rather than cohesion, since she is like a giant lodestone drawing

EUROPEAN ECONOMIC ALLIANCES, 1960

■ European Economic Community (Common Market) founded 1957

□ European Free Trade Association (EFTA) founded 1960

▨ Council for Mutual Economic Assistance (COMECON) founded 1949

with unequal degrees of force on each member state." He went on to say that British membership in the EEC would lead to "a unity that can transform the Western world." So with a mixture of anxiety over its economic and political position, fear that Europe would go it alone, and assurance that the United States approved, on August 10, 1961, Great Britain asked to negotiate with the EEC.

Fourteen months later, with the basis for British entry not yet completely settled, de Gaulle intervened. On January 14, 1963, he informed the world:

> England in fact is insular, maritime, bound by her trade, her markets, her supplies to countries that are very diverse and often far away . . . The nature, the structure, the situation that are peculiar to England are very different from those of the continental countries. How can England, as she lives, as she

produces, as she trades, be incorporated into the Common Market as it was conceived and as it works?

Fifteen days later the negotiations were brought to a close.

De Gaulle disapproved of British entry into the EEC for a variety of reasons. Perhaps most important was the likelihood that it would destroy France's domination of the organization. The EEC had made it possible for France to play a much larger role in the world than its own resources warranted. After the loss of its colonial empire, de Gaulle hoped to regain in Europe what it had lost in the world. Furthermore, de Gaulle resented Britain's close relationship with the United States. De Gaulle could not say in so many words that France did not want to share its leadership of the EEC, but he *could* say the British were acting as a "Trojan horse" for the Americans.

A final roadblock to British entry was a number of conditions that Britain wanted taken into consideration, including protection for its agriculture and special consideration for the interests of its Commonwealth and EFTA partners. De Gaulle was not alone in opposing the special conditions, for if every member had been given such consideration, there would have been no EEC. Still, it was the brusque manner of de Gaulle's rejection, without warning, that so embittered the British and impaired EEC operations in the mid-1960s.

The difference between de Gaulle's conception of Europe — as a springboard for French designs — and that of the European federalists became the subject of a 1965 struggle to decide which of the EEC governing bodies should have precedence. The focus of the conflict was a clash between de Gaulle and the head of the EEC Commission, Walter Hallstein. De Gaulle needed EEC support for his policy of grandeur (see chapter 3) but he did not want to have any economic decision making taken out of French hands. Therefore, he refused to give the Commission and Chairman Hallstein the authority they desired.

Hallstein, in turn, tried to move toward a federal Europe by lodging the authority to debate and reject the Community's budget in EEC's legislative body, the European Parliament. This de Gaulle opposed as an infringement on the rights of national government. In his turn, he prevented the establishment of a truly federal parliament of the kind favored by the EEC founders by keeping decision making primarily in the hands of the Council of Ministers.

Although the other EEC members stood firm against de Gaulle, they could not compel the French to accept an increase in the authority of the Commission. The crisis was resolved in 1966 when the six governments signed the Luxembourg Agreement stipulating that the EEC Commission consult the individual states before making major proposals. Further, the agreement provided that no member nation could be overruled in the

Council of Ministers on an issue that that nation saw as affecting its vital interests.

In July 1967 a new European Commission replaced the institutions of the EEC, Euratom, and ECSC's High Authority. But real authority remained in the hands of a new single Council of Ministers, which appoints the Commission members and takes its orders from the member governments. The conflict between de Gaulle and the federalists proved a serious setback to the supranational concept of Europe from which the EEC has never fully recovered.

The period from 1967 to 1971 was dominated by British attempts to enter the Common Market. Prime Minister Harold Wilson tried to reopen negotiations in 1967 and was turned back, but a series of later events combined to make British entry possible. Foremost among these events was the change of government in France when de Gaulle retired in 1969. His successor was Georges Pompidou, a supporter of a confederated Europe who was not as firmly opposed to British membership since his goals for France were not as exaggerated as those of de Gaulle.

Equally persuasive in shaping the new French attitude was the growing power and independence of West Germany. When de Gaulle and the francophile Konrad Adenauer were in power, France had little difficulty in dominating the EEC. But after forced wage increases in 1968 and a growing trade deficit, French financial reserves, once a threat to the United States, began to dwindle. De Gaulle tried to get Germany to revalue its currency higher so as to keep France from having to devalue. That he failed was a severe blow to his prestige and the first indication that West Germany's politics would no longer be tied to French coattails.

When the Social Democrat Willy Brandt came to power, the change became even more apparent. Brandt's *Ostpolitik,* or Eastern policy, pointed to an independence in foreign affairs that could unify Germany and make it an even stronger economic and political entity. In addition, Brandt's attempts to resolve difficulties with the Soviet Union and Eastern Europe stole the thunder from de Gaulle's attempts at détente.

The French reaction to Brandt's designs reflected growing fears with regard to Germany. A final blow to French pride was a German unilateral decision to let the strong German mark float against other currencies in May 1971. One Gaullist deputy was quoted as saying, "the importance of the power of Germany now makes the French people think that Great Britain will be very, very useful in the Common Market."

Britain's economic woes daily made entry into the Common Market seem more desirable. The hope was widespread that EEC membership could step up Britain's economic pace and cut its persistent trade deficits. Politically, Prime Minister Edward Heath realized that the EEC concept of confederation would mean no significant sacrifice of Britain's sovereignty. Now Britain's view was that the EEC, stripped of its supranational tendencies, could strengthen Britain's economy and restore a measure of its dwindling stature.

The negotiations for British membership, which began in July 1970, were concluded within one year. The British were now willing to forgo some special privileges; for example, instead of a six-year transition period before its agriculture had to meet all the requirements of membership, Britain now agreed to a three-year transition. It also accepted a diminished world role for sterling in order to insure the equality of all EEC currencies. In 1972 the remaining obstacles to entry were cleared up, and Britain joined two other nations, Ireland and Denmark, in assuming membership in the EEC.

Prospects of Further Integration

Despite the acceptance of Britain, it is difficult at this writing to be optimistic about a further integration of Europe. In fact, the economic unity achieved in the 1950s may even now be in jeopardy. A 1980 deadline for European union was agreed to at the Paris Summit Conference of the nine heads of state in 1972. A year later it had become a laughing matter as each country tried to find its own way out of the economic recession that began in that year. The common energy policy that was proposed at the Copenhagen Summit by the nine heads of state in 1972 has also failed to materialize.

When the member states have encountered difficult economic problems, they have refused to act like genuine economic partners. During the fuel crisis that was an aftermath of the Arab–Israeli War in 1973, the nine went their separate ways, trying to make unilateral deals for oil and refusing to stand behind Holland, which was denied Arab oil because of its support of Israel.

Nor did British entry promote further unity as expected; instead, it actually retarded integration until 1975. Britain dragged its feet on full economic integration because the new Labour government was dissatisfied with the terms of entry into the community and because British leaders feared that the EEC wanted a share of the oil discovered in the North Sea. Fifteen months after entry, Britain was still threatening a referendum on EEC participation unless the policy on agriculture was revised to let some Commonwealth products have preferential treatment, reduce the British contribution to the budget, and change the rules on regional policy and taxes. Similarly, severe economic problems in Italy in 1974 led Britain to impose import controls on goods from other EEC members.

A special fifteen-member EEC committee set up to investigate the outlook for economic and monetary union reported in April 1975: "Europe is no nearer to economic and monetary union today than when it was proposed six years ago, largely because of lack of political will." The report attributed this to the international monetary crisis that began in the late

1960s, the financial problems caused by the sharp rise in oil prices in 1973, and the tendency of each government to search for its own way out of its own troubles.

There seems to be little possibility of political integration at this time. Previous hopes that economic unification would lead to political union have not materialized. If the members' economies had been fully integrated, as the federalists desired, additional unification might have been a possibility.

Yet a measure of economic integration is now taking place on an even larger scale through international corporations, international military arrangements, and so on. International corporations, many based in the United States, now dominate various branches of trade and industry in Europe.

There may be as good a chance of integrating Europe into a larger Atlantic unit as into a European community. One West German official maintains that if Chancellor Helmut Schmidt is forced to choose between Europe and Washington, he will choose Washington. The Labour government in Britain warned its EEC partners in March 1974 that its ties with the United States were as important as those with Europe. As Foreign Secretary James Callaghan put it, "My country wishes to remain a member of an effective Atlantic alliance and there is therefore concern about the degree of disagreement between the Community and the United States."

One factor which may preserve at least economic cooperation among EEC members is the network of economic ties which have developed over the past two decades and the fact that a customs union does indeed exist. Between 1958 and 1968, trade quadrupled among the six original members of the EEC. Of the EEC's manufactured goods 61 percent was sold within the community in 1968. The Italians would be as reluctant to give up the huge tariff-free zone for their refrigerators and wine as the other members would be to lose this advantage for their own national specialties.

Perhaps France's Valery Giscard d'Estaing and Germany's Helmut Schmidt can provide the leadership necessary to maintain the community's economic cooperation. Both are pragmatic individuals who realize the importance of French–German cooperation for the continuation of an effective European Community. The fact that France came out in favor of direct elections to the European Parliament in 1975, rather than continuing to send delegates from existing national parliaments, seems to herald a new more cooperative French attitude. In addition, popular support for the EEC seems to be stronger than many Europeans realized. The Norwegian electorate's rejection of EEC membership in 1971 was far outweighed by the British electorate's approval of membership in 1975. When Britain's continued participation was put to a vote in 1975, two out of three voters backed British membership. After this vote, Harold Wilson told the community that Britain was ready for total integration within the Common Market. As a result, the prospects for continued economic cooperation seem favorable.

Further Reading

For standard thorough accounts of the early stages of European integration see Hans Schmitt, *The Path to European Union: From the Marshall Plan to the Common Market* (1962); Richard Mayne, *The Community of Europe*

(1962); Ernst B. Haas, *The Uniting of Europe* (1958); F. Roy Willis, *France, Germany and the New Europe, 1945-1967* (rev. ed., 1968); John Calmann, *The Common Market: The Treaty of Rome Explained* (1967); and U. W. Kitzinger, *The Politics and Economics of European Integration* (1963).

The following studies concentrate on the motives for integration: Charles A. Cerami, *Alliance Born of Danger: America, the Common Market and the Atlantic Partnership* (1963); Max Beloff, *The United States and the Unity of Europe* (1963); and Leon N. Lundberg, *The Political Dynamics of European Economic Integration* (1963).

Recent events are covered in S. J. Warnecke, *The Economic Community in the 1970's* (1972); and Richard Mayne, *The Recovery of Europe, 1945-1973* (rev. ed., 1973).

Great Britain and the EEC are treated in Miriam Camps, *Britain and the European Community* (1965) and *European Unification and the Six: From the Veto to the Crisis* (1966); and in Nora Beloff, *The General Says No* (1963).

An excellent analysis of the functioning of the EEC can be found in Stephen Holt, *The Common Market: The Conflict of Theory and Practice* (1967).

More optimistic accounts of the functioning and future prospects for the EEC than appear in this chapter are in Carl J. Friedrich, *Europe: An Emergent Nation?* (1969); and R. H. Beck et al., *The Changing Structure of Europe* (1970).

For the most recent information on the EEC see *European Community, The Atlantic Community Quarterly,* and the vast number of EEC publications and special reports.

9 European Society in the 1960s: The Managed

What people really pay attention to here is the same as in all the rest of France—TV, auto, and *tiercé* [the Sunday triple bet].

Lawrence Wylie, quoted in "The French Are In," Flora Lewis, *The New York Times Magazine,* October 28, 1973

Western European countries have entered a new socioeconomic and political era. There is a wide gap between prewar and postwar average income, standard of living, and ownership of consumer goods. And the programs of political parties make abundantly plain that it is political suicide to oppose the welfare state or to support a laissez-faire economic system. On the left of the political spectrum, even the Communist parties have dropped their revolutionary rhetoric and programs and now support the welfare state.

Despite the changes in conditions and attitudes, Western European society is still divided between a new managed class, including laborers and the lower levels of white-collar workers, and the new managers. Even though many workers are sharing in the new affluence, they continue to think in terms of "us" and "them." The emergence of the affluent society brought important socioeconomic changes but did not fundamentally alter the relationship between the managers and the managed. Now, as before, political power and industrial management rest solidly in the hands of the upper-middle and middle-middle classes.

An immediately apparent difference between prewar and postwar Europe is the occupational composition of the population. As Table 9-1 shows, the service class has outpaced the industrial class and left the agrarian sector considerably diminished. By 1972 the proportion of the working population engaged in service had surpassed the proportion employed in industry not only in France but in Great Britain, Belgium, the Netherlands, Switzerland, and Scandinavia as well.

The rapid growth of government bureaucracy and the increasing number of service industries in highly industrialized societies had meant

151

Table 9-1   Working Population

	France 1954	1962	1973	West Germany 1950	1962	1973	Italy 1954	1966	1973
First sector (agriculture, forestry, fishing)	28.2	20.7	12.2	24.6	13.5	7.5	39.9	28	17.4
Second sector (industrial)	37.1	40.1	39.3	42.9	49	49.5	32.8	41	44.0
Third sector (service)	34.7	39.2	48.5	32.5	37.5	43.0	27.3	31	38.6

SOURCE: Figures for 1973 are from *The OECD Observer,* No. 74, March-April 1975, p. 21. All other figures from M. M. Postan, *An Economic History of Western Europe, 1945-1964* (1967), p. 191.

proliferation of white-collar employment. It appears likely that Europe will continue to move in the direction of the United States, where the service class now comprises 63 percent of the working population. Such a change in the class structure makes it difficult to accept the polarization of society between bourgeoisie and proletariat predicted by Karl Marx unless a large segment of the service class is categorized among the proletariat. Indeed, many neo-Marxist writers view the bottom third of the service class as a new proletariat separated from the ruling class in terms of wealth and political power. A closer examination of the class structure, then, is fundamental to any understanding of the concept of a new European society.

Europe's Class Structure

Despite social change and unprecedented affluence, Western European societies can still be analyzed in terms of differences in income, education, housing, and sociopolitical attitudes. To be sure, these factors have become less clear indicators of social status for several reasons.

For one thing, income, educational possibilities, and the distribution of consumer goods have risen at all levels of the population. For another thing, the traditional isolation of social classes in their own neighborhoods, once a clear indication of class, has now given way in some Northern European countries to a widespread mixing of classes in the new suburbs and new towns. Whether this mixing has produced a classless mentality is of course a question that is yet to be answered. The final factor is demographic. As the number of young people in the population has grown, a youth cult has emerged that does not accept traditional class differences. This has tended to break down class attitudes somewhat.

Because of the wide socioeconomic gulf separating Northern and Southern Europe, generalizations about one are true only in part or not true at all for the other. Western Europe can be categorized into three separate socioeconomic regions: highly developed Scandinavia, the Benelux countries, Great Britain, France, West Germany, and Switzerland; developed Austria and Italy; and underdeveloped Spain, Portugal, and Ireland.

The increase in per capita national disposable income and the welfare state have blurred some former social class distinctions. Disposable income is the amount of money available to spend on food, clothing, or whatever, after fixed expenses such as taxes and rent have been paid. This amount rose considerably by the 1960s, especially in Scandinavia, the Benelux countries, Switzerland, and West Germany. As Table 9-2 indicates, the gap between the United States and Europe narrowed during the 1960s and 1970s as the European economies continued to grow at a rapid rate while that of the United States grew more slowly; in fact Sweden has outstripped the United States in disposable income. The most remarkable growth of per capita income has occurred in West Germany; from $320 in 1949 to $4,943 in 1973. Also notable are the exceedingly low per capita disposable incomes in Ireland, Portugal, and Spain.

Wide disparities also exist in occupational income and average income in Europe. Service class workers (white collar) generally had higher incomes

Table 9-2   Per Capita National Disposable Income (in U.S. dollars of 1974 purchasing power)

	1960	*1973*
Austria	803	3,360
Belgium	1,126	4,262
Denmark	1,187	5,029
France	1,179	4,221
West Germany	1,198	4,943
Ireland	628	2,009
Italy	633	2,303
Portugal	304	1,391
Spain	320	1,606
Sweden	1,860	5,562
United Kingdom	1,250	2,780
United States	2,546	5,523

SOURCE: United Nations, *Yearbook of National Accounts Statistics, 1974,* vol. II (United Nations Publications, 1975), pp. 16-18. Copyright, United Nations (1974). Reprinted by permission.

A newly affluent middle-class French family purchases the latest model washing machine.

Henri Cartier-Bresson

than manual laborers. Table 9-3, showing a slightly higher income for French white-collar workers in 1969, is somewhat misleading since the classification of white-collar employees encompassed highly paid top administrative positions.

A 1967 survey for Great Britain (see Table 9-4) shows that the bottom levels of the service class (clerks, for example) are paid less than manual laborers. The fact that 76 percent of British clerks earned less than $2,500 annually in 1967 lends credence to the left criticism that the only thing separating those in the lower levels of white-collar employment from the working class is their greater expectations.

Only professionals and managers have a significantly higher income than manual workers; the salary difference between manual workers and the top levels of the service class (administrators) are shown clearly in the incomes exceeding $3,744. However, the pay structure in the Scandinavian countries is much more egalitarian — especially in Sweden, where construction workers earn more than teachers.

The gap between the upper income groups and manual and service-class workers is narrowed somewhat by state benefits — tax rebates, pensions, family allowances, rent assistance, and so on — that go primarily to low income groups. These so-called fringe benefits reach as high as 60 percent of

154

Time seems to have stood still in this poverty-stricken village in Sicily as hens scratch in the street and an old woman hides her face from the photographer.

Alfred Gregory—Camera Press London

a worker's income in Sweden and 51 percent in Italy and France, and they average 37 percent for all the Common Market countries. Using data for 1972, the Organization for Economic Cooperation and Development calculated that state benefits increased the disposable income of a worker with two children and a nonworking wife to 106 percent of gross pay in France, 102 percent in Spain, and 96 percent in Italy. A married Swedish worker with two children and a yearly income of about $2,400 pays no taxes and receives $603 in child support and as much as $777 in housing support.

Table 9-3 Monthly Income by Occupational Level in France (1969)

	Under $160	*$160-$350*	*Over $350*
White collar	4.9%	50.9%	44.2%
Blue collar	13.0	65.5	21.5

SOURCE: Adapted from Stanley Rothman, *European Society and Politics* (New York: Bobbs-Merrill, 1970), p. 153.

Table 9-4   Income and Employment by Occupational Level in Great Britain in 1967 (percentages)

Yearly Income	Manual Workers	Shop Assistants	Clerks	Professionals, Administrators, and Teachers
Under $1,248	9	66	17	3
$1,248-$2,496	50	31	59	25
$2,496-$3,744	35	2	20	36
$3,744-$4,992	5	1	3	19
Over $4,992	1	0	1	17

SOURCE: Stanley Rothman, *European Society and Politics* (New York: Bobbs-Merrill, 1970), p. 185. Rothman's figures are from *Family Expenditure Survey, Report for 1967* (London: HMSO, 1968), pp. 96-97.

Status of Working Women

While the status of women has improved since 1945, they are still treated as second-class citizens in many European countries. Compared to the nineteenth century, when women were employed primarily in domestic service, they now make up a large segment of those employed in white-collar occupations and an increasing number of those in blue-collar occupations. In Sweden and Austria, women constitute about 60 percent of the labor force. However, recent investigations make it apparent, as shown in Table 9–5, that the differences in pay are still substantial. As late as 1974, Austrian women were earning an average of $275 per month, compared to $400 for men. Within the EEC, the differences *have* narrowed slightly. In 1974, the EEC rebuked Britain, Ireland, and Denmark for their unequal treatment of women. The other EEC states had established equal-pay-for-equal-work guidelines, although in practice the gaps had not been completely closed. Another hopeful sign is the decision by the otherwise conservative government of Giscard d'Estaing in France to establish a Ministry of Women's Affairs. Its head, Françoise Giroud, looks to the day when there will be no need for her new ministry, when there "will be no more women's problems, but simply human problems."

Status of Immigrant Laborers

Excluded from the new affluence are the thousands of immigrant laborers who flocked to Northern Europe's factories in the 1960s. When the employment of foreign workers reached its peak of about 10 million in Western Europe, before the economic recession led to mass firings, over one-third of the Swiss labor force consisted of foreign workers. By 1974

Table 9-5   Women's Earnings as a Percentage of Men's by Skill
Level (1970) (all manufacturing industries)

Skill Level	Belgium	France	Germany	Italy	Netherlands
Skilled	66.8	74.2	73.2	70.6	59.9
Semiskilled	71.3	80.6	74.4	76.0	60.1
Unskilled	75.0	84.4	78.2	90.9	68.7

SOURCE: Evelyne Sallerot, "Equality of remuneration for men and women in the
member states of the EEC," *International Labor Review* (Geneva: International
Labor Office, August-September 1975), p. 95. Reprinted by permission.

their numbers had declined to 7.5 million. Filling the least desirable jobs in
municipalities and on assembly lines, they now constitute an underpaid,
neglected segment of the working class. They sweep streets, collect garbage,
clean *pissoirs* (public urinals), do unskilled work in factories. About 80
percent of the assembly line tasks at the Renault factory near Paris are
performed by foreign laborers. Willing to accept lower wages than
Northern European workers, they are despised by the native populations.
To prevent a further influx of Italian workers, some Swiss have resorted to
fear tactics and hate slogans: "Would you like to share a hospital room with
a Sicilian?"

In order to save money to buy a car, support their families, and set
themselves up when they return home, many of them are willing to live in
slums. In France shantytowns, called *Bidonvilles,* have sprung up on the
outskirts of the major cities to house most of the 4 million foreign workers.
For the most part, Northern European workers show little concern for this
"sub-proletariat." A semiskilled worker in West Germany rationalized his
renting a small house to several families of these foreign workers with the
excuse that they were accustomed to such overcrowding in their home
countries.

Wages and Fringe Benefits

While the gap between rich and poor has remained wide (see chapter 10),
few would dispute that wages have increased more than costs since World
War II. In most European countries, government and industrial leaders
have adopted a new attitude toward labor because of their acceptance of
Keynesian economics. They now promote higher wages for laborers, in line
with the conviction that this will increase the demand for consumer goods
and avoid industrial conflict. This new attitude is often reflected in the
guidelines set by the government to guarantee wage increments. In Sweden,
labor leaders, employers, and government officials negotiate annual
contracts for the work force. This so-called incomes policy assures labor of

annual increases to meet rising costs. The 1963 labor contracts included an increase of 7.5 percent in the annual wage bill even though the gross national product rose by only 3.3 percent.

Not all governments were convinced of the benefits of higher wages. The Netherlands government deliberately kept wages low in order to increase exports. When this effort failed and there was a resultant labor surplus, brought about by a failure to raise exports, labor leaders cooperated in the government's effort to avert a serious economic decline. Similarly, in 1975 and 1976 British workers agreed to reduced annual wage increments so as to support government attempts to check a huge inflation rate and bring the country out of an economic crisis.

European wages increased most during periods of rapid economic growth and low inflation. Between 1953 and 1965, real wages rose 36 percent in Great Britain, 58 percent in France, 80 percent in Italy, and 100 percent in Germany. Despite these increases, wages remained comparatively low in France and Italy. Even after the Grenelle Agreements settling a rash of strikes in France in 1968, Table 9-6 shows that French wages have remained near the low Italian level. Although the table gives the average wage in manufacturing for each country, it does not include expenditures for social services or benefits received by workers, both of which are higher in European countries than in the United States. In Scandinavia and West Germany, where workers receive high fringe benefits along with high wages, workers' living standards have approached those of laborers in the United States.

The Standard of Living

Although Europe still trails the United States in level of consumer goods used, the more industrialized European states have entered what some are now describing as the affluent society. As smaller percentages of their wages have been used up on clothing, food, and rent, workers have had considerably more money to spend on the kind of consumer goods known as durables because they are long lasting. Ownership of telephones, refrigerators, television sets, and cars began to reach levels near that of the United States in the more developed countries. Not that the different nations had the same priorities for consumer goods. As a case in point, the Scandinavian countries, with a standard of living near that of West Germany, have about twice as many telephones per capita.

As Table 9-7 indicates, ownership of passenger cars is perhaps more reliable, although not conclusive, as an indicator of standard of living. Before World War II French workers spent half their income on food. By 1970 the outlay for food and drink had declined to one-third of income. Much of the change in the workers' standard of living has come about since 1960. For instance, food and drink took as much as 40.3 percent of the average Austrian's expenditures in 1962 but only 30.3 percent by 1972.

Table 9-6   Average Hourly Wages in Manufacturing (in current U.S. Dollars)

	1960	1965	1971	1974
United States	$2.28	$2.61	$3.57	$4.40
Sweden	1.14	1.67	2.88	4.02
Norway	.90	1.29	2.29	3.50
West Germany	.82	1.30	2.49	3.44
Great Britain	.82	1.28	2.14	2.66
France	.51	.65	1.24	1.86
Italy	not available	.69 (1966)	1.10	1.87

SOURCE: *Bulletin of Labor Statistics* (Geneva: International Labor Office, 3rd quarter, 1975), pp. 57-62.

Table 9-7   Ownership of Consumer Durables (number per 1,000 inhabitants)

	Telephones		Passenger Cars		Television Sets	
	1969	1972	1969	1971	1969	1972
United States	567	628	427	443	399	474
Sweden	515	576	275	290	300	333
United Kingdom	253	314	205	219	284	305
Luxembourg	314	361	251	296	183	220
Switzerland	457	535	206	233	184	239
West Germany	212	268	208	239	262	293
France	161	199	238	260	201	237
Italy	160	206	170	209	170	202

SOURCE: OECD *Economic Surveys* (1976); OECD *Observer*, No. 74, March-April 1975; *OECD Observer*, No. 56, Feb. 1972.

Nevertheless, it is important to remember that workers did not all share equally in this new affluence. Unskilled workers and low-paid white-collar workers who earn less than $160 a month still spend more than half their incomes on food and drink. John Ardagh estimates that nearly a quarter of the French population is still close to poverty. In less developed countries such as Italy, Spain, and Portugal an even larger share of the population is at the poverty level. Workers in these countries have had to migrate to the richer northern countries.

Both the improvement in the standard of living and the wide gap between Northern and Southern Europe are revealed in the rise in per capita private consumption since 1955. Table 9-8 shows the countries' rankings according to private consumption in 1973; the figures agree fairly closely with previous figures on income and the ownership of consumer goods. Although the higher prices in the top-ranked countries reduce the difference between consumers in the countries at the top and the bottom of the ranking, the figures show a great difference between the countries previously described as highly developed, developed, and underdeveloped.

The Work Week and Vacation

For most workers reduced working hours and paid holidays and vacations have relieved the boredom of the factory. The average working week has declined from 48 hours in the prewar period to about 43 hours in Great Britain and 47 hours in West Germany. The 40-hour work week became mandatory in Austrian industry in January 1975. In France the average working week has actually been lengthened. Before the war, Léon Blum's Popular Front government instituted the 35-hour work week; now a 44-hour week is commonplace.

Moonlighting is common throughout Europe. Longer weeks help workers to afford the consumer goods and costly four- or five-week vacations they prize. As an Italian printer explained, "Once a luxury becomes a necessity, there's no turning back." But luxury isn't the only motivation for moonlighting; extra work may be necessary to survival. In Britain family budgets were so dependent on overtime pay in the early 1970s, when inflation bit deep into paychecks, that workers reduced their

Table 9-8 Per Capita Private Expenditure (in 1973 U.S. dollars)

	1973
Denmark	$3,050
Switzerland	3,640
Sweden	3,240
France	2,913
Belgium	2,810
West Germany	3,000
Netherlands	2,430
United Kingdom	1,960
Norway	2,530
Austria	1,870
Italy	1,620
Ireland	1,370
United States	3,840

SOURCE: OECD *Economic Survey: Germany* (Paris: OECD, 1975).
International Comparisons.

output during the week in order to insure Saturday morning work at time-and-a-half pay.

Workers in low-level white-collar jobs do have one advantage over manual laborers: they put in shorter hours. In Paris the average is 41.5 hours a week.

Because of higher incomes and paid vacations, entire countries come almost to a standstill at certain times of the year. In Sweden, West Germany, and Italy, paid holidays and vacations totaled thirty-two to thirty-five days annually by the late 1960s. In the richest country in Europe, Sweden, three out of four residents take a vacation outside their place of residence each year.

Foreign tourism has risen sharply since the middle 1950s. Then, 30 million tourists crossed their own borders; now more than 125 million Europeans tour outside their own countries each year.

In August the only people left in Paris are the poorer workers, tourists, and those few unfortunates who are left behind to serve the tourists. Vienna has now worked out a staggered vacation plan so that the tourist trade will not be adversely affected by the en masse departure of the populace, and the windows of closed restaurants display signs directing tourists to nearby restaurants that have remained open.

The Voices of Labor

Affluence, full employment, and diminished economic crisis in the most developed European countries have changed the goals of labor unions and labor parties from revolutionary to reformist. Some unionists still pay lip service to Marxism, but unions and labor-oriented parties now concentrate their demands on higher wages, full employment, fringe benefits, and price stability. Only in France and Italy are the labor movements dominated by Communist parties, albeit reformist rather than revolutionary parties. French and Italian unions have changed their goals as reform-oriented British, German, and Scandinavian unions have succeeded in improving the position of the workers in their societies.

Swedish and German labor unions work closely with business leaders and government officials in negotiating working conditions, wages, and fringe benefits. Swedish unions, which represent 95 percent of the workers, have become a powerful interest group. German labor leaders sit on the boards of directors of the top German industrial enterprises. The Confederation of German Trade Unions (DGB), which speaks for about 30 percent of German workers, operates schools, banks, and insurance companies. The head of the DGB maintains, "you can't stop progress — our job is to see that workers get the benefit of it." Since the DGB is not affiliated with any political party, it is a strong independent political force. German labor leaders stoutly defend their gradualism against more militant unionists by pointing to the much larger number of workers organized in Germany, the much lower wages of workers in France and Italy, and the near absence of unemployment in Germany.

Swedish and German labor leaders believe industrial profits must be high so that they can negotiate for higher wages. They also do not try to keep workers on the job in obsolete industries. Workers who become unemployed because their jobs are mechanized or because their industries are in a decline are immediately retrained at union expense. Militant unionists fear that close integration with big business and government means labor can offer no democratic counterweight to the ruling groups and will eventually be controlled and emasculated by the state.

Labor unions that cling to their revolutionary goals have lost their effectiveness. In France, where unionism is dominated by the Communist Confédération Générale du Travail (CGT), only about one quarter of the workers are organized. Despite considerable theoretical militancy, in practice French labor unions have been much less militant than their rhetoric would indicate. In fact the CGT actually restrained workers during the 1968 Paris riots. Although France has more strikes than the United States, the number of working days lost per thousand employees is only one-third that of the United States. (See Table 9-9.) French strikes are of the short wildcat variety that make the average strike less than a day long, compared to fourteen days in the United States. In Italy, where unions are split among Communist, Socialist, and Christian federations, the number of days lost per thousand workers is seven times higher than in France. Yet Italy has by far the lowest wages among Common Market countries. British unions are suspicious of management and refuse to cooperate with industrialists or to amalgamate in a few strong unions. The 163 unions in the Trades Union Congress strike separately, often with little warning, over sometimes minor issues. In the United States, Germany, and Scandinavia, strikes are well organized and planned well in advance in order to permit management to meet their terms.

Predictions that unionization will decline as the various interests in society are fully integrated in the new Europe have not materialized. In fact,

Table 9-9 Number of Working Days Lost per 1,000 Workers in Strikes (1966)

Italy	1,700	United Kingdom	180
United States	934	Sweden	110
Belgium	310	Germany	34
France	240		

SOURCES: Anthony Sampson, *Anatomy of Europe* (New York: Harper & Row, 1970), p. 365; Stanley Rothman, *European Society and Politics* (New York: Bobbs-Merrill, 1970), p. 177.

the influence of labor unions may grow as workers defend their interests against proliferating organizations of teachers, renters, white-collar workers, students, and so on. In Sweden, not to be a member of an occupational organization is highly unusual. Organized labor may be hard put to justify its demands if it should be confronted by organized and lower-paid clerks. The militancy of white-collar workers and professionals can be expected to increase if the high inflation rate — averaging more than 10 percent in 1974 — is not reduced significantly. In most countries, even the organized laborers have not been keeping up with inflation since 1968.

Social Leveling

Much has been written on the blurring of class lines brought about by the improved standard of living of the working class and the growth of the service class. It is said that European society is undergoing an embourgeoisement — the word used for the drift of the working class into the middle class — and that classes as we know them now will cease to exist.

Service-class workers are salaried (a traditional status symbol) and usually have more education than blue-collar workers, but they often live in the same neighborhoods and buy the same status symbols that have traditionally divided the middle and working classes.

Studies have shown that there is growing social mobility between these two groups. Approximately one-third of the offspring of industrial workers in Western Europe rise into nonmanual categories, predominantly the service and professional classes. At the same time a smaller but not insignificant group of white-collar workers move down into working-class occupations. A survey of the social class background of nonmanual workers in 1959 showed that 30 percent in France and Great Britain, 29 percent in the United States, and 20 percent in West Germany came from working-class families.

Still, a 1966 survey conducted by the French newspaper *Le Monde* found that 74 percent of French workers are the children of manual laborers. But the continued growth of the service class and the relative decline of manual laborers in the total work force should reflect a rise in the number of workers who move into the service class.

New housing and intermarriage have also brought the service and working classes closer together. Living in the same areas, and no longer divided by dress as they were in the nineteenth century, youth ignore social class differences. Many new towns and suburbs are not socially segregated, as the major cities still tend to be. This is especially true in the more developed countries. In the new model housing areas in Sweden, middle- and lower-class families are deliberately mixed by providing the poor with rent supports. The pervasiveness of modern advertising and cheaper mass-produced goods have also reduced the differences between working-class and middle-class homes and furnishings. And the behavioral pattern of

New housing projects with apartments affordable to the average citizen sprang up in Europe during the postwar economic resurgence. This building, located in a suburb of Paris, France, has 450 apartments and houses 1,500 tenants. In 1959, when it was built, it was the longest building in France.

manual workers in their new surroundings has changed as well. They tend to spend less time in pubs and more time at home watching television. The fact that working-class children in socially integrated neighborhoods attend the same schools as middle-class children has a further leveling effect.

Despite this social leveling, class distinctions remain very much a part of European society, especially in Great Britain, France, and Southern Europe. There has been little mingling of working class and middle class in the South. Even within social classes in Europe, divisions continue to exist. Divisions between skilled and unskilled laborers are often greater than those between the working class and the middle class.

This is similar to the split found between the upper levels of the service class (administrators) and lower-level clerks. Most of the service-class workers consider themselves members of the middle class and pursue practices common to the middle class. In a recent French random survey, 51 percent of the respondents rated a lower-paid clerical worker higher than a foundry worker.

In 1969 Cambridge University sponsored a sociological study of seventy British working-class families. The report, entitled *The Affluent Worker in the Class Structure,* revealed that "no more than one or two of the seventy couples in question here could be realistically represented as being even on the road to a middle-class pattern of social life." This study, drawn from a relatively affluent working-class area, concluded that the embourgeoisement thesis has limited validity in Great Britain. The researchers found that only seven couples followed middle-class life-styles and had middle-class friends from other than family or work associations.

Political Attitudes and Social Class

Although there have been some changes, the political attitudes of the working class and the service class continue to differ. The service class tends to support moderate or conservative parties while the working class gives most of its vote to the political left. However, these voting patterns are beginning to change. Only in France and Italy does working-class support go overwhelmingly to left-wing parties. In Germany, half the working-class vote goes to the moderate Christian Democrats rather than to the Social Democrats. One-third of Britain's laborers support the Conservative party. Even in France, support for the Communist party has declined among workers; the labor vote for the Communists dropped from 49 percent of the total labor vote in 1951 to 36 percent in the mid-1960s.

Of course, to some extent the shift in the labor vote can be attributed to changes in formerly conservative parties. In most European countries the traditional laissez-faire parties have disappeared; in Sweden all parties accept the welfare state and Swedish socialism. The British Conservative party has accepted the welfare state and the nationalization of much of British industry. Workers in an inflationary period may support a more conservative party because it promises to fight inflation while still supporting the welfare state.

Among the unskilled and semiskilled, working-class attitudes have changed very little. People at this level still believe that society is divided between those with and those without power and that for the have-nots there is little chance of escape. In a 1967 poll of French workers, 44 percent of those questioned believed that class war was still a reality. Members of the working class still tend to think more collectively than members of the service class. The latter, thoroughly imbued with middle-class values, think in terms of individual rather than group achievement.

Compared to manual laborers, white-collar workers are much less satisfied with their occupations and put considerably more money into education so as to prepare their children for jobs that "lead somewhere."

These service-class attitudes have now been adopted by many skilled and semiskilled workers in Western Europe, who hope to see their children rise into lower-middle-class or professional positions. These members of the working class now tend to think in terms of personal betterment rather than improvement of one's class.

Labor Dissatisfactions

That the worker is not at peace with society has been amply demonstrated by recent challenges to authority in factories even in the advanced societies of Northern Europe. In Holland, workers recently drew a chalk line around a corner of their factory and forbade entry to anyone who could not give a satisfactory explanation of his or her mission. Swiss and Swedish workers are demanding — and getting — joint participation with management in the determination of work schedules, duties, and salaries.

Paradoxically, the highest paid workers in Europe, the Swedes, have one of the highest industrial absentee and turnover rates in Europe. An enterprise with plants in Sweden and Germany reported a 1969 labor turnover of about 41 percent for the Swedish plant as against 4.8 percent for the German plant. The Volvo automobile factory in Torslanda reported a similarly high turnover rate in its plant, compared to 16 percent for Daimler–Benz in Germany. Absenteeism and turnover are lower in German factories primarily because the affluent society developed later in Germany. In Sweden, labor dissatisfaction seems to be an outgrowth of the contrast between the high standard of living and assembly line work in the factories.

A French sociologist explains, "The threshold of tolerance is dropping," and "What was accepted years earlier, like physical discomfort on the job, has now become unbearable because workers have seen for too long the way others in society are living."

In an attempt to come to grips with the so-called new worker, the Organization for Economic Cooperation and Development (OECD), to which all developed Western countries belong, has conducted seminars for personnel directors and management officials to devise solutions for what has been described as worker alienation. Management is now trying to make workers a more integral part of the factory by giving them a say in management decisions and by eliminating the routine in their work. At the Volvo plants, workers now change their places of work six times a day in order to relieve the boredom of the production line. At the Lunby truck factory, workers decide at the beginning of the week how the work is to be apportioned, when duties are to change, and when rest periods are to be taken. They have also done away with the traditional assembly line by assigning to groups of workers the responsibility for assembling sections of automobiles within their practically autonomous work area. Since these changes were instituted, worker absenteeism and turnover have declined markedly while production has improved.

The French student and worker riots in 1968 provided the clearest indication that workers do not yet see themselves as full participants in the new affluent societies and that the gap between skilled and unskilled workers is wide. French workers, primarily the young, joined the student rioters to protest low wages, poor working conditions, authoritarian factory managers, and a spiraling i flation that ate into their wages.

The protest began with a strike at the Renault plant at Boulogne–Billancourt, where one-third of the workers were migrant laborers. As a consequence of the disturbances, the minimum hourly wage was raised from 2.22 francs to 4.64 francs in 1973, more workers were paid by the month rather than by the hour — a prestige factor — and automatic pay increases were promised whenever prices rose. In effect, the unskilled workers were given what the skilled laborers were already receiving. But much of the wage increase has been eroded by inflation, and French workers are still dissatisfied.

In Sum . . .

It is difficult to generalize about the thesis of a new European society throughout Western Europe because of the wide variety of conditions and attitudes. However, one can draw certain conclusions. In Scandinavia and the Netherlands a new society *has* emerged. The standard of living and the social relationships between the classes bear little resemblance to the prewar period. Workers are no longer underpaid, overworked, and without voice in the determination of their working conditions or wages.

A Swedish worker's income is now comparable to that of a laborer in the United States. Perhaps more important, workers in Sweden have more autonomy and a greater share in management decisions than workers in the United States, and workers' representatives already sit on all companies' boards in Sweden. One observer's assertion that Sweden is becoming a trade union state may be an exaggeration, but there is no denying that labor and capital now deal with one another as near equals. Trade union officials in Sweden are quick to point out that they do indeed have more power than industrialists when deciding wages, but industrialists are dominant in all other matters pertaining to the business. However, Sweden's ruling Social Democratic party, in its 1975 program, promised to increase labor influence in industrial management even more.

The concept of a new Europe is considerably less applicable to Great Britain, France, Germany, and a number of smaller developed states. Certainly, a much larger section of the population now is upwardly mobile and is sharing in the new-found affluence. Yet 20 to 25 percent of their populations live near the poverty level — even more, if the foreign workers are included — calling to mind visions of the old Europe.

There is considerably less mixing of social classes in these countries than in Scandinavia or the United States. Nevertheless, remarkable progress has been made since the war. The majority of their populations now have vastly improved housing, more consumer goods and the money to buy them, more free time, and income enough to enjoy "le weekend" and annual vacations that amount to a month in most countries.

Southern Europe's nineteenth-century class structure is sufficient proof that new societies have not emerged there. With a large segment of the population still at the poverty level, despite the emigration of thousands of workers, talk of an embourgeoisement of society has little justification. In Spain and Portugal, incomes and working conditions compare with those of Northern Europe before World War II. With U.S. economic aid and a growing reform movement, Spain has recently begun to modernize its economy. Still, it will be some time before any Southern European country achieves the social transformation characteristic of Northern Europe.

FURTHER READING

Two important surveys that contain extensive information on European society are Stanley Rothman, *European Society and Politics* (1970); and Stephen Graubard (ed.), *The New Europe?* (1963). Unfortunately, Rothman's Europe is limited to Britain, France, West Germany, and the Soviet Union. The Graubard study contains several interesting and informative articles on labor and society. One of them, Ralf Dahrendorf's "Recent Changes in the Class Structure" takes the position that the growth of white-collar employment has led to the emergence of the service-class society in Western Europe. Another, Seymour Martin Lipset's "The Changing Class Structure and Contemporary European Politics" argues that affluence has moderated class conflict and ideological differences. Politics has been reduced to the "politics of collective bargaining," according to Lipset, and modernization has reduced worker hostility toward management by changing managerial behavior. Alain Touraine's contribution to Graubard's study, "Management and the Working Class in Western Europe," maintains that postwar changes in industry and management make it impossible to support the simple dichotomy between an oppressed working class and a politically and economically dominant ruling class.

M. M. Postan, in *An Economic History of Western Europe, 1945–1964* (1967), believes the working class is gradually becoming middle class in the advanced Western European states and says the division between manual and nonmanual workers is decreasing as modern technology transforms skilled workers into technicians. Ralf Dahrendorf, in *Class and Class Conflict in Industrial Society* (1959), contends that industrial society has not evolved the way Marx believed it would. The development of an intermediate white-collar stratum has prevented the polarization of society between proletariat and bourgeoisie as Marx predicted. Moreover, Marx did not foresee the massive role of the state in modern capitalist society.

A number of works disagree with the embourgeoisement theory. Andre Gorz in *Strategy for Labor* (1964) argues that capitalism alienates labor and molds workers into mass production robots whose minds are diverted from the reality of their condition by mass consumerism. The theme of alienation is common to left criticism of modern industrialism. Herbert Marcuse, in *One-Dimensional Man* (1964), has one of the clearest explanations of the alienation theme. Marcuse believes that the mass consumerism promoted by affluent societies satisfies only a few material needs while it destroys what should be humanity's ultimate objectives: the humanization of social, productive, and work relationships.

The disagreement concerning the impact of the modern industrial state is continued in studies of individual countries. F. Zweig's *The Worker in an Affluent Society* (1961); R. Miller's *The New Classes* (1966); and Josephine Klein's *Samples from English Cultures* (1965) agree that the working class is moving toward middle-class values and existence. Zweig argues that as the distinctive economic characteristics of the working class have changed under neocapitalism, so has its cultural distinctiveness. Miller maintains that, in performing technically complicated tasks in modern industry, the skilled worker is functioning as a technician rather than as the traditional industrial worker. Three studies edited by John Goldthorpe et al. — *The Affluent Worker: Industrial Attitudes and Behavior* (1968), *The Affluent Worker: Political Attitudes and Behavior* (1968), and *The Affluent Worker in the Class Structure* (1971) — reject the embourgeoisement thesis. He maintains that the worker has generally not accepted middle-class cultural values and has not been accepted socially by white-collar employees. A stimulating study of the attitudes of the British white-collar worker is provided in David Lockwood's *The Blackcoated Worker* (1958).

Valuable studies of French labor are Val Lorwin's *The French Labor Movement* (1954); and Richard F. Hamilton's *Affluence and the French Worker in the Fourth Republic* (1967). Serge Mallet in *La Nouvelle Classe Ouvrière* (1963) sees advanced technology leading to cooperation among workers, technicians, and managers against plant directors and executives that will in turn lead to worker control of factories, to democratization of industry, and to the decline of worker alienation. Alain Touraine in "La Vie Ouvrière" in Alain Touraine (ed.), *Histoire Général du Travail* (1961), is critical of the embourgeoisement thesis. While he agrees that a certain segment of the working class is now living a middle-class existence in an economic sense, he does not believe that the working class has adopted middle-class life-styles and attitudes. Michael Crozier in *The Bureaucratic Phenomenon* (1964) and *The World of the Office Worker* (1971) has provided excellent insights into the world of the white-collar worker and

French society. He believes that French society resists change until the last possible moment, when only a violent change will relieve the situation.

Some other important studies of European labor are Daniel Horowitz, *The Italian Labor Movement* (1963); H. P. Bahrdt, *Industriebürokratie* (1958) and "Die Industriearbeiter" in Marianne Feuersenger (ed.), *Gibt es noch ein Proletariat?* (1962). Bahrdt accepts fully the embourgeoisement thesis.

Recent statistics and studies can be found in the OECD *Observer,* OECD *Economic Surveys, International Labor Review,* International Labor Office *Bulletin of Labor Statistics,* and the many publications of the United Nations.

10 European Society in the 1960s: The Managers

> If property was the criterion of membership in the former dominant classes, the new dominant class is defined by knowledge and a certain level of education.
>
> Alain Touraine, *The Post-Industrial Society*

Despite the spread of economic rewards and political rights in the postwar period, some people are, in George Orwell's words, more equal than others. Although government and administrative positions have increased, only in a few countries do those who occupy positions of power and influence in contemporary European society come from the lower-middle or working class. Even among Socialist party leaders, the number of workers has in fact decreased substantially since the late 1940s. Government and industry were once viewed as providing a way for the lower classes to move up into positions of wealth and power. But top positions are now reserved for those whose power and authority are based on skill — called a meritocracy. And there is not an increased role for the lower classes primarily because the middle class has dominated the educational institutions where the people with the skill, called technocrats, are trained.

On the other hand, the emergence of the meritocracy has brought important social and political changes at the top. The increasing need for the highly skilled in government and politics has reduced even further the role of the aristocracy. Parties with a traditionally conservative political program have ceased to exist in Northern Europe; all political parties now reject a hierarchically organized society and are increasingly controlled by those with training in one of the professions.

The New Ruling Class

The life-styles of this new privileged managerial stratum remain distinct from those of the lower strata. Although it is now difficult to distinguish classes by traditional measures such as dress and ownership of consumer goods, sizable differences remain in occupations, educational attainment, wealth, and housing, as well as in life-styles.

No single term is used to describe the ruling classes in Europe and the United States. Some people still subscribe to the idea of a ruling class. Others have adopted one or another of the more sophisticated concepts: an establishment, or a military–industrial complex, or a power elite. Some have adopted C.W. Mills's description of the rulers of the United States — a conspiratorial power elite of business, military, and government officials — to describe European societies.

However, the European countries are sufficiently different from the United States and from one another to warrant the use of several descriptions of their societies. For instance, one can speak of an establishment in Great Britain and France because of the continued influence of former elites and the similar training of government leaders. The leaders of British government and society have been trained primarily in the same schools — private secondary schools, then Oxford or Cambridge — and retain their social ties (the old-boy network) long after their formal schooling ends.

In France, the ruling circles are trained in bourgeois-dominated secondary schools (*lycées*) and exclusive professional schools (*grandes écoles*). In both countries, individuals who follow the prescribed path to power may fill a diversity of government and economic positions merely because they have been initiated and accepted into the ruling circles.

In the other developed nations in Europe, only Italy has an establishment similar to that in Great Britain and France. However, Italy has no old-boy ties that bind the ruling circles together. For the remaining developed European countries, it seems best to adopt the theory of a more accessible but still intact ruling stratum.

The Rise of Pluralism

In some European societies, business, labor, agriculture, and other groups compete with the ruling elites for power. Under this state of affairs — known as pluralism — leaders of the various interest groups bargain with each other and with the government for a larger share of national expenditures and for legislation favorable to members of their own groups. However, in several important aspects this pluralistic competition does not appear to have produced what some thought it would: a more democratic exercise of political power and a fairer division of wealth.

Pluralism has had a limited impact in France and Great Britain, where the different elites are dominated by a single old-boy network. Also, where one interest group has prevailed, as was long true of the German business elite, the pluralistic thesis has had limited applicability. In Italy not only have the business interests dominated but the various interest groups are too antagonistic to engage in the kind of collective bargaining that makes interest-group politics effective.

Where pluralism has worked best is in the smaller, less complex European societies. In Sweden, where everyone is a member of a strong interest group, there has been a more democratic sharing of political power. A small business elite is countered by a large and well-organized labor group, led by the Social Democrats, that has great influence in the government. One observer has described government in Sweden as a permanent barter between the technocratic officialdom and the interest groups, with politicians limited to a presiding role.

Austria also has a fairly balanced sharing of power between the various interests. There is even an interest-group committee that brings together interest groups and traditional chambers (commerce, labor, and so on). A federal chancellor is in attendance to prevent conflict. The committee provides a forum for the groups that want to be heard and insures that their opinions are given due consideration when deciding on future government policy. A supporter of the Austrian system boasted that in no other country is there as much interest for the common good.

Composition of the Ruling Class

Although the composition of the ruling stratum has changed since 1945, power is still exercised by a small, privileged elite in most European societies. A 1961 study of 2,000 eminent people in France showed that 68 percent were recruited from the top 5 percent of the population and 81 percent from the top 15 percent of the population. Studies of German ruling circles have produced similar findings. Nearly one-third of all German higher civil servants are the children of higher civil servants. As Table 10-1 indicates, the top levels of government have little worker representation. Since 1965 the number of working-class deputies has declined even further.

Guttsman's study, *The British Political Elite,* showed that about "two-thirds of the members of the highest occupational groups, comprising less than three percent of the population, are the sons of men who belonged to the same group." Moreover, in most European countries there has been a reversal of an immediate postwar trend to choose parliamentary members from the working class. Now more and more British Labour party leaders are chosen from the professions. Lewis J. Edinger's 1964 study, *Politics in Germany,* indicates that of all elite members only 1 percent was drawn from the lower class.

A similar pattern has been found in Austria, where the number of workers in parliament has declined from 55 in 1956 to 29 in 1968. Here, as elsewhere, the number of representatives chosen from the service class has climbed sharply: from 47 in 1956 to 66 of a total of 165 in 1968. Only in Sweden, where politicians lack the authority of their counterparts elsewhere

Table 10-1   Socio-occupational Composition of German
Legislature, 1961-1965 (in percentages)

Occupation	All Bundestag Deputies	CDU (Christian Democratic) Deputies	SPD (Social Democratic) Deputies
Government officials and employees	22.3	22.7	23.1
Professions	20.5	17.5	25.1
Employees of political parties and labor unions	16.1	9.6	28.1
Entrepreneurs, executives, business association officials	15.5	16.7	8.4
Farmers and members of farm organizations	11.5	18.3	1.5
Small businessmen, artisans	6.0	8.0	3.5
White and blue collar workers	5.6	4.8	7.4
Housewives	2.5	2.4	2.9

SOURCE: Arnold J. Heidenheimer, *The Governments of Germany,* 3rd ed.
(New York: Thomas Y. Crowell, 1971), p. 168.

in Western Europe, has there been a democratization of the political elite. More than half the ministers serving in the Social Democratic cabinet from 1956 to 1968 had lower-class social origins.

Anthony Sampson sums it up perhaps best of all: "The chances of the son of a working man reaching a position of power are almost — but not quite — as remote as they were in 1789."

The New Managers

Liberal hopes that the new managers — also known as the meritocracy — might form a separate elite distinct from the upper and middle bourgeoisie were soon disappointed. In France the new managers have not only merged with the *haute bourgeoisie* (upper-middle class) but have also been drawn primarily from this class. A recent study of British top management personnel revealed that 43 percent came from the two highest occupational groups in the registrar-general's classification of society — groups that formed only 15 percent of the population.

Such social exclusiveness has not been restricted to France and Great Britain. A study conducted in the 1950s revealed that only 1 percent of Swedish managers came from the working class, whereas 92 percent came from the families of businessmen, civil servants, and members of the professions. In Germany, however, the selection of managers has been more democratic. Out of a sample of 537 German managers, 5 percent came from lower-class homes and 49 percent from lower-middle-class homes.

Another factor that has prevented the establishment of a separate technocratic elite has been an extensive horizontal mobility between government and industrial managers. Many Frenchmen who have been trained for government service in the *grandes écoles* have received top industrial posts because of their old-boy connections with economic leaders.

Even within the ranks of new managers the layers of authority and wealth are clear to see. Only the top managers wield significant economic and political power. As in the United States, the differences are reflected in the private possessions of the various strata. Middle management officials buy less expensive automobiles — BMWs instead of Mercedes, or Renaults instead of Citröens — and do not live in the same areas as their superiors. As Alain Touraine observed in *The Post-Industrial Society,* "A hierarchical continuity among bureaucrats and technocrats may appear to exist but it is a rare case when the members of a great organization cannot recognize the line that separates them." In Germany the top government and management officials — ambassadors, generals, big business leaders — come predominantly from the upper-middle class whereas middle management officials come primarily from the middle class.

Education of the Ruling Class

At first a thorough democratization of Europe's ruling circles seemed imminent as more elite positions — especially those requiring advanced training — were filled by students from presumably more democratic educational systems. Confirming that the route to the top was indeed through higher education, recent studies have shown that in 1961 nearly 85 percent of a large sample of the French ruling stratum had received a university education and that 63 percent of a smaller group from German ruling circles had had at least some university training. However, postwar Europe lags far behind the United States in access to higher education, and the number of lower-class children in the upper levels of European education has increased only slightly. As tables 10–2 and 10–3 show, some European countries permit few to go on to higher education; and, with the exception of Great Britain, the increase in the number of manual workers' children attending the universities has been minimal.

Advanced schooling continues to be the preserve of children of the upper-middle and middle classes. However, even in the most class-based

Table 10-2   Access to Higher Education (percentage of relevant age group)

Austria	15.6	(1972)	Norway	27.5	(1970)
Belgium	28.5	(1970)	Portugal	6.6	(1970)
Denmark	34.3	(1973)	Spain	27.1	(1972)
France	30.0	(1971)	Sweden	31.1	(1972)
Germany	15.8	(1970)	United Kingdom	21.3	(1971)
Italy	28.2	(1970)	United States	43.8	(1972)
Netherlands	20.5	(1971)			

SOURCE: *OECD Observer*, No. 74, March-April 1975.

Table 10-3   Percentage of Manual Workers' Sons in University Student Bodies

	1960	*1964*
Great Britain	25.0 (1961)	—
Sweden	14.0	—
Italy	13.2	15.3
Denmark	9.0 (1959)	10.0
Holland	8.0 (1958)	6.0 (1961)
Austria	6.0	5.0
France	5.3	8.3
West Germany	5.2	5.3

SOURCE: UNESCO, *Access to Higher Education* (Bucharest, 1968), p. 49.

educational system, the wall of social privilege started to break down in the late 1960s and early 1970s. Nevertheless, the various European countries differ sufficiently to necessitate the separate study of the major educational systems.

British Ruling-class Education   Success in British government has normally led through the exclusive "public" schools — Eton, Winchester, and so on — then Oxford or Cambridge universities. In 1964, slightly over one-third of the House of Comnons members had attended Oxford or Cambridge — or Oxbridge, as they are referred to collectively. These schools are even more closely connected to the Conservative party. Four-fifths of the university-educated Conservative candidates for parliament between 1950 and 1966 were Oxbridge graduates. A recent study by the National Foundation for Educational Research has shown that efforts to reduce the influence of privately educated individuals in the ruling circles have not had much success. This study, completed in 1973, showed graduates of the twenty-six leading private secondary schools had had as large a share of the elite positions in Britain in 1939 as they had some thirty years later. Edward Heath's 1971 cabinet of seventeen, for example, included fourteen members who had attended Oxbridge.

Some Labour party leaders have concluded from such evidence that the only way to break the hold of the private schools is to abolish them. This view has of course raised howls of indignation from most Conservative party members and from the *London Times.*

Although Oxbridge graduates retain an inordinate share of the important positions of power in Britain, changes in education, even at Oxbridge, indicate that such a monopoly does not have the same social significance as it once did. For one thing, a quarter of the university student body now comes from working-class homes. For another thing, university education is becoming a decisive factor in the competition for positions of power and influence. So graduates who have working-class backgrounds will undoubtedly fill a greater share of the important positions in society.

Most working-class students attend the less prestigious universities, some of them not established until after the war, but Oxford and Cambridge have

Uniformed and hatted students at Harrow, one of England's elite secondary schools, leaving chapel.
Keystone Press Agency, Inc.

enrolled a larger number of students from working-class homes. Yet those colleges within Oxford University that have a large working-class enrollment, such as Wolfson College, lack the prestige of the older colleges, nor do the Wolfson graduates have the same occupational opportunities.

At the secondary level, comprehensive schools are gradually increasing their share of students from that age group. But the comprehensive schools have not achieved the academic excellence of the grammar schools or most of the independent public schools. Labour's attempts to put all secondary students in comprehensive schools have encountered stiff opposition from the middle-class-dominated grammar and public schools. The opponents maintain that placing all students in comprehensive schools of the American type will mean the end of excellence in British education. The comprehensives have themselves promoted some of this opposition because of their diverse organization and often suspect pedagogy.

French Ruling-class Education   As in Great Britain, both France's top industrial positions and its government service have been dominated by the upper-middle and middle classes. Anthony Sampson is convinced that "if there is such a thing as a power elite, then they [the *haute bourgeoisie* or upper-middle class] are in the middle of it." The *haute bourgeoisie* now dominates government service not merely because of social position but also because of the children's better education, which their wealth and social position make possible.

The persistence of social divisions in France can be attributed directly to this ruling stratum's monopoly of an elite educational system. The domination begins in the state *lycées.* John Ardagh says in *The New French Revolution,* "State *lycées,* though in theory free and open to all, are in practice still largely a preserve of the middle class, and they alone provide a passport to higher education and the best jobs." Bourgeois society itself is divided between those who have obtained a *lycée* diploma (*le baccalauréat*) and those who have failed. With *le bac* the student is prepared to attend the university or — for the fortunate 15 percent of those who proceed beyond *le bac* — one of the *grandes écoles,* where the future leaders of the nation are trained.

Leaders of business and government have long been recruited from these bastions of privilege, especially the *Ecole Polytechnique,* the *Ecole Normale Superieure,* the school of civil engineering, and the newer national school of administration (ENA). Graduates of the *Ecole Polytechnique,* affectionately called "X" because of its emblem of two crossed cannon, have long had their choice of the highest positions in government and business.

Both the students' brilliance — the selection process is one of the most rigorous in the world — and their connections make such a choice possible for them. In fact, an old-boy network similar to the British one exists for *grande école* graduates. In 1967, seven of the eleven top positions in the

Ministry of Finance and sixteen of the twenty-nine cabinet minister positions were held by ENA graduates. One must agree with Sampson that ENA now provides "an old-boy net or a 'Mafia' which makes others — the Harvard Business School, Balliol, or even the *Polytechnique* — seem amateurish."

The majority of top business executives have university degrees. Table 10-4, based on a representative sample of 2,500 chairmen and chief executives of large companies who received university degrees, indicates how the *grandes écoles* dominate the business community. More than 50 percent of the sample of university-educated businessmen came from the *grandes écoles*.

Of those entering the *grandes écoles* in 1967, only 2 percent came from the working class and 4 percent from the peasantry. In the same year, 57 percent of the students in higher education had professional parents and 17 percent came from the industrial and commercial bourgeoisie. Philip Williams has calculated that only one child of farm workers in a thousand reached the university in the late 1960s.

German Ruling-class Education In Germany no schools or families unite the ruling circles. Entry into the ruling stratum has come primarily through study at a university and, more specifically, through the study of law; Ralf Dahrendorf, in *Society and Democracy in Germany,* has calculated that more than half the top civil servants have law degrees. Since university study is restricted to the upper and middle classes in Germany even more than in France, the narrow social basis of the ruling stratum is readily apparent.

Table 10-4 Educational Background of French Businessmen

Type of Institution	Percentage of Sample Attending
Ecole Polytechnique	21.4
Other engineering schools	34.5
Science faculties	3.8
Arts faculties	3.8
Law faculties	8.8
Political science faculties	9.6
Commercial schools	1.7
Military schools	2.6
Other schools	10.1
No answer	3.7

SOURCE: F. F. Ridley, "French Technocracy and Comparative Government," *Political Studies,* (14 February 1966), 499. © 1966 Oxford University Press, reprinted by permission of Oxford University Press.

Higher education has long been considered appropriate for only the talented few; four-fifths of the students leave school at age fourteen. As in France, few children from working-class homes pass from the primary school (*grundschule*) into the select secondary school (*gymnasium*). Table 10–5 shows the low percentage of entry into the *gymnasium* of children in the province of Baden-Württemberg whose fathers earn less than 1,000 *deutschemarks* a month.

Scandinavian Ruling-class Education   The Scandinavian countries have the most socially progressive educational systems in Western Europe. Modeled on that of the United States, Swedish education is free and open to all up to the university level. All students receive their primary and secondary education in the same common *gymnasium,* but here the similarity with the United States ends.

Despite thirty years of Social Democratic party rule, the percentage of working-class children obtaining a university education has risen very little. The cultural deprivation of lower-class children has prevented them from performing as well as middle-class children in secondary schools. However, the government's policy of social equalization and the existence of a common secondary school should increase the number of working-class children attending universities in the future.

The Aristocrats

The aristocracy has received little attention thus far in this study not because it has disappeared but because it has become less important in the

Table 10-5   Rates of Transition from Primary to Secondary Education by Monthly Income of Father in Baden-Württemberg in 1968

Monthly income (deutschemarks)	Total leaving Grundschule	Thereof entering		
		Hauptschule	Realschule	Gymnasium
- 600	100	79.9	12.5	7.6
600 - 799	100	75.4	15.9	8.7
800 - 999	100	73.2	14.7	12.1
1,000 - 1,249	100	59.9	15.3	24.8
1,250 - 1,499	100	45.7	20.6	33.7
1,500 - 1,999	100	34.9	13.7	51.4
2,000	100	28.4	4.8	66.8

SOURCE: "Germany: On the Brink of Educational Reform," OECD *Observer* No. 58, June 1972. Information for this table was supplied by the Work Group for Empirical Educational Research, Heidelberg.

power structure of most European countries. It no longer rules as it did in most of Europe in the nineteenth century but has become a part, usually a minor one, of a new enlarged ruling stratum. With the exception of the Southern European countries, aristocrats do not dominate the top military and diplomatic posts as they did before World War II. In most of the developed states the aristocracy no longer sets social standards for the bourgeoisie to emulate; instead, it has adopted a life-style much like that of the middle class. Many aristocrats can no longer live on the income from their estates and must take salaried positions in the senior civil service, in banks, sometimes even in industry.

In 1966, Britain's top hundred enterprises had ninety-one peers (members of the nobility) on their boards of directors, thirteen of them in the post of chairman. However, because of their sizable landholdings and traditional flexibility, aristocrats have preserved their social and political preeminence better in Britain than in any of the other highly industrialized countries. The peers and old established gentry remain among the largest landholders in Britain. Although some estates have been sold or diminished, increased land values — fourfold in the last twenty years — have raised the value of the remaining aristocratic holdings. Many of the wealthiest aristocrats own residential property. The Duke of Westminster owns most of Belgravia, in the middle of London, as well as estates in Canada, Australia, and South Africa. Included in the Duke of Hamilton's estates are the industrial towns of Motherwell and Cambusland, where development land is worth £3,000 an acre. In terms of political influence, the British aristocracy approaches the authority exercised by the aristocrats in Southern Europe.

The aristocracy retains an elite forum in the House of Lords, which stands as convincing evidence that Britain still has a social and political hierarchy. Although the House of Lords has lost almost all its direct political power, it has retained indirect political influence and social preeminence. According to one peer, Lord Balniel, "Although the class has long ago shed the mantle of a ruling class, it has inherited a tradition of public service which gives it influence in the higher reaches of political and executive government." In the House of Lords, in exclusive social clubs, and to some degree in the Conservative party, the aristocracy exercises a degree of influence that it has lost in most of Northern Europe.

French aristocrats, never as receptive to change as the English, have much less influence in society and politics than their English counterparts. They were never willing to engage in mundane occupations before World War II. As their financial position worsened after the war they could no longer disdain to take positions in industry, banks, and the civil service. They have now merged with the *haute* (upper-middle) and *bonne* (middle-middle class) bourgeoisie to form a new privileged elite, but socially they remain rather exclusive.

The Plutocrats

In the prewar period the upper-middle class, numbering 2 to 3 percent of the population, was distinguished primarily by its dominance of political power, its wealth, and its life-style. Now it has to share power with a much broader segment of the middle class. This new ruling stratum, comprising at most 10 percent of the population of any Western European country, has at its disposal a major share of the wealth. Table 10–6 indicates that its share of total income has changed little between 1954 and 1964.

Other indicators of wealth, such as taxable income and possession of private property, confirm the existence of a relatively small plutocracy in most European countries. According to the British Inland Revenue Board's estimate of ownership of wealth (based upon inheritance taxes) from 1960 to 1968, the number of those owning over £50,000 had doubled while the number owning less than £5,000 had declined by only 16 percent.

From 1950 to 1970 the share of real wealth in Germany held by employees declined from 30 to 15 percent of the total wealth. The top 3 percent of all taxpayers had 42 percent of all taxable wealth at their disposal in 1967. Of the real wealth, 80 percent is in the hands of the self-employed, employers, and national institutions; about 30 percent is publicly owned. In 1967, 17 percent of all West German families owned over 70 percent of all private property.

On the other hand, in Scandinavia and several smaller countries there has been a redistribution of income in favor of employees. Sweden, paradoxically, has the most egalitarian allocation of wealth and the smallest group of extremely wealthy families; fifteen families and two banks control 90 percent of the country's private industrial capital. This situation came about primarily because high income taxes prevented the bulk of the population from investing in industry and because many Socialists wanted

Table 10-6 Portion of Total Income Received by the Top
10 percent of Families Before Taxes

	1938	*1954*	*1964*
United Kingdom	38	30.4	29.3
France	—	34.1[a]	36.8[c]
West Germany	39[a]	44.0[b]	41.4
United States	36	30	28

[a]Data for all Germany in 1936.
[b]French data for 1956, German for 1955.
[c]Data for 1962.

SOURCE: Stanley Rothman, *European Society and Politics*
(New York: Bobbs-Merrill, 1970), p. 137.

to keep the moneyed aristocracy intact but small so that it would offer little resistance to Socialist programs. Sweden's taxes are so high that a jump in income from 20,000 to 40,000 kroner a year will produce a real income increase of only 3,000 kroner.

In Norway, even higher taxes on income and property forced about 2,000 wealthy Norwegians to pay taxes in excess of their 1973 incomes. Now, however, the Socialist majority in parliament has apparently decided to return to an earlier law limiting taxes to a maximum of 80 percent of one's income.

In West Germany, where class lines are not as distinct as in France or Great Britain, there are reports of the beginnings of a service-class society. According to this view, all who hold service jobs — soon to be the majority of the employed — from the clerk to the top government minister, are involved in the exercise of power and can no longer be divided into distinct social classes. Yet service-class workers do not behave as a class or think as a class; they behave and think as individuals. Although the German class structure is certainly less distinct than those in France and Great Britain, the service-class thesis seems somewhat premature.

Class demarcations in wealth and the exercise of political power remain clear in West Germany. In a study entitled *Die Reichen und die Superreichen in Deutschland (The Rich and the Superrich in Germany),* Michael Jungblut, relying primarily on more scholarly studies by others, has singled out a new "oligarchy of wealth" numbering some 50,000 families. Each family has more than 10 million marks, and as a group they control 16 percent of the country's capital shares and 7 percent of the individual wealth. A slightly larger group, 1.7 percent of the population, possessed 35 percent of the country's wealth in 1960. Later studies have tended to bear out these findings.

Housing and Life-style of the Ruling Class

There are still immense gaps between the life-styles of the middle and working classes, as the differences in their housing make particularly evident. The bourgeoisie and aristocracy inhabit distinct bourgeois or aristocratic sections of the cities or suburbs as well as having villas in the countryside.

The Austrian government had to enact laws to prevent rich West Germans from buying up much of the Tyrol for vacation cottages. In Paris the aristocrats live primarily in the St. Germain district. For the bourgeoisie there is, according to John Ardagh, "a chic new town flat in Neuilly (Paris) at half a million francs, a modern 'maison de campagne, style anglais' in the woods of the Ile-de-France." This housing pattern is similar for top French administrators, who are primarily drawn from the upper bourgeoisie. A study of 347 of them found that 103 lived in the middle-class district of Passy and 42 in the elegant suburb of Neuilly.

In London the expensive West End is far from the cramped quarters of the working-class section. Similarly, the housing of the Viennese bourgeoisie on the edges of the nineteenth district (Döbling) amid parks, vineyards, and portions of the Vienna Woods bears little resemblance to the crowded working-class housing in the tenth district (Favoriten). The life-style of the bourgeoisie — including smart new apartments or modernized villas and sleek new cars — is a constant reminder that class distinctions remain important in Europe.

The suburban areas that have been developed around Europe's major cities, like those in the United States, have catered to the bourgeoisie. West of Paris, American-style housing estates with tennis courts, boutiques, and discotheques are fast filling the landscape. Named *le Parc Montaigne* or *le Residence Vendome,* the new homes feature sun terraces and built-in barbecues. The estate of 520 villas built by the American firm of Levitt and Sons southwest of Versailles was subscribed twice over in three weeks, primarily by engineers, doctors, and middle management officials.

Housing developers are proving that the Parisian does not always prefer an apartment; indeed, many French feel that these new suburban homes enhance their social status. Now they can bring prospective clients or friends to their new villas, whereas before they may have been unable to accommodate guests in their crowded Paris apartments. Every morning they follow a routine much like that of an executive from New Jersey or Long Island who works in New York City as they climb into their new Citröens or Peugeots or crowd into the early morning trains for the trip to their Paris offices.

The differences in life-style extend to leisure activities as well. England's upper class prefers rugby and tennis; the lower class enjoys soccer. Certain ski resorts cater primarily to the middle class, providing expensive accommodations, après ski rituals, and smart shops. The wealthy often make two or three visits a year to St. Moritz, Davos, or Kitzbühel.

As the lower-middle class and even the working class began visiting the Spanish and Italian coasts, the wealthy sought more exotic retreats. German tourist agencies now offer safaris in Kenya, gold-digging holidays in Alaska, and camel caravans in the desert. One tourist organization, the Club Mediterranée, offers holiday camps where one can live in a well-organized "primitive" environment.

To cater to wealthy European travelers, expensive hotels have multiplied throughout Western and Eastern Europe. The Hotel Intercontinental chain now provides a luxurious home away from home throughout Europe, where the hotels dish out native culture in small, acceptable doses so that the wealthy guests, watching local folk dances and trying one meal of local delicacies in the security of their hotel, will have the impression that they are indeed in another country.

The Technocrats

Still, European society in the 1970s is not what it was in the prewar period. As more and more industrial ownership has passed into the hands of governments and corporations, a new technocratic elite has replaced the traditional industrialist as the manager of these transformed enterprises. The directors of Italy's two major public corporations exercise more authority than any industrialist, including the owner of Fiat.

Despite this change the power structure has been transformed very little, since the vast majority of the new managers have come from the middle class. In addition, those few technocrats who rose from the lower-middle class or lower class quickly adopted the life-style of the bourgeoisie and no longer considered themselves a part of their former social class.

Yet the possessors of economic power are not altogether free to use it for their own political and economic gain. On the contrary, they must contend with increased government intervention and the demands of other interest groups, especially labor. Although they have managed to maintain or even increase their share of national wealth, the members of this new ruling stratum no longer have the political authority previously exercised by the leaders of business and industry.

Of course, there are important differences from country to country. Technocrats and entrepreneurs have considerably more political influence in France and Great Britain than they do in the Scandinavian countries. Managers in Sweden must contend with a Social Democratic government that guarantees wage increases and similar benefits to the labor force. In France and Italy, on the other hand, management decisions are not so circumscribed.

With the exception of the Scandinavian states, postwar European society has experienced only a limited shift in educational opportunity, equalization of wealth, and access to positions of power and influence. However, there is strong pressure for a further democratization of education, and plans are being made. Since the important positions in business and industry are going to the well-trained managers, educational democratization could one day lead to greater social mobility. But the opposition of traditional interests will probably prevent full educational democratization of the kind that has been achieved in the United States. It appears that a greater equalization of wealth will be impossible to accomplish. The lower income groups have increased their incomes in the postwar period, but not as dramatically as the middle and upper classes have done. So the income gap between the two groups has actually widened since the war. Because the lower classes own little property and do not invest their money, a large percentage of their income is taxed. The rich, on the other hand, have managed to avoid paying their proper share of the tax burden since most of their income comes from property and investments, not from a salary. The statistics on income presented in this chapter cannot tell the whole story of the disparity in wealth between the two groups because a large portion of the wealth of upper income groups is not reported.

FURTHER READING

Two interesting and informative surveys of Europe since 1945 are Anthony Sampson, *Anatomy of Europe* (1968); and Stanley Rothman, *European Society and Politics* (1971). Although acknowledging a general improvement in the standard of living, Sampson is critical of Europe's failure to institute more far-reaching educational and social reforms. Rothman's study — a competent survey of the relationship between politics and society in Britain, France, West Germany, and the Soviet Union — is especially valuable for its many excellent tables. The most up-to-date and thorough study of the relationship between social background and educational opportunity is Torsten Husen, *Social Background and Educational Opportunity* (1972). Stephen Graubard's *A New Europe?* (1963), cited earlier, is invaluable on many aspects of postwar society.

There are many valuable studies of postwar British society and politics. Anthony Sampson's *The New Anatomy of Britain* (1972) is an up-to-date, critical survey. E. A. Johns, *The Social Structure of Modern Britain* (1965), is a more thorough study. M. Young's *The Rise of the Meritocracy* (1958) finds that education is replacing the family as the avenue to power. D. V. Glass (ed.), *Social Mobility in Britain* (1954), is a somewhat dated study that discerned little social mobility, having found that sons normally had the same status as their fathers. W. L. Guttsman in *The British Political Elite* (1963) has noted little change in the social background of British political leaders. Two highly critical studies are R. M. Titmuss, *The Irresponsible Society* (1960); and Michael Shanks, *The Stagnant Society* (1961). A more recent study is Pauline Gregg, *The Welfare State* (1969). The studies listed in the bibliography for chapter 9 can also contribute to an understanding of British society and politics.

A sound and very readable survey of the impact of economic modernization on French society is John Ardagh, *The New French Revolution* (1969). For another perceptive study see Edward Tannenbaum, *The New France* (1961). Stanley Hoffmann and his associates, in *In Search of France* (1963), say the French Third Republic was characterized by a social stalemate that permitted only gradual change and thereby preserved the position of the dominant social groups in society. But they believed that the social stalemate was collapsing from the shock of World War II, the postwar economic modernization, and the strong Gaullist state.

More critical studies of French society are Michael Crozier, *The Stalled*

Society (1973); A. Girard, *La Réussite Sociale en France* (1961); and M. Dogan, "Political Ascent in a Class Society: French Deputies 1870–1958," in D. Marvick (ed.), *Political Decision-Makers* (1961). Crozier contends that France still suffers from a stalemate or a stalled society and discerns two opposing social forces: the desire for authority and an extreme individualism. The rigidity of society fosters periodic crises during which the French act collectively under dynamic leadership, but then they revert to rigidity. Girard sees little change in the social composition of those in positions of power and influence in politics and society. Dogan advances a similar hypothesis. A competent study of French education is W. R. Fraser, *Reforms and Restraints in Modern French Education* (1971). For a scholarly analysis of French local politics see Mark Kesselman, *The Ambiguous Consensus* (1967).

For good introductions to German politics and society see Louis J. Edinger, *Politics in Germany* (1968); and Arnold J. Heidenheimer, *The Governments of Germany* (3d ed., 1971). Edinger considers German interest groups and the persistence of a German political elite. Heidenheimer compares East and West Germany and finds greater social equalization in the East but greater political liberty in the West.

For a more critical study of modern German society see Ralf Dahrendorf, *Society and Democracy in Germany* (1968). Dahrendorf believes that West Germany must institute a greater social equalization and political democratization. W. Zapf, in *Wandlungen der deutschen Elite, 1919–1961* (1965) and *Beiträge zur Analyse der deutschen Oberschicht* (2d ed., 1965), finds a relatively rapid turnover of German political leaders in the postwar period but a low turnover for civil servants and business leaders.

Also highly critical is Michael Jungblut's *Die Reichen und die Superreichen in Deutschland* (1971). Similar to its American counterpart, *The Rich and the Superrich,* by Ferdinand Lundberg, Jungblut's study describes the monopoly of wealth and power exercised by a relatively small plutocracy.

A sound study of social and political change in postwar Sweden can be found in M. Donald Hancock, *Sweden: The Politics of Postindustrial Change* (1972). For a severely critical, sometimes polemical, study of postwar Sweden see Roland Huntford, *The New Totalitarians* (1972).

Recent statistics are available in publications of the OECD, United Nations, and UNESCO.

11 Economics and Society in the Communist World

[In East Germany] the society of inherited status has largely given way to a society of achieved status.

Ralf Dahrendorf, *Society and Democracy in Germany*

In the years since 1945, social changes in the East European states have exceeded those in the West, but only East Germany has undergone a dramatic economic change. Economic modernization and communism have wrought changes both in the society and in the economy. Eastern Europe and the Soviet Union were overwhelmingly agrarian states in 1945. But by 1974, only Bulgaria and Albania were not yet industrially developed. Socially, the Soviet Union and the Eastern European countries insist, the equalization of educational opportunity, the abandonment of private ownership of property, and the imposition of government control of industry have transformed these states into classless societies. Whether Eastern Europe and the Soviet Union are in fact free of a privileged stratum is a question that merits examination.

Although the Soviet Union had made considerable progress in the interwar years, World War II set back its industrialization severely. With its industry reduced to a quarter of the prewar output, its war effort was heavily dependent on American aid. Nevertheless, the war provided some lasting benefits to Soviet industrialization, for entire industries had been set up beyond the Urals to escape German destruction. With these industrial areas intact and the older ones rebuilt, the country's industrial potential was immensely increased. In 1953 the Soviet Union regained its prewar levels of production. Concentration on heavy industry put the nation in a position to challenge the United States in the production of raw materials and producer goods — though not consumer goods — in the late 1960s.

Khrushchev's Decentralization

But Soviet economic growth has not been continuously strong in the postwar period, nor has the Soviet Union been able to challenge the United States in total industrial output, as Nikita Khrushchev boasted would happen. Since Josef Stalin's death the Soviet economy has experienced two markedly different periods of development, the first under Khrushchev and the second under his successors, Leonid Brezhnev and Aleksei Kosygin. Of course, both periods were influenced by the rigid centralization under Stalin. Khrushchev's policies were in fact a reaction to Stalinist centralization and his concentration on heavy industry.

Beginning in 1958, Khrushchev instituted a major reorganization of the Soviet economy along regional lines. The rationale for this decentralization was sound. The extreme Stalinist centralization was adequate for a small developing economy but not for an increasingly complex developed one. The rigid centralized plans, long-term goals, and resource allocations meant waste of resources and shoddiness of manufactured goods.

However, because Khrushchev's decentralization was hastily instituted, it created new difficulties. Overall coordination and control of 100 regional areas was extremely difficult. Local factory managers were hampered by greater interference than they had endured under Stalin, since they now received endless directives, many of them conflicting, from the newly empowered local and state agencies. Nor was the factory manager freed from the exaggerated production goals typical of the Stalinist period, since Khrushchev was equally determined to catch up with American industrial output. Because production goals were still couched in terms of volume or weight, managers went on meeting their quotas by hoarding materials, falsifying records, and turning out shoddy products. The Soviet publication *Krokodil* once lampooned the system of output measurement and factory management by showing a nail factory that had met its quota by producing one giant nail. Since transport goals were expressed in ton-kilometers, transport firms made useless trips in order to fulfill their quotas.

Khrushchev's determination to raise agricultural production also misfired. The concentration on increasing corn and wheat production forced local officials to adopt monoculture. To raise production, fallowing was banned almost entirely. This led to weed infestation, wind erosion, and falling yields. And Khrushchev's emphasis on raising production in certain fertile areas left the land in less fertile areas with little fertilizer and little capital.

When Khrushchev realized that his policy of decentralization was failing, he resorted to haphazard remedies — even to recentralization of authority. In 1962 he divided the party into agricultural and industrial groups, thereby further complicating an already confused situation. Local Communist party officials were extremely resentful when the new division of responsibility deprived them of half their authority. Nor were things better at the national level, where both the Soviet *Sovnaskhov* (economic council) and the Supreme Council of National Economy were given the authority to issue directives in the same industrial sectors.

Other factors contributed to the lag in Soviet economic growth under Khrushchev. In the first place, the expansion of the space and military programs diverted capital from industry and absorbed the best scientists, engineers, and managers. In the second place, a serious shortage of skilled labor occurred during the Khrushchev years because the birthrate dropped during World War II. Increasing the supply of industrial labor entailed shifting workers from agriculture and reducing enrollment in schools. Finally, the shift to new technologies and new energy sources was not rapid enough to sustain high growth rates. On top of all that, Khrushchev himself created a coal shortage by insisting on a rapid transition away from solid fuels. For several years, neither coal nor new fuels could be turned out in sufficient quantities. Because he had by now alienated a large segment of the party, his opponents had little difficulty in removing him from power when he suffered reverses in foreign policy as well (see chapter 7).

Economic Policy of Kosygin and Brezhnev

The second major shift in economic policy began after Kosygin and Brezhnev instituted reforms in 1965. They abolished regional administration and returned to centralized direction of the economy. But this was not a Stalinist centralism with its complete control over all aspects of production, investment, and resource allocation. To be centrally determined were major investments, volume of sales, basic assortment of output, total wages fund, amount of profit and profit rate on capital, and payments to and allocations from the state budget. Local managers were to have the authority to handle most factory labor questions except gross wages and to authorize all minor investments out of their profits. Most important, volume of sales and profitability replaced gross output as indicators of the success of enterprises. Central controls now tended to be indirect rather than direct: taxes, subsidies, interest rates, rents, price ceilings, and profit rates. To avoid the dislocation that accompanied Khrushchev's changes, the reforms were implemented gradually; in 1967 only one-third of the industrial labor force was working in firms under this new system.

The economic lag of the early 1960s has come to an end as a measure of order has been reestablished in the economy. Moreover, Brezhnev and Kosygin seem intent on achieving a balanced economy and avoiding too great a concentration on heavy industry and military goods. More emphasis has been on the consumer goods industry, including major deals with Fiat and Renault to provide Soviet citizens with passenger cars.

Competition with the United States means more to Kosygin and Brezhnev than merely equality in the production of military and heavy industrial goods. The sharp difference in the living standards of American and Soviet citizens has certainly not been a good advertisement for the superiority of communism. Kosygin is concerned with creating an affluent society in the Soviet Union more than with winning an ideological battle with the United States.

Soviet Economic Modernization

Soviet businessmen and industrial managers have recently won the grudging respect of their Western counterparts for their economic bargaining with Western governments and businesses. According to an editorial in the Chase Manhattan Bank's biweekly *East-West Markets,* the Soviet manager "would do anything that gets him ahead." In economic negotiations, U. S. businessmen have begun to recognize that Soviet industrial leaders are no longer merely plodding government functionaries. Since 1965, Soviet factories have paid incentive bonuses to managers who increase productivity and sales; however, they must work within an overall plan and a resource allocation that prevents them from operating a factory according to strict supply and demand factors. Therefore, using profit as a measurement of economic success and of bonuses is not a move toward a capitalist system but merely a way to increase output.

The basis for much of the transformation of Eastern Europe and the Soviet Union in the postwar years has been economic modernization. Most of the countries have made the transition from peasant societies to diversified economies. Having a good economic balance of agricultural and industrial output, East Germany has made particularly rapid strides since the war. With a population of only 17 million, East Germany has become the tenth leading industrial country in the world. Despite the loss of over a million skilled workers to the West, East Germany has maintained its reputation as one of the world's leading producers of optical and photographic equipment and has become a leading producer of chemicals, iron and steel, and automobiles.

Romania, with its important mineral resources, has also made impressive economic gains since 1945: its economic growth rate averaged 10 percent annually between 1950 and 1973. Romania's rejection of the role of mere raw materials supplier to the Soviet Union and the other members of Comecon led it to develop its own manufacturing industries, with apparent success.

The economic development of the other Eastern European countries has been more checkered. In the 1960s their output fell far behind their goals. Czechoslovakia, with an advanced manufacturing sector, has suffered from overzealous planning, political turmoil, and a labor shortage. Although political stability in recent years has promoted economic improvement, highly planned resource allocation still inhibits rapid economic growth.

In the 1970s Poland and Bulgaria, two countries that had lagged behind East Germany and Romania, began to achieve industrial growth rates near 10 percent. As a whole the Eastern European economies are maintaining a rapid advance; for 1971 to 1973 every country's industrial growth rate topped 6 percent. Per capita GNP has risen steadily since the early 1960s. But, as Table 11-1 shows, there is considerable variance from one East European state to another. Only East Germany, the Soviet Union, and Czechoslovakia can be considered fully developed industrial societies.

Agricultural Problems

Some of the Soviet Union's industrial progress, particularly in the Stalin period, has been at the expense of agriculture. Arcadius Kahan has called it a policy of calculated subsistence for agriculture. As a result, Soviet agriculture was marked by a high input of manpower and land and a low input of technology; the Soviet Union used only about 30 percent of the tractors and 40 percent of the fertilizer used in the United States. With about 75 percent more sown land, in the early 1960s the Soviet Union produced about 63 percent of the U. S. crop of major grains. Only under extremely favorable climatic conditions can the Soviet Union feed its population.

Khrushchev's attempts to raise agricultural production failed because they were primarily restricted to tilling new marginal virgin land and trying one short-term project after another to raise production, instead of undertaking long-term efforts to modernize farming methods and provide adequate machinery and fertilizers. The post-Khrushchev planners have begun to invest more in agriculture and to raise the wages of agricultural

Table 11-1   Per Capita GNP (1965 U.S. dollars)

	1965	1973
East Germany	$1,574	$2,871
Soviet Union	1,288	2,648
Czechoslovakia	1,554	2,705
Hungary	1,100	1,846
Poland	962	1,820
Bulgaria	690	1,826
Romania	757	1,832

SOURCE: U. S. Department of Commerce, *Selected Trade and Economic Data of the Centrally Planned Economies,* May 1975, p. 2.

workers, but despite their efforts, Soviet food needs cannot be covered completely without optimum weather conditions. From 1971 to 1973, the average growth of Soviet agricultural output was only 3.4 percent. The failure of the Soviet grain crop in 1972 necessitated huge grain purchases from the United States.

Soviet planners have been faced with another major agricultural problem — the migration of agricultural workers, especially the young, to the cities. A 1967 survey showed that 65 percent of those described as job transients were under thirty years of age. The Communist youth organization, Komsomol, has not been able to slow this migration. A 1966 survey of the Smolensk region showed that the number of Komsomol members working on state farms had halved in five years; on collective farms it had dropped even more, from 21,043 to 8,778.

The disparity between the drabness of life on a rural collective and the livelier life-style possible in a larger city is symbolized by the difference in the clothing styles available in each. So the arbiter of Soviet men's fashions — in an attempt to keep them down on the collective — recently advocated that a return to Cossack styles with dashing boots, embroidered shirts, and flared trousers could provide an alternative to the coveted Western fashion trends while retaining a traditional mode of dress that offers beauty, comfort, and timeless appeal.

Agriculture underwent a deeper transformation than did industry in Eastern Europe after the war. From an agrarian system of large privately owned estates, most land has now become divided into state-owned and cooperatively owned sectors. The exceptions are Poland and Yugoslavia, where the bulk of the land is still held by the peasantry.

In an attempt to satisfy land-hungry peasants, land was first distributed in small private plots. Later, as governments came under Communist domination, the land was either taken over by the state or organized into cooperatives. The cooperatives range from those where the peasant owns nothing and is paid a wage to those where property is individually owned but cooperatively farmed. Fierce peasant resistance to collectivization in Poland, combined with the leaders' reluctance to collectivize, has led to the establishment of over 3 million small private farms.

Such population density on the land, the primary problem in the interwar period, retards the development of agriculture; one study fixed the population density in the private sector at forty to fifty workers for every 250 acres. In Western Europe the agricultural population is under 20 percent of the working population, but it remains near 40 percent in all East European countries except East Germany.

Collectivized agriculture has not yet provided the answer to East Europe's agrarian problems. In fact, Poland's agricultural output has risen more than that of any other East European country because of its small farms, whereas output in collectivized East Germany, Czechoslovakia, and

Hungary is actually lower than the 1938 production. A Polish farmer recently remarked, "It is amusing to us to see high-ranking Russian officers going home carrying sacks of potatoes." Among the countries with collectivized agriculture, only Romania has shown a slight increase in agricultural production since the war. The average growth from 1971 through 1973 was highest in Romania and Poland (9.2 and 6.6 percent) and lowest in Bulgaria, Czechoslovakia, and East Germany (3.3, 3.8, and 3.5 percent). Collectivized agriculture in Yugoslavia provides a higher yield mainly because the most fertile land is in large state farms in the Voivodina area north of Belgrade whereas individually owned farms (not larger than twenty-five acres) are located in infertile mountainous terrain.

Living Standards

Economic changes have not brought about a standard of living in the Soviet Union and Eastern Europe similar to that in Western Europe. Two major studies of living standards conducted in the early 1960s, the Russet and Niewiaroski scales, ranked the Soviet Union no better than twentieth among the 88 (Niewiaroski) to 107 (Russet) countries studied. Based upon the nine economic and five social variables in the Niewiaroski scale the English-speaking countries, Western European countries, East Germany, Czechoslovakia, Finland, and Israel ranked well ahead of the Soviet Union. The Soviets' high ranking in terms of social equality offset somewhat their much lower ranking in the economic scale. It is doubtful that the Soviet Union's position on the scale changed much by 1970 since its per capita national income of $1,000 compared unfavorably to $1,800 in Western Europe and $3,500 in the United States.

In terms of equalizing income, the Soviet Union has surpassed most of the West European states with the exception of Scandinavia. Table 11–2 indicates that top managers, physicians, and lawyers are not paid the huge sums characteristic in the West but that political leaders receive a much higher salary than the average worker. Since Stalin renewed income differentiation in the early 1930s to promote production, Soviet leaders have apparently felt that wage differentials are necessary in an industrialized society. It is noteworthy that men constitute only 40 percent of physicians, probably because of the extensive training required and the comparatively low salaries.

The concentration of Soviet resources on heavy industry and the armaments and space programs, has left little for consumer goods. Until recently Soviet leaders were little interested in providing consumer goods: Khrushchev asserted, "A person cannot consume, for example, more bread and other products than are necessary for his organism. . . . Of course, when we speak of satisfying people's needs, we have in mind not whims or claims to luxuries, but the healthy needs of a culturally developed person."

Table 11-2   Base Wage Differentials in the Soviet Union, 1963
(U. S. dollars per year, before taxes)[a]

Cabinet minister, republic government	9,125
University professor	7,070
Factory director (machine building)	6,240
Doctor of science, head of department in a research institute	5,730
Master foreman (machine building)	5,028
Engineer (oil industry)	4,238
Technician	3,724
State farm manager	3,530
Average for all workers and employees	1,445[b]
Lawyer	1,376
Physician	1,260
Coal miner	1,092
Steel worker	872
High school teacher	824
Construction worker	746
Machine tool operator	746
Textile worker	679
Office typist	588
State farm worker	586
Collective farmer (1962)	574

[a]Rubles converted into dollars at 1:1.11 ratio.
[b]Total wages received, *including bonuses.* Bonuses are not included in the other figures in the table.

SOURCE: J. P. Nettl, *The Soviet Achievement* (New York: Harcourt Brace Jovanovich, 1967), p. 254. Reprinted by permission.

As late as 1962, Soviet per capita consumption of consumer goods was only 40 to 60 percent of that in France, West Germany, and the United Kingdom.

It is of course important to remember that consumer goods are more equally distributed in the Soviet Union than in France, West Germany, and the United Kingdom. For example, in housing there are no socially and economically differentiated neighborhoods like those in the West. The size of a dwelling usually depends on the size of the family. Since rents are low — only about 4 percent of an individual's income is spent on rent, fuel, and light — there are no economic barriers to entry into certain neighborhoods as there are in the West.

As in Western Europe, the standard of living varies considerably among East European countries, being highest in East Germany, Czechoslovakia, and Yugoslavia. Tito boasted in 1974 that every fifth Yugoslav had a car.

Typical Yugoslavs now spend only 37 percent of their income on food and drink compared to over 50 percent in the early 1960s. There is little doubt that these figures would not be so favorable if many Yugoslavs did not become guest workers in more affluent countries in the north.

Within Yugoslavia there is a radical difference in the standard of living between north and south. The north, with a standard of living near that of Austria, resents having to help the underdeveloped areas of Macedonia and Montenegro in the south. In Czechoslovakia the standard of living varies too, being much lower in the primarily agrarian Slovakian east.

Regional differences have been a long-standing problem in Eastern Europe, especially in Czechoslovakia and Yugoslavia. During the interwar years the Bohemian–Moravian areas in Czechoslovakia, like Croatia and Slovenia in Yugoslavia, had much more developed economic areas and considerably higher standards of living than other sections. The inhabitants of the Czech lands also held most of the government positions during the interwar years and in the postwar Communist government.

This political–economic imbalance was to be one of the factors leading to the emergence of Alexander Dubček as Communist party leader during the "Prague Spring" (see chapter 12). In Yugoslavia, political power has normally been in the hands of Serbs rather than Croatians or Slovenians. The result has been internecine warfare, especially during World War II, as the Croatians attempted to gain a greater share of power.

Although no Eastern bloc country has a living standard comparable to Western Europe, there has been rapid improvement since 1955. In East Germany in 1953 and Poland in 1956, workers rioted against low wages and a low standard of living. The riots were indications of poor existing conditions and heralds of change. The riots forced Communist party leaders to allocate more funds for raising agricultural and consumer goods output. When conditions worsened at times, as they did in Poland in 1970, the workers again took to the streets and demanded changes. Only Romania is still restricting the development of the consumer goods industries in order to develop its heavy industry.

A characteristic of the Communist bloc countries has been low-cost housing and services. In East Germany and Hungary, apartments and houses cost an average of $14.50 per month; public transportation costs are a fraction of those in the West; and medical services are free. However, the low costs are often offset by poor quality goods and inadequate housing. In 1961, for every 1,000 inhabitants Poland had 580 rooms and Bulgaria 545 rooms. Many apartments lack bathrooms, kitchens, and other amenities common to housing in Western Europe.

Because consumer goods are still expensive and of poor quality, visitors from Western Europe often find that their clothing attracts interest and sometimes prospective buyers. There *is* evidence that the quality of consumer goods is now improving. For instance, Polish clothing and

Russian vacationers driving up to a cottage in a resort area near Kiev.
Camera Press London

Yugoslav shoes are now being sold in huge quantities in the United States. And what is more, self-service stores are reducing the interminable waiting in lines.

Despite Soviet and East European efforts to upgrade the status of the worker, the gap between theory and practice remains. The prestige of many jobs is little different from that of the same positions in the West. Service-class jobs, especially those of the new technocracy, continue to be more respected. A Hungarian woman's choice of a lower-paying administrative position over that of a textile worker became a *cause célèbre* in 1973. Industrial progress naturally demands highly trained experts; their jobs are more prestigious and their incomes higher.

An increase in leisure time is one device used by Eastern European countries to meet workers' demands for a life-style similar to that in the West. Every worker now receives one month's paid vacation per year. Factory-owned resorts in the mountains and on the Baltic Sea and Black Sea give workers the kind of vacation they could only dream about fifteen years ago; an East German worker can spend two weeks on the Baltic for as little as $20. Eastern European travelers, a few workers included, are being seen in increasing numbers in the West. However, the West is still too expensive for most East European workers.

The Role of Women

Despite the egalitarian ideals of Communism, women possess no more real power in the Soviet Union than they do in the West. The 15-member Politburo, headed by Brezhnev, has no female members. Only 8 women are among the 287 full members of the Central Committee of the Communist party. Men head all the government ministries and committees. Larger numbers of women are employed in the professions — about 60 percent of the Soviet physicians and 72 percent of the secondary school teachers are female. But these are low-paying professions that are not desired by men. The heads of hospitals and schools are invariably male. Women still occupy an inferior place in the home. Even among those who hold jobs on the outside, most still do all the housework. And because they lack labor-saving devices and don't often go out to eat, their household work is much more arduous than in the West.

Added to the household duties are the ubiquitous lines in the shops. Soviet women have been found to spend as much as two hours each day waiting in lines. It is true that childcare centers leave wives free to work but this often simply means that a woman works both day and night without the satisfaction that comes with raising her own child. Except for the annual vacations leisure is an unknown concept for Eastern European women.

Social Structure

Postwar economic modernization and Communist-inspired social changes have transformed the East's social structure. In the Soviet Union the former ruling classes were destroyed during the interwar period. In Eastern Europe they lost their privileged positions after 1945.

Poland provides a clear example of the decline of a former ruling aristocracy. Those aristocrats who did not flee Poland as World War II drew to a close have lost both their property and their political power. Some are now part of the professional and service classes. Perhaps the best example of this transformation is the experience of the famous Potocki and Radziwill families.

In the interwar period the Potocki family owned 9 million acres of land and eighteen towns and employed countless peasants. When the Communists expropriated their land after the war, one member of the family, Ignacz Potocki, became a common laborer. But he had had a superior education, and by the late 1950s the government's fear of the former aristocracy had declined. So Potocki, who was an expert on medicinal springs, became chief geologist of the Ministry of Health and Social Welfare. Many of the prominent Radziwills have also found employment — as engineers, accountants, and book publishers.

Hungary and Romania, which had had large and wealthy aristocracies, experienced a similar social revolution. But in Bulgaria, Yugoslavia, and

Albania, where land was owned primarily by the peasants, no social transformation occurred.

All the Eastern European countries were primarily agrarian — 60 to 75 percent of the working population was engaged in agriculture at the end of World War II. The nationalization of industry therefore had far less impact on the social structures than did the destruction of the aristocracy. Only in Czechoslovakia and East Germany did the nationalization of industry displace a significant segment of the populations.

Changes in Education

Nowhere have the social changes been more dramatic than in education. Some Eastern states were ruthless in their determination to eliminate social privilege in education. In East Germany, which Ralf Dahrendorf called the first modern society on German soil, at least half the student populations in all secondary schools had to be workers' and peasants' children. This requirement succeeded in eliminating the grasp of the upper classes on advanced education. By 1963, one-third of all university students and half the students in technical colleges came from working-class families.

This change has meant that a much larger percentage of professors, judges, generals, and industrial managers now come from a working-class background. In comparison with the West, especially France and West Germany, Table 11–3 shows clearly that the number of children from laboring-class backgrounds in universities is much higher in Eastern Europe.

Table 11-3 Percentage of Manual Workers' Sons in Higher Education

	1960	1964
Yugoslavia	56.0	53.3
East Germany	—	40.0
Czechoslovakia	39.3	37.9
Romania	36.6	31.5
Poland	32.9	35.0
Bulgaria	28.0	—
Great Britain	25.0	—
Italy	13.2	15.3
France	5.3	8.3
West Germany	5.2	5.3

SOURCE: UNESCO, *Access to Higher Education* (Bucharest, 1968) p. 49.

However, Soviet and East European leaders have retreated from the view that working-class children should have preference in higher education. Soviet leaders feel that all citizens are now socially equal; therefore, tests no longer have to consider the different social backgrounds of the applicants for higher education. In addition, influential white-collar families have obtained preferential treatment for their children. These practices have tended to favor the children of the service class and intelligentsia. In 1971, children of blue-collar workers — numbering about 60 percent of the population — comprised 36 percent of those in higher education compared to almost 60 percent for children of white-collar workers. East Germany has dropped the 50 percent clause in order to provide sufficient competent managers for its rapidly industrializing economy.

The Soviet Union now has an obligatory two-year work period between secondary school and higher education, which has tended to divert some young people from pursuing an education. In spite of this trend to select future leaders from a more privileged sector of society, the number of children from working-class homes still considerably exceeds that of the West.

The Communist Ruling Class

The trend toward favoring children from the service class, including those from families engaged in politics, illustrates one of two widely held views about contemporary society in the Communist bloc countries. The view that is by far the most popular in the West is that a new class of privileged Communist bureaucrats has replaced the former ruling elites throughout the Communist world. This new class not only monopolizes political power, but also receives a major share of the wealth of each country. In some descriptions, the ruling stratum has been depicted as a new plutocracy with riches that compare with the former nobility.

The other view, held by a few Western intellectuals, is that Eastern societies provide a social equality that is missing in the West. Proponents of this view maintain that it does little good to provide people with political rights, as is done in the West, as long as there are huge social and economic gaps between the various classes.

Central to the question of a new class is the distribution both of rewards and of power. Is there in fact a small privileged elite that siphons off a major part of the wealth of the Soviet Union and Eastern Europe? The Communist ideal was that what each person gets is determined by his or her need. Has this been changed so that what each person gets is determined by his or her relationship to the ruling elite? Is power monopolized at the top in a totalitarian fashion, or is it distributed among various groups within the society? In sum, have the promises of Communist society been realized?

There is no escaping the fact that a new ruling stratum has replaced the old ruling classes. But it is similar to the old ruling groups only in its control of political power, not in its monopoly of wealth. No individuals in the East compare with millionaires in the West. Property and inheritance are limited to personal real estate and belongings, and it is impossible to profit from personal savings; therefore, inherited wealth cannot be the basis for a new capitalist class. But what of the concept of a new class popularized by Milovan Djilas, a close associate of Tito and formerly vice-president of Communist Yugoslavia? If the new-class label is restricted to those who exercise political power and benefit more than others from their favored position, then the theory has some validity.

Marshal Tito has become highly critical of the life-styles of some people in the Yugoslav ruling stratum. In 1973 he said it was time for Yugoslavia to rid itself of the deformations that had "brought shame to a Socialist society." To avert the development of a new oppressive class, Tito stole a page from Chairman Mao's book. He removed about 100,000 members from the League of Communists and ordered all elected officeholders to retain their previous jobs while carrying out their new duties in their spare time. Whether he succeeded in enforcing this order is not yet clear. In any case, he acknowledged the existence of a major social problem for a Communist society.

Like political parties in the West, Communist parties are becoming more professionalized and less worker-oriented. In a recent survey, 70 percent of the Communist party members in one Soviet province were found to have come from white-collar occupations — managers, technicians, and government and party bureaucrats. It is doubtful whether any of the Eastern societies will be able to change this trend radically since they cannot industrialize without leaders who have the knowledge and training that can be provided only by the professional classes.

The Beginnings of Pluralism?

A final important question concerning Communist bloc countries is whether these new ruling strata are relatively open. Do they monopolize power in totalitarian fashion as former rulers did, or do they receive political inputs from interest groups that have no strong party connections? Again, as in our analysis of interest groups in the West, we find that leaders of the various interest groups are often closely affiliated with the Communist parties. However, as these various interest groups become more professionalized, they tend to be less closely associated with the party.

The dominance of the Communist parties over decision making seems to be tied rather closely to economic development. Where the economies can still be described as underdeveloped, as in Bulgaria, Albania, and Romania, the party still dominates political and economic decision making. But in the more developed societies, such as the Soviet Union, East Germany, Czechoslovakia, Poland, and Hungary, decision making has spread beyond the narrow confines of the party bureaucracy.

Even though it is premature to speak of pluralism in the Soviet Union, the various interest groups are starting to have an impact on politics. Political decision making has moved far from the narrow court politics of Stalin. Whereas Stalin issued orders after consulting only his closest associates, Khrushchev found it necessary to open up debate to a much larger segment of the society.

More and more party decisions reflect conclusions arrived at by experts and interest groups. Debates on economic policy are often aired in newspapers like *Pravda* and *Izvestia*. A debate carried on in 1962 on planning and management resulted in a decision two years later to introduce a kind of market relations between trade organizations and firms producing about one quarter of all clothing and shoes. The need to base decisions on expert advice and not purely on political considerations will probably enlarge the decision-making strata even more as time goes on.

In the developed Eastern European states the decision-making process is considerably more democratic. In countries such as Poland, the Communist party never achieved complete control over the Roman Catholic Church, the peasantry, or labor. Opposition to agrarian collectivization was so stout that the political authorities eventually had to drop their plans to eliminate private farming.

Labor unions and business groups are much more powerful in Poland than in the Soviet Union. Unions nominate business leaders who have a veto power over the decisions of the state economic planning executives. The violent strikes of 1956 and 1970 and the changes they precipitated are a further indication of the limits of the party's power.

In Yugoslavia, where economic decision making has been decentralized, the League of Communists has even less power. Tito has in fact had second thoughts about decentralization since in his opinion it has led to a revival of regionalism and "social democratic" thinking. He removed most of the Croatian party leaders in the early 1970s because of their desire to concentrate on Croatian rather than Yugoslav development. They opposed sending a part of the profits from Croatian industry and tourism to the poorer areas in the south. Finally, without the intervention of the Soviet Union, Czechoslovakia would long ago have developed a pluralistic society in the pattern of Western Europe.

In the course of time, change in the Soviet Union and Eastern Europe will grow out of conflict between institutions and interest groups, not out of decisions by a small clique of party functionaries. Public debate over national priorities will also increase. Eastern European societies have already had to step up the production of consumer goods in the face of increasing public demand. However, whether the Eastern European countries will be able to carry out the decisions they arrive at without provoking Soviet intervention is not clear.

FURTHER READING

Several edited studies have been particularly helpful in the preparation of this chapter: Allen Kassof (ed.), *Prospects for Soviet Society* (1968); Alexander Dallin and Thomas B. Larson (eds.), *Soviet Politics Since Khrushchev* (1968); Alex Inkeles and Kent Geiger (eds.), *Soviet Society* (1961); and Abraham Brumberg, *Russia Under Khrushchev* (1962). Kassof's volume is a comprehensive treatment of Soviet society until the mid-1960s. The consensus of the seven contributors to the Dallin and Larson study is that Brezhnev and Kosygin have taken a more cautious and realistic approach to problems than Khrushchev did. But they admit that the many uncertainties about the present government must reflect the contradictions and ambiguities of the Brezhnev–Kosygin regime itself. The contributors point to the absence of a monolithic view among the party leaders, which may in fact be the reason for Western uncertainty about Soviet policies. Inkeles and Geiger have put together a good introduction to social problems in the Soviet Union, but it is now somewhat dated.

The views expressed by Alex Inkeles and Raymond A. Bauer in *The Soviet Citizen* (1959) are still voiced in more recent works. They maintained that Soviet citizens accept the Soviet way of life even though they may reject certain leaders. They want the security that comes with collectivism, central planning, comprehensive socialization, and single-party rule. More recent studies of Soviet society are John G. Eriksen, *The Development of Soviet Society* (1970); David Lane, *Politics and Society in the U.S.S.R.* (1971); Milton G. Lodge, *Soviet Elite Attitudes Since Stalin* (1969); and J. Strong, *The Soviet Union Under Brezhnev and Kosygin* (1971).

Criticisms of Soviet society from Soviet citizens include the sharp denunciations of Andrei Amalrik, *Will the Soviet Union Survive Until 1984?* (1970); and the many works of Aleksandr Solzhenitsyn. For less polemical criticisms see Roy Medvedev, *On Socialist Democracy* (1975) and *Let History Judge* (1971). The most important non-Russian criticism has come from Milovan Djilas in *The New Class* (1957) and *The Unperfect Society: Beyond the New Class* (1969). In *The New Class* Djilas contends that a new privileged group of party officials reaps the major rewards in Communist society and refuses to institute true communism since it would destroy their privileged position. In *The Unperfect Society* Djilas contends that Communist ideology is disintegrating and is no longer accepted even by Communist leaders as a means of social organization. As a disillusioned former Communist vice-president of Yugoslavia, Djilas would like to see a form of democratic socialism in Communist countries.

The standard work on the Soviet economy is Alec Nove, *The Soviet Economy* (rev. ed. 1966). See also Harry Schwartz, *The Soviet Economy Since Stalin* (1965); and the Marxist critique by M. Dobb, *Soviet Economic Development Since 1917* (rev. ed. 1966). A more recent study is Michael Ellman, *Economic Reform in the Soviet Union* (1969). A somewhat dated but still valuable study is David Granick, *The Red Executive: A Study of the Organization Man in Russian Industry* (1960).

The Soviet worker can be studied in A. Brodersen, *The Soviet Worker* (1966); Robert Conquest (ed.), *Industrial Workers in the U.S.S.R.* (1967); and Emily Clark Brown, *Soviet Trade Unions and Labour Relations* (1966).

Two recent accounts of Soviet life by journalists are Hedrick Smith, *The Russians* (1976); and Robert G. Kaiser, *Russia: The People and the Power* (1976). Both contend that the classless society is a myth in the Soviet Union, that Soviet industry is inefficient, and that the Soviet population is influenced by a pervasive collectivist mentality. Both agree with Inkeles and Bauer that Soviet citizens equate freedom with danger and disorder and believe the state has given them the security they yearn for by providing cheap housing, sufficient food, guaranteed employment, free education and medical care, and pensions for the old and disabled.

There are few studies in English on Eastern European societies. A valuable broader synthesis of politics and society is Ghita Ionescu, *The Politics of the European Communist States* (1967). Ionescu believes that the West has underestimated the extent of political dissent in Eastern Europe. He feels that the Eastern European countries have at this point an embryonic form of pluralism and that they will continue to become more European and less communistic. Nenod Popovic, in *Yugoslavia: The New Class in Crisis* (1968), applies the Djilas thesis to Yugoslavia. Jan F. Triska (ed.), in *Communist Party States* (1969), looks at the nature of Communist rule throughout Eastern Europe. Some important articles are contained in Stephen Fischer-Galati (ed.), *Eastern Europe in the 60's.* Wayne Vucinich's contribution questions some of Djilas's assumptions. He maintains that a new middle class of technocrats is numerous in Eastern Europe and that Djilas's static picture of Eastern European societies needs revision.

There are many more studies of the Eastern European economies. An important study of the workings of Comecon is Michael Kaser's *Comecon: Integration Problems of the Planned Economies* (1965). There are many studies of the Yugoslav economic system, especially of the Workers' Councils. Competent studies are George W. Hoffman and Fred W. Neal (ed.), *Yugoslavia and the New Communism (1962); Jiri Kolaja, Workers' Councils: The Yugoslav Experience* (1965); M. J. Broekmeyer (ed.), *Yugoslav Workers Selfmanagement* (1970); Joseph T. Bombelles, *Economic Development of Communist Yugoslavia, 1947–64* (1968); and Ichak Adizes, *Industrial Democracy: Yugoslav Style* (1971). John Michael Montias, in *Economic Development in Communist Rumania* (1967), has detailed Romania's attempts to establish a diversified economy. The general works listed in the bibliography following chapter 7 contain information on economics and society in the other East European states. Jean Edward Smith, in *Germany Beyond the Wall* (1967), describes the rapid economic growth in East Germany and the transformation of society. See also A. Zauberman, *Industrial Progress in Poland, Czechoslovakia and East Germany, 1937–1962* (1964); and J.F. Brown, *The New Eastern Europe* (1966).

12 1968: Year of Crisis

> To speak of repression in the case of an institution possessing no
> "physical" repressive power, such as a university, may seem
> paradoxical. This repression is part of the very functioning of the
> institution, its structure, which makes the student passive, because
> he interiorizes its norms and requirements. . . . This passivity kills
> all real desire and all creative spirit, the expressions of a
> nonalienated life.
>
> Daniel Cohn-Bendit, *The Action–Image of Society* by Alfred
> Willener

> We have introduced the specter of liquidation of the absolute power
> of the bureaucratic caste, a caste introduced to the international
> scene by Stalinist socialism. . . . But bureaucracy, even if it has not
> the dimensions of a class, still shows its characteristics in anything
> that concerns the exercise of power. It takes preventive measures to
> defend itself and it will do so to the bitter end. . . . We do not
> endanger socialism: to the contrary. We endanger bureaucracy
> which has been slowly but surely burying socialism on a worldwide
> scale.
>
> "The Luxury of Illusions," *Prague Reporter,* July 31, 1968

> The internal hierarchy is to be abolished. Every employee, no matter
> what his job, will receive the same pay . . .
>
> French workers' pamphlet, Assurance Générale de France, 1968

On its way toward the affluent society, Western Europe was shocked by a
series of student-led riots in 1968 that ultimately brought into question
much of what Europe's leaders had been trying to achieve since 1945.
Before the riots began, some political scientists had suggested that the
relative absence of serious political turmoil could only be explained by an
"end of ideology" brought about by the inappropriateness of radical
solutions in the modern welfare state. Both in Europe and in the United
States during the 1950s students seemed to have little interest in politics.
Although American students became more active in the early 1960s in
response to the civil rights movement and then to the Vietnam War,
Europe's students remained quiet. Even if students had been dissatisfied, no
one expected that their activities could harm the stable advanced European
societies, let alone nearly bring down the government in France. Unrest was
not confined to Western Europe. In Czechoslovakia, students and reform-
minded Communist party members overthrew an ossified bureaucratic
party leadership and blew a breath of fresh air into the party before they

206

themselves fell to Soviet forces in late 1968. Despite the obvious political differences between France and Czechoslovakia, both were perceived by the demonstrators as authoritarian, bureaucratic states that were unresponsive to the needs of the citizenry.

Danger signals had already begun to appear in Western Europe in the early 1960s. Dissatisfaction and unrest, first evident in Italy, were directed at the overcrowding in universities, the outdated curriculum, and the authoritarian attitude and archaic teaching methods of the professors. The medieval university, where students could select and fire professors, provided a model for students dissatisfied with the overcrowded, bureaucratic Italian universities. In 1967 the ratio of students to professors was 105 to 1, as against 13 to 1 in the United States and 23 to 1 in French universities.

The problem was one not merely of numbers but also of the attitude of European professors. A privileged small professorial elite opposed increasing the number of full professors and making curriculum changes, especially those aimed at instituting new disciplines such as sociology. Sociology was being taught in faculties of architecture, because of its relevance to urban planning, but professors in general refused to acknowledge sociology as a genuine discipline.

Student Unrest in Italy and Germany

As early as 1965 students rioted at the University of Milan and the University of Trento, demanding reforms in the curriculum and a voice in university government. The most militant students at Milan were those in the faculties of architecture, where courses on sociology were taught. At Trento, where the only faculty of sociology existed, students demanded that the university be more closely related to the demands of the modern world. Clearly, the professors had been correct in fearing the consciousness-raising potential of sociology.

Neither the Italian nor the German student movement seriously challenged the stability of the respective governments. Unrest was expected even less among German students than among Italian students. Most Germans were satisfied to share in their country's growing prosperity. In fact, a major reason advanced for Germany's prosperity was the docility of its population. The stereotype German students were passive information gatherers who would later take their places as good bureaucrats. While the stereotype may have been true for a large segment of the population, it did not fit the considerable number of university students who, according to one interpretation, wanted to atone for their elders' past submissiveness to authority.

Radicalism was at first restricted to a few students who had American connections: Karl-Dietrich Wolff had taken part in civil rights marches and anti-Vietnam War demonstrations in the United States; Rudi Dutschke (Red Rudi) has an American wife; and Ehkehart Krippendorf had studied in the United States. German and other student movements borrowed the methods as well as the language of American protesters: sit-in, teach-in, establishment, military–industrial complex. But in time the German student movement spread to a much larger group of students and developed its own ideological positions. Among the many primarily German and European reasons for student dissatisfaction were the extreme authoritarianism of full professors, the failure of European universities to change their antiquated curricula, and a widespread interest in various forms of Marxism.

Throughout Europe, extremist student groups lashed out at established authority and a growing consumerism that they felt manipulated the poor and filled the pockets of the rich. In their minds, modern society had destroyed all that was noble in people by channeling their desires solely to material possessions. Primarily from middle-class backgrounds, the student radicals perceived a wide gap between their own background and that of the lower-income groups. Their model was not existing Communist parties in the West or East since they rightly observed that these were bureaucratic, authoritarian entities (see Daniel Cohn-Bendit, *Obsolete Communism).* Instead they chose Che Guevara, Fidel Castro, Ho Chi Minh, Mao Tse-tung, or Leon Trotsky, all of whom represented rebellion against such perceived evils as U.S. imperialism, Communist bureaucratization, and inequality. This radical fringe would have been of limited effectiveness had it not become intertwined with the protests of a larger group of students concerning conditions within European universities — and had the political authorities not disregarded their legitimate protests.

German Student Protests

In 1966 the formation of the Grand Coalition, a political partnership between the Christian Democrats and the Social Democrats, ignited the first German student protests. Student leaders of the German Socialist Students' Federation (SDS) felt betrayed by the Social Democrats' actions. They now considered the SPD an integral part of the establishment and therefore uninterested in reform.

The students gave voice to their discontent in widespread protests against the Shah of Iran's repressive regime during his visit to West Berlin in 1967. Underlying this outburst was hostility over German and American support of the shah. The death of one student, Benno Ohnesorg, in the riots steeled the students in their determination to bring down the establishment.

The next target was the conservative newspaper–magazine empire of Axel Springer, whose publications had viciously attacked student leaders such as Dutschke. When Dutschke was shot by a deranged man at Easter, masses of students rose against Springer and succeeded in disrupting the distribution of his newspapers and magazines. This seemed to promise even greater successes in the future. But unlike French students, who almost toppled the Gaullist regime, German students confined themselves to discussing revolution and engaging in isolated minor confrontations.

The students' inability to act on a major scale has been interpreted as reflecting the German inability to act decisively or, more correctly, as resulting from insufficient public support. Older Germans, with their memories of postwar shortages, were afraid of any challenge to the stability of the government. So an SDS member had good reason to say, enviously, "It isn't that the French students are stronger; it's just that the public is more sympathetic."

Although German students were unable to mount a serious challenge to government policies, they did achieve important changes in the universities. They now have a share in university governance and have impelled most professors to change their teaching methods. As a result of chaotic disturbances in the universities during the height of the turmoil, many professors were actuated to leave the classrooms for good. And it is now commonplace in Germany universities to have student-suggested courses in which professors are participants rather than lecturers.

Protest in France

Until 1968, French universities remained so calm that students from Italy and Germany began to doubt the presumed revolutionary mentality of the French. Yet when the explosion came in 1968, it rocked not only the universities but also the Gaullist government. A number of extreme left student groups — Trotskyites, Maoists, and anarchists — had existed since early in the decade. But they could speak for only a minority of the students and had no support at all among the remaining population.

Another surprising thing about the events of 1968 was that they came at a time of unquestioned prosperity and national grandeur. De Gaulle and France played a far greater role in the world than was justified by the nation's resources. Why, then, did the student-led protests in France spread to a much larger segment of the population than elsewhere and lead, despite a resounding election triumph in late 1968, to de Gaulle's resignation?

The immediate causes of protest in France were little different from those in Italy and Germany. For French students the Vietnam War became a symbol of the misplaced priorities of all military–industrial complexes, including the Gaullist regime. Especially annoying to students was de Gaulle's concentration on foreign affairs and his failure to respond to the often deplorable conditions in the universities. Classes at the famed Sorbonne sometimes had nearly 1,000 students enrolled; those students who did not arrive early enough had to listen to lectures on closed-circuit television or buy copies of the lectures. The curriculum was filled with obsolete courses. There was little attention to sociology, or modern social problems, or career preparation for those not going on for advanced degrees.

Students directed their dissatisfaction at the French Ministry of National Education and local faculty governing bodies, which, in their opinion, were more interested in training a few researchers than in preparing the mass of students for less exalted careers. In response to student demands for relevance and participation in determining curriculum, the Ministry of Education fell back on tradition and repression. Another major issue grew out of the ministry's attempt to reduce overcrowding in the universities by making examinations more difficult. Therefore, the student demand for an end to examinations was an attempt to prevent the selection of only the gifted few for advanced degrees.

The Events at Nanterre   Paradoxically, the protests began at the new university at Nanterre, which had been established to relieve the overcrowding at the Sorbonne. Despite the excellent facilities and lower student–teacher ratio, Nanterre became the center for student dissatisfaction because it gave students a greater opportunity to question and sometime embarrass their teachers. Classes were interrupted often by questions about the Vietnam War or Franco's Spain. Young instructors and assistant professors, having only recently completed the traditional course of instruction, were hard put to answer these questions. Many of the younger faculty members were won over to the idea of reform of the education system. Moreover, the location of Nanterre near one of the shantytowns housing immigrant laborers promoted debate beyond purely university and academic matters. The contrast between the students' almost entirely middle-class backgrounds, and the living conditions they saw around them convinced many students that the government was impervious not only to the need for change in the university but also to the plight of the poor.

The first incident occurred in November 1967 when sociology students at Nanterre, one of the few universities with a separate sociology faculty, resisted the introduction of a reform plan — called the Fouchet Plan — by the Ministry of Education. Student opposition to the plan foreshadowed the later more violent conflict over the role of the student, in university governance. Although the Fouchet Plan responded to some student complaints by providing one course of study for those pursuing the *license* (roughly equivalent to our bachelor's degree) and another for those going on for advanced degrees, the course of study was lengthened by one year for some students. However, it was not merely the Fouchet Plan that aroused dissatisfaction. Both the Ministry of Education and the deans of the faculties refused to let students discuss the changes or participate in the faculty committee governing the school of sociology that debated the plan.

This incensed the students and triggered the eruption. The Nanterre protest failed, but it paved the way for the more violent reaction that was to come because it convinced student radicals that a moderate demand for a student voice in university governance was doomed to fail.

During the four months following the initial incident at Nanterre, student radicals (*enragés*) gradually brought together the four major issues of what came to be called the March 22 Movement: opposition to Gaullism; rejection of the organization and structure of the university system; student freedom; and protest against the Vietnam War. While the Maoists and Trotskyites concentrated on the Vietnam issue, Daniel Cohn-Bendit led other students at Nanterre against all forms of administrative, political, intellectual, and sexual repression.

Cohn-Bendit's support for sexual freedom was a part of the much larger issue that students should be free to decide their own living conditions on campus. It was also a challenge to the repression that Cohn-Bendit found throughout the society. His campaign instilled a desire for action into a left that had theretofore limited itself to the discussion of revolutionary objectives.

When the university attempted to expel Cohn-Bendit, the conflict enlarged beyond the revolutionary left. First the sociology department assembly, composed of faculty and students, came out in support of Cohn-Bendit. Gaining confidence as they picked up student and faculty support, student leaders became more outspoken and disruptive. When the Vietnam Committee leaders were arrested on March 22, students invaded and occupied the administration building at Nanterre.

From this point onward, many rooms at Nanterre became meeting places for student groups engaged in discussing the university structure, Vietnam, and student–worker relations. By April many instructors and assistant professors had joined these discussion groups. This breakdown in the traditional relationships among faculty members unnerved the dean of the faculty of letters. Then student leaders proposed two anti-imperialist days for May 2 and 3 at Nanterre, and a rightist student group began gathering support for an attack on the student radicals. At this point the dean decided to close the university on May 2. With this decision, Nanterre ceased to be the center of agitation. The supporters of the March 22 Movement then moved to the Sorbonne and the potentially more volatile Latin Quarter.

The Events at the Sorbonne   The protest at the Sorbonne might have been confined to the university community had not the violent reaction of the police enlarged the scope of the "events of May" to other groups in the society. Cohn-Bendit and other leaders of the March 22 Movement had been notified that they were to face the disciplinary council of the University of Paris on May 6. More than 400 leftist students, including the March 22 Movement leaders, met at the Sorbonne on May 3 to discuss their course of action at Nanterre. The rector at the Sorbonne, acting on the advice of the Ministry of Education, decided to call in the police in the hope that such a move would break the back of the student protest movement.

The sight of students being thrown into police vans on university grounds spread the protest beyond the original student activists, since a centuries-old tradition guaranteed the security of students within university walls, and the police had not entered any university grounds since 1791.

In the Latin Quarter that night, police battled thousands of students who were demanding that the imprisoned students be freed. Three days later, on Bloody Sunday, thousands of students and faculty sympathizers armed with cobblestones battled police around the Sorbonne. Although 435 policemen and an untold number of demonstrators were injured, battles continued day after day in the Latin Quarter.

From May 3 to May 13 the protest movement was predominantly a student struggle, fought out in the streets. As the injury toll mounted, public opinion swung to the students. The police were stymied. The more they attacked, the greater grew the number of demonstrators and the popular support for the insurrection. The government turned a deaf ear to student demands to remove the police, open the faculties at the Sorbonne, and grant an amnesty to the imprisoned demonstrators. The confrontation continued.

Ultimately, on the Night of the Barricades — May 10–11 — students surrounded the Sorbonne and the police with makeshift barricades. The barricades symbolized the students' refusal to abandon the Latin Quarter to the police and provided the psychological boost to keep the protest alive. The police attack on the barricades, followed by beatings of students in the police vans and at police stations, had several aftermaths: it launched the general strike of May 13; it brought on the government's capitulation; it triggered the student occupation of the Sorbonne; and it spread the protest far beyond the original student nucleus.

From Student Protest to General Strike   It was at this point that the French upheaval went beyond the student uprisings elsewhere. Whereas German students had had to face the wrath of workers, French students got their support. This cannot be explained by wages alone since the French workers refused to accept a wage increase negotiated on May 27. What is more, the Communist party, as head of the largest labor union, had not approved of the workers' joining the students.

Workers, especially the young ones, were protesting their lack of decision-making power in an ever more complex bureaucratized world. Among other things they were asking for greater delegation of authority — the right of co-management — just as the students were. French industry, led by the major federation of French employers, the *Conseil National du Patronat Français* (CNPF), resolutely supported its traditional authoritarianism. Most industrialists, with CNPF backing, had withstood

The courtyard of the main building of the Sorbonne in Paris, France, filled with left-wing demonstrators during the student protests of 1968.
Magnum Photos

the labor ministry's attempts to institute factory management–workers councils, *comités d'entreprise.* Although these councils had no real share in management decisions but were limited to overseeing welfare activities and conferring with management, by 1965 only 6,000 and 25,000 firms had complied with a 1945 ordinance to establish them. During the demonstrations, the *Confédération Français et Democratique de Travail* (CFDT), a labor union with strength among both blue- and white-collar workers, made its position plain:

> The student struggle to democratize the university and the workers' struggle to democratize industry are one and the same. The constraints and institutions

213

against which the students are rebelling are paralleled by even more intolerable forms in factories, or worksites, in offices and workshops. . . . Industrial and administrative monarchy must be replaced by democratic institutions based on self-management.

Some of those who joined in the protest were white-collar workers who also desired a change in the bureaucracies that governed them. Striking workers at the Assurance Générale de France (AGF), the second-largest French insurance company, demanded that those in positions of responsibility "be accountable for their actions to the entire staff," that they be subject to dismissal "by those who have appointed them," and that AGF property and stock become "the property of all, managed by all."

To protesting workers and intellectuals the Gaullist regime seemed the prime example of an overbureaucratized, technocratic, soulless institution. With the Communist party becoming a part of this mammoth bureaucracy, workers saw little hope for change. Workers' slogans during the uprising, such as "down with alienation," and "co-management," expressed their sense of estrangement.

The strike of producers and journalists at the nationalized French television stations characterized the rebellion of many, including young physicians and other professionals, and showed that the events of May were not restricted to students and workers. Television producers saw the May riots as their opportunity to end the centralization of programing and to gain a measure of local autonomy. Everywhere it was the same — a reaction against the centralization of authority that had stripped the individual of his right to make decisions. As former premier Pierre Mendès-France explained in 1968:

> The dispute is not simply over personalities or institutions. It also dramatizes the determination of Frenchmen no longer to be considered impotent subjects in a harsh, inhumane, conservative society, but rather to perform their own role freely in a society they can look upon as really their own.

With the power of the workers thrown into the fray, the Gaullist regime was soon on the verge of collapse.

On May 13 a twenty-four-hour labor strike brought Paris to a standstill. Nearly 300,000 people marched in a Paris without transportation, electricity, or postal service. Throughout France workers occupied factories, set up strike committees, even established worker management of factories. Everywhere, the organization and management of the firms were criticized more than the workers' material conditions. Signs appeared proclaiming, "The boss needs you — you don't need him." By May 17 nearly 10 million workers were out on strike and hundreds of young workers had joined the demonstrators in the streets. Action committees and student soviets sprang up all over France. The massive worker response finally forced the Communist party to support labor's demands for reforms. Even the Socialist party, led by Mitterand, joined the protest movement when it appeared that the Gaullist regime could be toppled.

De Gaulle's Counterattack Until May 30, when de Gaulle finally acted, the protestors had good reason to believe that the government would fall. Except for the beleaguered police in the streets, little had been heard from the government. When de Gaulle left Paris on May 29, many expected him to relinquish power. Only his close associates knew that he had gone to West Germany to assure himself of the support of French troops stationed there.

Some of the causes for the discontent were not clear to the government when de Gaulle began his counterattack. He was inclined to the belief that worker demands for higher wages and student excesses were primary causes of the unrest. In any case, he had no intentions of tolerating what he considered to be anarchy or allowing his plans for French grandeur to be put in jeopardy.

After visiting the commander of French troops in West Germany, de Gaulle returned to Paris and announced new parliamentary elections for June and firm measures to end the anarchy. In a television address on May 30, in order to rally all anti-communist forces to his side he unjustly accused the Communist party of instigating the outbreaks. Then he presented France with a choice: communism or Gaullism. As the students feared, his pleas were answered with massive support from most of the bourgeoisie and from the provincial areas. Immediately following his speech, 1 million French, including many from the provinces, staged a mass demonstration in Paris in favor of de Gaulle. This outpouring of support for de Gaulle demoralized the rioters. Workers ended their occupation of factories and students left the colleges they had seized. De Gaulle arrested radical leaders and outlawed leftist student groups. The same forces that rallied to de Gaulle, which had been afraid to speak out during the height of the crisis, gave de Gaulle an impressive majority in the June elections; Gaullists increased their representation in the legislature from 200 to 299 while the left's representation dropped from 194 to 100.

De Gaulle's victory was short-lived. Within a year he felt it necessary to resign. His popularity had begun to fade even in the formerly strong Gaullist areas, and his party opposed his authoritarianism and concentration on foreign rather than internal affairs. The Gaullists remained in power for five years more, losing the presidency in 1974, partly as a result of a changed attitude in France brought about by the events of 1968 (see chapter 13). Even during the presidency of de Gaulle's successor, Georges Pompidou, national priorities had been moving toward happiness (*bonheur*) and away from grandeur. This in itself meant greater attention to pressing domestic problems and less attention to France's world mission.

For the students and workers, the results of 1968 can be measured with greater accuracy. University students have gained many of their demands.

Overcrowding has been relieved by increasing the number of universities from twenty-two to sixty-five. Students achieved a measure of joint management in most universities. Greater autonomy, although much less than students fought for, has permitted universities to avoid some of the rigid centralization of instruction under the Ministry of Education. The more radical demands for the abolition of exams and an end to the Ministry of Education itself have not been granted.

Laborers received increased pay following the riots (see chapter 9), but they are still among the lowest paid in Western Europe. Unions won the right to be represented in each enterprise; union representatives are now given some free time to carry out union duties during working hours. But workers have not achieved joint management, which was so important an aspect of their demands in 1968. French managers, incapable of overcoming their hierarchical conceptions of factory relations, resolutely oppose giving workers a share in factory management. Most of the firms in France that have granted a measure of self-management are foreign-owned.

Unrest in Czechoslovakia

Although there are many differences between the unrest in the West and in Czechoslovakia in 1968, there was one major similarity: the revolt against centralized, bureaucratic, authoritarian structures. Under the leadership of Antonin Novotny, Czechoslovakia had instituted rigid centralization by the early 1960s. Even though two Communist parties existed in the country, one in Slovakia and one in the Czech lands, all areas of the country were ruled dictatorially from Prague. Economic growth was slowed by rigid planning and resource allocation. No important decisions of any kind could be made without the approval of the Communist party in Prague.

Novotny was very popular when he came to power in 1957 because he had rid the party of Stalinists, but his brand of authoritarian national communism soon became as oppressive as the Stalinism before him had been. Changes in Moscow, however, soon weakened his control over the party. The Soviet Union's continued denunciation of Stalin, Khrushchev's desires to decentralize economic decision making at home, and Yugoslav decentralization provided convenient excuses for Czech reformers. The cultural division of the country into Czech and Slovak segments further weakened centralization.

Slovak demands for economic decentralization soon received support from some Czech party members who sought to overcome a severe economic crisis that had begun in 1962. Because of the decentralization in the Soviet Union, Czech and Slovak reformers felt they could try similar reforms at home. The Slovak party ousted its Stalinist leader, Karol Bacilek, in 1963 and replaced him with the reformer Alexander Dubček. from 1963 until 1968, Novotny and the conservatives fought a losing battle against the reformers.

The conservatives' Achilles' heel proved to be the country's economic weakness. Led by economic expert Dr. Ota Sik, the reformers forced Novotny to accept decentralization of the economy in 1966. The reformers had managed to convince the party members that excessive planning, excessive resource allocation, and inattention to the consumer goods industry were responsible for Czechoslovakia's economic ills.

Novotny had been trying to fulfill Czechoslovakia's assigned role in Comecon as the producer of heavy industrial goods and had neglected to develop light industry. The economy had also suffered from a typical East European economic policy: instead of improving factories to overcome low output, Novotny merely built new factories and thus spread raw materials and labor even thinner. The reformers, following changes already instituted in Yugoslavia and the Soviet Union, succeeded in pushing through a system of profit accountability whereby industrial production could be measured more accurately (see chapter 8).

By 1967 Novotny's position as party chairman had been seriously undermined by the reformers, and his suppression of student demonstrators protesting dormitory living conditions further damaged his position. The reformers, who had now gained a majority in the Central Committee of the party, compared Novotny's treatment of the students to his opposition to all reformers within the party. With his base of support eroded, it was a simple matter to replace Novotny as party chairman in December 1967. The selection of an outspoken reformer, Dubček, as his successor indicated the extent of the reformers' victory. In March 1968 Novotny lost his position as president of Czechoslovakia to a moderate, the military hero General Ludvik Svoboda.

. With Novotny gone, a relaxed and joyous mood set in throughout the country. By June 1968 the changed attitude was immediately evident. Caught up in the euphoria, Czechs informed visitors that they needed American economic and diplomatic aid, not military help. The press, carried away with its new-found freedom, was given to exaggerating the changes contemplated by the new leadership. There was discussion of a viable political opposition and a political system that, to the rest of the Communist world, smacked of Western parliamentary government.

This euphoria turned out to be one of Dubček's major problems. Had he tried to prevent such discussion — and he may not have been able to do so — he might have lost the support of his countrymen; but unless he controlled the enthusiasm, he risked losing the support of the Soviet Union. Dubček was never able to free himself from this problem. To illustrate Dubček's difficulties, most newspapers published an extremely liberal manifesto, "The Two Thousand Words," written by the most liberal elements in the country. The manifesto promised military support to Dubček if other East European countries or the Soviet Union should invade, and it questioned the achievements of communism in

Czechoslovakia. When Dubček did not publicly denounce this manifesto, the other Eastern European states, all of them Warsaw Pact members, assumed that he approved it.

Despite Dubček's repeated protestations of loyalty to a Communist-dominated state, his actions hardly served to allay fears in other Eastern capitals. In April Dubček permitted non-communist political groups to form. Although he assured Moscow that these organizations would not become independent political parties but would be a part of the Communist-dominated National Front, it is easy to see why the Soviets would be suspicious. Further, the Communist party promised to bring to trial all those responsible for the Stalinist-inspired political trials in the 1950s, a move that threatened to incriminate Soviet officials. Some papers had in fact demanded an investigation into Soviet involvement in the apparent suicide of Czech Foreign Minister Jan Masaryk during the Communist coup in 1948.

From April until the Soviet invasion on August 20, 1968, the "Czechoslovak experiment" became hopelessly entangled with Polish and East German fears that a similar "democratic" contagion might spread to their countries and Soviet fears that Dubček's policies might eventually lead Czechoslovakia out of the Warsaw Pact. As early as March Poland's leader Wladyslaw Gomulka had been upset by students' shouts of "We want a Polish Dubček." But East German party secretary Walter Ulbricht was not merely upset; he feared that his weaker authoritarian regime could be overthrown by similar reformers.

Czech leaders had already established contacts with West Germany in order to open trade relations between the two countries. The Soviet Union was willing to permit more internal liberalization in Czechoslovakia than in East Germany or Poland, but was afraid that Czech reformers might eventually demand an independent foreign policy similar to that of Romania. Soviet hard-liners conjured up visions of an anti-Soviet alliance of Yugoslavia, Romania, and Czechoslovakia.

Certainly Soviet military experts had much more to fear from a Czech withdrawal from the Warsaw Pact than they did from Romanian disaffection. Not only did Czechoslovakia border on Western Europe, but its withdrawal from the Warsaw Pact would have cut Eastern Europe in two and would have severely complicated military strategy in case of war with the West. The Czech reform was also ill-timed. Stung by the Soviet humiliation in Cuba in 1962, the Sino–Soviet imbroglio, Albanian support for China, and Romania's withdrawal from the Warsaw Pact, Soviet hard-liners were adamant in their opposition to Czech liberalization and possible loss to the Warsaw Pact countries.

Soviet and East European leaders, with the exception of those of Romania and Czechoslovakia, began their offensive against Dubček with the Warsaw Letter of July 14–16, ordering that Czechoslovakia reestablish

Defiant Czechs carry their flag through the streets of Prague during the Soviet invasion of 1968.

Magnum Photos

the dictatorship of the Communist party or face invasion. Dubček stoutly rejoined that the Communist party was still in control, and he convinced the Soviet leadership. Still, it took a meeting between Dubček and Soviet leaders at Cierna in Slovakia to avert the intervention of Warsaw Pact armies that just appened to be on maneuvers in Czechoslovakia at the time.

Even though Dubček convinced the Soviets that the Communist party was still in control and that Czechoslovakia had no intention of pulling out of the Warsaw Pact, East Germany and Poland were not convinced. These two states demanded a meeting of all East European leaders at Bratislava in Slovakia on August 3. At that meeting Dubček was forced to sign the Bratislava Declaration promising not to go beyond the Polish reforms instituted by Gomulka in the late 1950s.

Between the Bratislava meeting and the invasion on August 20, several decisions by Dubček were seen by other Communist governments to have violated the Cierna and Bratislava agreements. When Tito and Romanian leader Nicolae Ceausescu were given warm receptions in Prague, the action was taken to indicate that Dubcek was not going to adopt the attitude of other East European states toward Yugoslavia and Romania. More damning was a Czech draft of new party statutes permitting the existence of factions within the Communist party. Such actions hardly convinced Ulbricht and Gomulka that Dubček was opposing ideological heresy even in the Communist party.

However, Soviet leaders may already have decided on intervention as early as the Bratislava meeting. To Soviet leaders, the advantages of an invasion seemed to outweigh the disadvantages. They realized that they would suffer a bad international press for a time, but they were convinced that it would not last much longer than the 1956 outburst following the invasion of Hungary.

Because of the policy of détente with the United States with its recognition of mutual spheres of influence, they did not fear American intervention. On the other hand, the military and political example that Czech disaffection would have established was intolerable to many Soviet leaders.

After Dubček had been taken into custody by invading Soviet forces, President Ludvik Svoboda refused to appoint as new premier a conservative opponent of Dubček's and a man already approved by the Soviets, Alois India. The adoption of passive resistance by the majority of the population further frustrated Soviet designs to make the invasion appear to have been no more than a change of government. Some Czechs did throw Molotov cocktails or stones at Soviet tanks, but for the most part they merely tried to place obstacles in the way of the Russian advance. Svoboda's refusal to negotiate with the Soviet Union until Dubček was released probably saved Dubček's life, but nothing could be done to save the Czech experiment. Leaders subservient to Moscow were soon installed in office — Gustav Husák as party secretary and Lubómir Strougal as prime minister — press censorship was renewed, and Soviet troops were kept on Czech soil to protect the country against imperialism.

Common Protest Themes

Many themes united the protest movements of 1968. Students in Paris and Prague lashed out at a repressive society and yearned for greater participation. Political repression was more direct and more in evidence in Czechoslovakia, but French students, workers, and intellectuals had similar feelings of frustration and powerlessness under Gaullist paternalism.

Although the French state did not engage in direct repression, it did centralize decision making at the top in all administrative, economic, and cultural institutions. In the eyes of the Parisian demonstrator, there was little difference between a Communist party bureaucracy in Prague and the bureaucratized institutions in France, including the French Communist party.

In both countries, demonstrators hoped to weaken or destroy the isolated bureaucratic structures with participation from below. Czech students' desires for greater intellectual freedom in combination with the antibureaucratic efforts of economic reformers, brought down the government. Similar objectives in France nearly toppled the Gaullist regime in May 1968, contributed to the subsequent disenchantment with de Gaulle's authoritarianism, even among Gaullist deputies, and compelled his resignation in 1969.

FURTHER READING

Although a large number of works have appeared on the 1968 French upheaval, only a few are of major importance. Probably the best general coverage is in Adrien Dansette's *Mai 1968* (1971). The most complete coverage of the workers' role is Pierre Dubois et al., *Grèves Revendicatives ou Grèves Politiques* (1971). On the role of the Communist party see Daniel Cohn-Bendit's left-wing denunciation, *Obsolete Communism: The Left-Wing Alternative* (1968); and Richard Johnson's balanced study, *The French Communist Party versus the Students* (1972).

A highly critical treatment of the student rioters can be found in Raymond Aron, *The Elusive Revolution* (1968).

Four generally favorable treatments of the actions of the rioters are Daniel Singer, *Prelude to Revolution* (1970); J. J. Servan-Schreiber, *The Spirit of May* (1969); Alain Touraine, *The May Movement: Revolt and Reform* (1971); and Alfred Willener, *The Action–Image of Society* (1970). Singer believes the 1968 upheaval proved that a full-scale Socialist revolution is still possible in the developed Western countries. He maintains that there were valid reasons for the upheaval in France. He unfortunately spends much of his time arguing for revolution and outlining the proper revolutionary strategy to achieve a Socialist society.

J.-J. Servan-Schreiber argues that the upheaval was caused by French cultural and social rigidity. This theme is similar to the one presented by Michael Crozier in *The Stalled Society* (1973). Touraine feels that the upheaval was a legitimate response to the advanced capitalist societies and their managers, who manipulate and control in an authoritarian manner all aspects of society. The events in France were therefore merely one instance of many possible revolts against post-industrial societies. Willener believes that a combination of political and cultural resistance gave the upheaval its intensity. The student demands for a new culture included action, egalitarianism, antiauthoritarianism, self-management, and imagination. However, many will find his book to be unreadable and inconclusive.

The most comprehensive treatment of the Czech upheaval is H. Gordon Skilling, *Czechoslovakia's Interrupted Revolution* (1976). A short treatment by an expert on Czech history is Z. A. B. Zeman, *Prague Spring* (1969). A general survey of Czechoslovakia that covers 1968 is Zdenek Suda, *The Czechoslovak Socialist Republic* (1969). An eyewitness account is provided in *A Year Is Eight Months: Czechoslovakia 1968* (1970). While William Shawcross has provided some insights into the character and policies of Dubček in *Dubček* (1970), a full understanding of his role may never be available because of the lack of information, especially on his meetings with Soviet leaders. Two recent studies that attempt to place the Czechoslovakian revolt into a broader perspective are Vojtech Mastny, *Czechoslovakia: Crisis in World Communism* (1972); and William I. Zartman, *Czechoslovakia: Intervention and Impact* (1970).

13 To the 1970s and Beyond

The Cold War, as far as we are concerned, is over.

Leonid Brezhnev, June 1973

Although Brezhnev's assertion that the Cold War is over may have been somewhat premature, recent actions indicate that the Soviets are operating as if the era of brinkmanship and confrontation with the United States is indeed over. This new attitude has not only lessened tensions and therefore the threat of war between East and West; it has also contributed to a political transformation in Western Europe.

As the inhabitants of Western Europe became less fearful of a Soviet invasion, their political attitudes began to change. Voters tended to reduce their support for anti-Communist parties on the right, usually Christian Democratic parties, in favor of the formerly suspect parties on the left, the Communist and Socialist parties.

It is tempting to view the postwar political change as the completion of a full political cycle from left to right and then back again. However, such a view would be an oversimplification since the Socialists and Social Democrats in the 1970s are dominated by reformers, with the once large revolutionary element providing only token opposition to the majority. Moreover, Communist party election gains have come as a result of a stated adherence to parliamentary government and the incompetence of ruling parties on the right.

Western Europe's foreign policy also reflected the relaxation in international tensions. As the need for American military protection lessened, Western Europeans began to shape their own foreign policy: de Gaulle pulled France out of NATO and West Germany formulated its own *Ostpolitik* (Eastern foreign policy).

The 1970s brought hopeful signs for democratic forces in Southern Europe. After years of dictatorial rule, both Greece and Portugal reestablished a semblance of constitutional government; and in 1974 Portugal overthrew its rightist dictatorship. Portugal also brought to a close centuries of European colonialism by freeing its colonies in Africa.

Europe is not, however, without problems. The political instability in Italy, accompanied by the growth of extremist groups, has severely handicapped attempts to solve long-standing economic and social problems and, in some cases, even to carry out normal government functions. Growing nationalist feelings have retarded European unity (see chapter 8), and an energy crisis that began in 1973 because of the Middle East conflict convinced many Europeans that their prosperity is more precarious than they had previously believed.

De Gaulle's foreign policy aim of détente with the Soviet Union and elimination of U.S. influence in Europe fell victim to the Soviet expectation that more harmonious relations with the United States would bring greater rewards. But the Soviet–American confrontation in Cuba in 1962 convinced both sides that a dreaded nuclear confrontation was a possibility.

The events leading to the confrontation began when Khrushchev was faced with mounting economic problems in the Soviet Union brought about by the failure of his agricultural policies (see chapter 11), and was also faced with Communist Chinese disaffection. To counteract these, Khrushchev needed a victory to maintain his position atop the Soviet leadership. Fidel Castro's overthrow of the U.S.-supported government in Cuba and the subsequent establishment of a Communist Cuban government offered Khrushchev the opportunity to increase Soviet influence in an area that was inside the U.S. sphere of influence.

Soviet technicians and advisers were rushed into Cuba, and Khrushchev was enticed by the possibility of installing missiles close to the U.S. borders, as the United States had done in countries ringing the Soviet Union. Because of strong Latin American criticism of any U.S. attempt to overthrow the Castro regime, Khrushchev thought the United States would be reluctant to act against Castro or any country that sought to help him. The failure of an invasion by anti-Castro Cuban refugees at the Bay of Pigs in April 1961, and the worldwide denunciation of the invasion, convinced Khrushchev that the United States would not send its own forces into Cuba. Khrushchev secretly sent missiles and bombers into Cuba in 1962. But early U.S. detection of the incomplete Soviet bases led to a U.S. blockade of Cuba. Faced with the blockade, Khrushchev backed down in October 1962.

This crisis had a sobering effect on both Soviet and U.S. leaders. Having come so near to nuclear war, both sides now moved toward reducing the tensions that had brought them to the brink of war. Only one year after the Cuban crisis, they agreed to ban the testing of nuclear devices in the atmosphere, sea, and outer space. Moreover, the emergence of China as a new superpower in the 1960s demanded that the two superpowers bury their differences to meet this new challenge.

There were also compelling domestic reasons for the Soviet move toward détente. In order to develop the economy fully, Soviet leaders wanted to reduce defense appropriations — possible only if an understanding with the United States could be reached — and to obtain financial and technical aid from both the United States and Europe. Commitments in Vietnam made the United States desirous of achieving a *modus vivendi* with the Soviet Union. Events after the Czech invasion in 1968 — which proved to be only a mild setback to the policy of détente — indicated that the Soviet Union had become a status quo power.

In addition to a multitude of cultural and economic agreements with the West, the Soviet Union became one of President Richard Nixon's staunchest supporters during his unsuccessful attempt to escape the consequences of the Watergate scandal. Afraid that a new president might reverse the Nixon policy of détente, the Soviets charged that anti-Soviet forces in the United States were hoping to use the scandal to change American foreign policy. In the 1974 national elections in France, the Soviet Union favored the ultimately victorious Liberal party candidate, Valery Giscard d'Estaing, over the candidate of the Left Coalition, François Mitterand, on the ground that Mitterand's election might lead to turmoil in France and thus upset the many economic and diplomatic arrangements between the two countries.

Both the reduced international tension and internal political developments slowly eased conservative parties out of office in Germany, Austria, Luxembourg, and Great Britain and reduced their majority in France and Italy after 1969. To many voters, including a majority of the young, conservative parties were identified with the bureaucratic, hierarchical Europe that had caused the outbreaks of 1968. Moreover, the parties on the left had become more acceptable to the masses because of Soviet détente and their own adoption of a reformist rather than a revolutionary position. Socialist parties all had accepted the welfare state, and the Communist parties had paid lip service to parliamentary government and the welfare state. Many leftist groups had become such an integral part of the establishment that new groups evolved to fill the political void on the left.

West German Political Transition

West Germany provides one of the earliest examples of this political transition. After the German Social Democratic party dropped its revolutionary program in 1959, as Table 13–1 shows, it slowly increased its representation in the *Bundestag,* first at the expense of the Christian Democratic party and later of the Free Democratic party. The election gains in the 1960s show clearly the result of the SPD adoption of a reform rather than a revolutionary program.

Table 13-1   Bundestag Seats

Party	1957	1961	1965	1969
CDU-CSU	270	242	245	242
SPD	169	190	202	224
FDP	41	67	49	30

Despite outspoken student criticism of SPD opportunism, the majority of the newly enfranchised voters cast their ballots for the SPD. The SPD first gained a share of power in 1966 as a part of the coalition put together by CDU Chancellor Kurt Georg Kiesinger. It was Kiesinger who wanted the SPD in the coalition because the FDP would be unwilling to support the strong economic measures he considered necessary to bring Germany out of a recession. Also, he did not want the CDU to shoulder all the blame for the unpopular tax increase he was going to institute. The coalition solved the economic problems by raising taxes, cutting military spending, and encouraging investment.

An unfortunate aspect of the economic crisis and the coalition was the growth of right-wing radical groups. An extreme nationalist group, the National Democratic party (NPD), with many former Nazis as members, won forty-eight seats in provincial elections in 1967. Although it won another twelve seats in 1968 by playing on the fears of those who had been upset by the student demonstrations, the return of economic stability soon halted the NPD growth. Moreover, once the CDU was in opposition after 1969, voters registered their complaints by voting for the CDU rather than the NPD.

In foreign policy, West Germany began to break away from American tutelage under Kiesinger. With Brandt as foreign secretary, the first steps were taken to establish normal diplomatic relations with the East. But it was not until Brandt became chancellor in a coalition with the FDP that West Germany's *Ostpolitik* (Eastern policy) began in earnest. Brandt's policy went beyond the reopening of diplomatic relations with East European states to the recognition of East Germany and an acceptance of the boundaries set up between Poland and East Germany after World War II.

This recognition, vehemently opposed by German conservatives and never even contemplated by earlier Christian Democrats, convinced most East Europeans that Brandt was sincere in his efforts to normalize relations with the East. The possibility that his *Ostpolitik* might ultimately lead to a reunification of the Germanies was looked upon with considerable trepidation by other Western European countries (see chapter 8).

Brandt remained in power until 1974, when he stepped down because of his disappointment with the failure of European unification, the slow pace of social reform, and the discovery of an East German spy among his advisers. His successor, Helmut Schmidt, representing the technocratic element in the SPD, is ideologically far from the postwar revolutionaries' brand of socialism or even Brandt's dedication to the concept of social improvement. Brandt told the German people to prepare for long-term social reforms that he was contemplating, whereas Schmidt speaks only about the solution of present problems. One of his first moves was to drop several of Brandt's reform proposals, but in an effort to satisfy the left wing of the party, he had decided to push Brandt's proposals for giving workers a say in the management of large businesses.

Although Schmidt's policies may lead to greater problems in the future, they were apparently helpful in overcoming an economic slowdown that lasted from 1973 to 1975 and pushed unemployment up near the 1967 level. By 1976, the West German economy was once again growing rapidly as other economies, especially that of the United States, began to recover from the worldwide recession of the 1970s and to stimulate German exports.

Italy's Political Transition

The growing popularity of the left is nowhere more apparent than in Italy, even though the left's political fortunes have been thwarted by its ideological divisions. The Socialists (PSI) and the Communists (PCI) have refused to cooperate, thereby preventing the left from exercising an effect on politics and society commensurate with its popularity. The non-Communist left, although sharing in centerleft coalitions between 1963 and 1969, never had the strength to alter the policies of the ruling Christian Democratic (DC) majority significantly.

The center–left coalition failed to meet the expectations of the public. In five years it had done little to modernize Italy's schools, hospitals, or law courts. The public, primarily the lower classes, suffered from poor public transportation, inadequate housing, and the lowest wages in the developed European countries. The nationalization of electricity, a major achievement of the coalition, aided the former owners and only burdened the government. A plan to decentralize administration by setting up regional administrators did not become effective until the early 1970s. Nor had Italy yet begun to profit from two agreements Fiat made to build car factories in the Soviet Union and Poland.

Unfortunately for the Socialists, only the DC gained political favor from the coalition. In the 1968 elections, the United Socialist Party (PSU) — formed when the PSI and the Social Democrats (PSDI) had merged in 1966 — lost twenty-nine seats. As Table 13–2 shows, twenty-three seats were won by the Socialist Party of Proletarian Unity, the former left of the PSI that had broken away in protest against PSI leader Nenni's cooperation with the DC. These changes and a Communist party gain indicated that the trend to the left had not ended. The losses led the PSU to break-up in 1969: in protest against the coalition, the PSU split into the former PSI and PSDI factions. Although a majority of the PSI remained loyal to the new DC premier, Mariano Rumor, his unwillingness to meet their demands reduced the coalition to a policy of muddling through. In 1972 the center–left coalition collapsed.

Since 1969, Italy has been beset with political corruption, student unrest, wildcat strikes, and the growth of extremist groups on the right and left. Economic instability has added to a sense of decline. Increased costs for oil and food imports have produced an enormous trade deficit, reaching to $8.5 billion in 1974. The tourist trade, usually a means to offset a trade imbalance, has been set back by the growing violence. Extremist groups such as the neo-Fascist Black Order have resorted to indiscriminate bombings in order to bring down the government and end parliamentary democracy. *La Stampa* of Turin, one of Italy's leading newspapers, wrote in 1974, "Italy is shaken by turbid ferment; it runs the risk of becoming a country on the outskirts of civilization and reason."

In 1974 a loan from Germany and austerity measures saved Italy from an immediate economic imbroglio, but steps of this kind are not likely to achieve long-term economic stability. It also seems impossible that the traditional kind of political coalition, CD-dominated, can succeed. Whether an ever more reformist course followed by the Communist party will reduce political acrimony and promote cooperation remains to be seen. Since 1970 Communist rule in Emilia–Romagna, Tuscany, and Umbria,

Table 13-2   Seats in the Italian Chamber of Deputies

Party	1958	1963	1968	1972	1976
Communist Party	140	166	171	171	227
Socialist Party of Proletarian Unity (PSIUP)	—	—	23	0	—
Socialists (PSI)	84	87	91 (PSU)[a]	61	57
Social Democrats (PSDI)	22	33	—	29	15
Republicans (PRI)	6	6	9	15	
Christian Democrats (DC)	273	260	265	265	263
Liberals	17	39	31	20	5
Monarchists	25	8	6	0	—
Neo-Fascists (MSI)	24	27	24	56	35
Others	5	4	—	8	—

[a]The PSU (United Socialist Party) existed from 1966 to 1969. In 1969 it divided into the PSI and the PSDI.

three of Italy's twenty units of limited self-government, has been efficient, democratic, and free from corruption. Local elections in 1975 gave the Communists control of three additional semi-autonomous regions, a number of major cities including Rome, and a total vote of 32.4 percent of the electorate compared to the DC's 35.6 percent.

The lack of corruption among Communist officials, the support of young voters, and the continued immobilism and corruption in the DC-dominated government were primarily responsible for the Communist gains. Communist party spokesmen have offered their aid in resolving Italy's severe economic crisis and have promised to "act within the framework of a specific international geographic and political reality." This statement implies an acceptance of NATO and Italy's mixed economy and may be the initial step in what Communist leaders have been calling a "historic compromise" with the DC. The 1976 parliamentary election resulted in large gains for the PCI, but the DC remained the largest party with 263 seats in the 630-seat Chamber of Deputies. In exchange for important posts in the legislature, such as speaker of the Chamber of Deputies, the Communist party acquiesced to the formation of a minority DC government under Prime Minister Giullo Andreotti. Since the former allies of the DC said they will no longer automatically support a DC government, passage of legislation will normally require Communist abstention or support. Only a rapid economic recovery will keep the DC in power. At this writing, Italy is at a major turning point in its postwar history.

French Political Transition

In France the establishment of the Fifth Republic under the powerful presidency of de Gaulle upset the traditional political balance between right and left. Both the fortuitous economic situation and de Gaulle's adept handling of the Algerian rebellion swung support to the right during the 1960s. In the 1964 elections, the Gaullists alone received 44 percent of the vote, whereas the Left Federation of Communists and Socialists, headed by Mitterand, got only 31 percent of the vote.

Despite the election success, de Gaulle's popularity had already begun to decline by 1964. His blocking of British entry into the EEC in 1963 made many French turn their backs on him. Others dropped their support when it became apparent that de Gaulle wished to reduce French democracy to a façade. A growing number felt that France should not try to develop an independent military deterrent but should concentrate on domestic problems.

The elections began to shift toward the left after 1964. In the 1967 parliamentary elections, the Gaullists' vote declined from over 50 percent in 1962 to 38 percent of the total. The overwhelming Gaullist victory in 1968 following the student–worker riots proved a temporary response when many voters believed their only choice was between Gaullism and communism. The election victory only temporarily overshadowed the shortcomings of de Gaulle's regime. With his policies often verging on megalomania — for example, his disregard of his own ministers — most Frenchmen breathed a sigh of relief when he retired in 1969. Although de Gaulle's successor, Georges Pompidou, continued Gaullist policies, he stripped them of their authoritarian character.

Subsequent elections revealed a renewed leftist trend. In the presidential elections in 1974, the Left Federation under Mitterand received 48 percent of the vote. The Gaullist candidate for president ran a poor third to Mitterand and the Liberal party candidate, Valery Giscard d'Estaing, in the preliminary runoff election. Only the complete cooperation of the right secured the election for d'Estaing.

British Political Transition

Britain experienced a similar shift to the left in the 1960s. Conservative party supporters soon discovered that they had little to fear from the Labour party and Prime Minister Harold Wilson, elected in October 1964. Almost as many Labour as Conservative members of parliament had gone to the "proper" schools. Wilson, a former Oxford economics don, represented the right reformist wing of the Labour party. Its left wing, desiring a fully socialized economy with the nationalization of all industry, was in the minority.

Wilson chose to fight the economic problems through the traditionally conservative policies of cutting back on government spending and increasing taxes. After he received a larger majority in the 1966 parliamentary elections, Wilson reduced government spending on both military and welfare programs. Both the increased social security payments and the freezing of prices and wages angered workers and the left wing of the party. Labour popularity declined even further when Wilson was forced to devalue the pound 14 perce t to raise British exports and reduce imports; devaluation raised the price of such necessities as bread.

By 1969, devaluation had started to have the desired effect: instead of deficits, the economy now had a sizable surplus. However, Wilson called an election in an attempt to take advantage of the improved economic conditions, and the attempt failed. The Conservatives led by Edward Heath won a thirty-seat majority in 1970. Perhaps the economic improvement was not as apparent to an electorate that had suffered through the economic emergencies and devaluation.

For the next four years the Conservatives tried to end inflation and put the economy on a healthy footing. Instead, Prime Minister Heath had to declare a state of emergency five times in less than four years in office. Moreover, the confrontations between Heath and the coal miners brought serious disruption to Britain's economy and a loss of support for the Conservatives. Labour, under Wilson, returned to power in February 1974. With only a small majority, Wilson was not able to act decisively to overcome the economic problems. He resisted the left wing's demands for more nationalization by pointing out the precariousness of Labour's majority.

A controversy has developed over Labour's long-term plans for massive nationalizations, including perhaps a hundred of the largest companies. The Labour industry manager, later energy minister, Anthony Wedgwood Benn, who made known the contents of the proposal, contended that private industry had failed to make adequate capital investments. Heath derisively referred to the industry minister as "Commissar Benn" and to his department as the "Gosplan department," Gosplan being the Soviet planning agency. There is some fear that business leaders are going to cut investments drastically since their firms may be taken over if Labour gets a big majority in the next elections.

As the economic uncertainties reduced confidence in the pound throughout the world, Britain's currency steadily lost ground against other currencies. In June 1976 the pound's value had declined to a record low of $1.71. Only a month earlier a tired Harold Wilson had relinquished the prime minister's post to James Callaghan. Many in Britain are now questioning the ability of the traditional party system to deal with the economic problems, and they have suggested a government of national unity similar to the World War II coalition to put party politics aside and focus on the economic problems.

Britain is alone among the major European countries in not shaping its own independent foreign policy. Ever since the Suez debacle, Britain has fashioned its policy after that of the United States. This is both a recognition of Britain's now limited resources in a world of superpowers and an acknowledgment of the close relationship between Britain and the United States. Britain hoped to become a mediator between the United States and Europe. Britain's 1960 decision to stop development of its own rocket, the Blue Streak, and purchase missiles from the United States emphasized the decision to stop developing its own deterrent. However, in the age of summit conferences between the Soviet Union and the United States, Britain was never able to play its chosen role as middleman between the Soviet Union and the United States as well as adviser to America. The Labour reluctance to oppose the American involvement in the Vietnam War cost the British government prestige at home and abroad.

Political Transition in the Smaller Nations

Among the smaller European countries, a right-to-left political pattern was equally clear. After having shared political power with the Social

Democrats for two decades, Austria's Christian Socialist party decided to end the coalition when it received a small electoral majority in the 1966 elections. The victory, however, was short-lived. In 1969 the Social Democrats, under the leadership of Bruno Kreisky, came to power. But the postwar Austrian Social Democratic party bore no more resemblance to the interwar party than did the other European Social Democratic parties. The party's major aim was to establish a modern industrial state rather than to achieve a completely egalitarian society. The party's fear that higher taxes would reduce economic investment made it refuse to shift any more of the tax burden onto the wealthy. As in Sweden in the 1970s Austria decided that future government expenses would be borne by the poor as well as by the rich.

In Luxembourg, the conservative Christian Social party's domination of political office came to an end in 1974 after half a century of rule. Thus the country's voters were saying what was being repeated all over Western Europe: The Christian Socialists had been in power too long. Young people between eighteen and twenty-one, voting for the first time, cast their ballots for the Socialists. A center–left government of Liberals and Socialists took power in June 1974, with a Liberal as premier because the Socialist leader was defeated in the May elections. In Scandinavia, popular dissatisfaction with the costly social welfare programs swept the Socialists from power in Denmark and Norway and reduced their majority in Sweden. But the programs of the various parties are so much alike that there has been little significant change in government programs. In Southern Europe, Greece might well have followed the Western European political pattern had it not been for a military coup in 1967. A center–right coalition under Constantine Karamanlis gave way to George Papandreou's Progressive Center Union (EPEK) in 1964. Papandreou could have formed a coalition government with the EDA, a Communist front organization, but chose instead to call an election in which he gained a majority for the EPEK. The army, sensing in Papandreou's victory a challenge to its authority, took a stand in opposition to the EPEK immediately. When it became clear that the EPEK would win the 1967 elections, the army carried out a coup d'état and set up a right-wing military dictatorship. Papandreou and other center–left politicians were forced to flee the country.

Despite worldwide criticism, often led by Greeks in exile, the military maintained its dictatorial rule. An abortive attempt by the deposed King Constantine to overthrow the military junta ended with his flight into exile. During its seven years of authoritarian government, the military junta tried to establish Greek suzerainty over Cyprus to satisfy the Greek majority on the island and the Greek nationalists at home. When its attempt to oust the ruler of Cyprus, Archbishop Makarios, brought Greece close to war with Turkey and close to civil war, the junta was forced to recall Karamanlis. Karamanlis's center cabinet, which restored the 1952 constitution, won

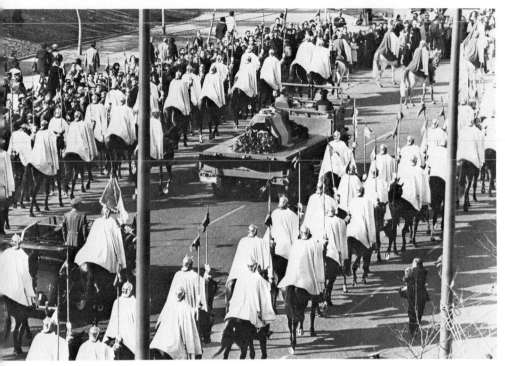

The funeral procession of Generalissimo Francisco Franco, dictator of Spain for almost forty years until his death in 1975, heads for the Valley of the Fallen in Madrid.
Photo Trends

victory in the 1975 elections. Greeks have opposed the return of King Constantine, who was never happy with truly constitutional government, but the center forces of Papandreou can be expected to play a major role in future governments.

The Iberian peninsula, despite recent changes in Portugal, has remained under authoritarian control since World War II. General Francisco Franco in Spain, supported by the Catholic Church, the army, and the Falange, made only enough concessions to avert rebellion. Many liberals were appeased in the 1960s by the relaxation of press censorship, the abolition of military courts, and the election of an opposition comprising one-sixth of the parliament.

In Spain's future, change is predictable. More and more influential people want economic and political modernization. Numbered among the reformist elements are young army officers and a Catholic reform group, *Opus Dei,* which includes members of the government. Change was also inevitable after the death of Franco in November 1975. His successor, Don Juan Carlos, has attempted to institute gradual reforms but has encountered stiff resistance from a conservative legislature. Since a large segment of the population expected dramatic changes in the post-Franco period, turmoil can be expected as the new government tries to establish a more democratic political system in a country that has experienced almost forty years of dictatorship.

Portugal's Political Transition

The difficulty in interpreting contemporary history is starkly revealed in attempting to explain the recent events in Portugal. In 1974 the seemingly impregnable rightist dictatorship of Premier Marcelo Caetano, successor to Antonio Salazar, was suddenly overthrown in a coup d'état carried out by junior army officers and a few sympathetic generals. These officers had been forced to serve repeated tours of duty in Portugal's African colonies of Angola, Guinea–Bissau, and Mozambique; they had received low pay and few promotions; and they had been given inferior equipment with which to fight Soviet-armed guerrillas.

To make matters worse, a new government policy permitted university students to obtain second-lieutenant's bars after undergoing a short course at the military academy. This debasement of their stature was what drove the officers to form the *Movimento das Forces Armadas* (MFA), or Armed Forces Movement, which was responsible for toppling the Caetano regime.

The political views of these young officers had been shaped by constant contact with disgruntled Portuguese university students who had been compelled to serve in Portugal's African territories and by captured African guerrilla leaders. These people convinced many of the officers that they were no less manipulated and suppressed than the native Africans. The students and captured guerrilla leaders, many of them Communists, persuaded these junior officers that only a thoroughgoing change in Portuguese society and leadership would improve the position of the military. This explains the strong Socialist–Communist sympathies of the original military leadership.

These captains and majors became convinced that they could not win the colonial wars and that they were going to be blamed for the defeat in Africa, as they had been blamed for the loss of Goa to India in 1961. At that point they began to question their support for what they believed to be a corrupt, inefficient, reactionary government in Lisbon that was prepared to sacrifice the army in order to save itself.

The revolt in April 1974, euphorically dubbed the "flower Revolution" because the revolutionaries wore carnations, brought to power General Antonio de Spinola. He had recently been dismissed from his post as the army's deputy chief of staff because he had openly urged the political democratization of Portugal and an end to the costly colonial wars in Africa. Because of Spinola's widespread popularity among the Portuguese population, the MFA threw its support to him in order to achieve some respectability for the military junta.

The government of Spinola, filled with conservative older officers, stood well to the political right of the MFA leaders who had planned and carried out the military coup. Although Spinola and the twelve-man Coordination Committee of the MFA immediately began to disagree over colonial and domestic policy, the MFA did not want to replace him until it had secured its own power in Portugal. Spinola opposed immediate independence for Guinea–Bissau and Mozambique and opposed giving the Communist party a role in the government, both of which were MFA policies.

Spinola lost the first round when the MFA forced him to accept a member of the Coordinating Committee sympathetic to the Communists, Vasco Gonçalves, as prime minister. When the MFA and the Communist party forced Spinola to cancel a rally of his supporters in September 1974 — considered a coup attempt by the MFA — Spinola resigned the presidency. He apparently hoped he would be called back to power, not an impossibility, when the Communist influence among the military leadership was overcome by the country's predominant conservative and center forces.

Portugal's military leaders have been guided by their conviction that a powerful parliament, dominated by the Socialists and parties to their right, would halt the military's policy of nationalization and impede the movement toward greater equalization of wealth. But the Communist party had supported the military's economic and social program, and it therefore exerted a major influence on the military leadership until November 1975. At that time the removal of the Communist-backed Gonçalves because of Western pressure, coupled with the opposition of more conservative military leaders, led military units sympathetic to the Communists to attempt a coup. Its failure reduced Communist influence among military leaders and in the country as a whole.

Nationalization of the Communist-dominated television and radio stations and reorganization of the Communist-influenced, state-owned press severely weakened the Communists. The now-moderate Council of the Revolution, the executive authority led by General Francisco da Costa Gomes, acted rapidly to remove leftist military officers from the armed forces.

The authority of the military has declined as a result of the ideological differences among military leaders and the parliamentary election victories of the Socialist party (led by Mario Soares), and the bourgeois parties. The Socialist victory in the April 1976 parliamentary elections and the demand for a return of parliamentary government have put the Socialist party in a dominant position in the newly formed legislature. The Socialists will share power with newly elected President Antonio Ramalho Eanes, the army chief of staff, who won 61 percent of the presidential vote in the June 1976 elections.

The results of that election show how far the political leadership has moved to the right since the revolution. A once-popular leftist military leader, Major Otelo Saraiva de Carvalho, received only 16 percent of the presidential vote, whereas Eanes, who was responsible for crushing the rebellion of leftist military units, won easily. The original revolutionaries, whose goal was a complete revamping of society, are now disillusioned and powerless.

Nationalism in Europe

By 1976 Europeans could point with pride to the achievements of three decades: the reemergence of Europe as a powerful economic and cultural force, the growth of affluence, the fading of authoritarian government in the South and East, the reduction of antagonisms between East and West, and the end of European colonialism. Despite these obvious achievements, pessimists point to a resurgence of nationalism that prevents the political and economic integration of Europe, a spreading terrorism, a growth of bureaucratic and executive power that threatens to make a mockery of parliamentary government, a loss of distinctively European culture, and an economic crisis from which they say Europe will ultimately not recover.

Has there, in fact, been a resurgence of nationalism in Europe and thus a decline in the support for a united Europe? Some have singled out the strengths of neo-Fascist parties, the NPD in West Germany and the MSI in Italy, as proof of rising nationalism. However, the experience of the NPD suggests that their growth may be transitory. After winning a number of local elections in West Germany, the NPD has now lost most of its support. Despite predictions of continued victories, these extremists were never able to win a single seat in the West German parliament. The NPD appears at this writing to be no more significant than the traditional extreme rightist fringe represented by the German Party of the Right from 1946 to 1949 and by the Reich Social party. And in Italy the MSI has failed to increase its representation in the Chamber of Deputies since 1958.

It seems more accurate to say that nationalism has not regained strength but has never been eliminated. The support for and opposition to a united Europe seem to have changed little in the past thirty years. The Benelux countries were then and are now the strongest advocates of European unity. De Gaulle never favored a truly united Europe except insofar as it enhanced French prestige and power.

The declining support for European unification in the 1970s is more closely tied to economic phenomena. Italy is unsure of its industry's ability to compete with those of Germany and France in a customs-free European community, and many British leaders still are anxious about a complete economic integration in the EEC.

In Eastern Europe, nationalism was only temporarily silenced by Soviet might. The increasingly independent course taken by Eastern European Communist parties was symbolized by the July 1976 Communist summit meeting in East Germany, where the Soviet Union was pressured into acknowledging the independence of the various Communist parties in Eastern and Western Europe. However, among the young there is considerably less nationalism than there once was. A common youth culture extends even into Eastern Europe and the Soviet Union.

Although Europe has recently experienced an increase in terrorism, the source of the conflicts have been long standing. The turmoil in Northern Ireland (Ulster), in Cyprus, and in the Basque region of Spain originated before World War II. The Ulster violence can be traced back to a centuries-old conflict between the native Catholic Irish and the primarily English Protestant settlers. Whether its source is essentially socioeconomic (as asserted by the Irish Republican Army, or IRA) or religious (as asserted by the British and by the Ulster Protestants), the enmity has been a part of the European experience for generations.

In the 1970s, desperation has driven the IRA to extend the terrorism to the streets of London. Unable to overcome the Protestant majority in Ulster, and confronted by British tanks and soldiers, the IRA hopes to paralyze both the Ulster and British governments in order to attain its goals of equality for the Ulster Catholics and the incorporation of Ulster into the Irish Republic.

In Cyprus the conflict between the Greek and Turkish inhabitants centers around the Turkish Cypriote charges that they are a mistreated minority, in both an economic and political sense, and the Greek Cypriote desire to incorporate Cyprus into a larger Greece. After Cyprus achieved independence from the British in 1960, a complicated political arrangement agreed to in a compromise between Greeks and Turks was the basis for a division of responsibility in local government. This broke down in 1963 when the Greeks tried to take over, and hostility was minimized only through the presence of a United Nations peacekeeping force.

A 1974 attempt to oust the Cypriote president, Archbishop Markarios, and join the island to the Greek mainland to satisfy Greek nationalists led to a Turkish invasion of Cyprus and an intensification of the civil war. Only the presence of Turkish troops in Cyprus and the fall of the military junta in Greece have preserved a modicum of peace on the island.

In Spain, Basque separatist terrorism against Madrid is the result of a long-standing Basque desire for more autonomy or independence for the four Basque provinces, as against the Franco regime's desire to eliminate the separatists. The conflict is ultimately a matter of the language and cultural uniqueness of the Basque regions and the failure of previous Spanish rulers to fully integrate the area into the Spanish nation.

While these conflicts may be among Europe's major problems, they are not of recent origin, nor are they more violent than the terrorism that has spread throughout the world in the last decade.

The New Europe

There can be little doubt that the authority of national governments and the executive branch of governments has increased since 1945. In France, the constitution of the Fifth Republic is a clear example of a strengthened executive. But the executive branch of government has increased its power in most European states. As populations and economies have grown, economic and social problems have become more complex, and national governments rather than local governments have tended to deal with them. This has created vast, impersonal, centralized bureaucracies that are more often than not unresponsive to local and individual needs. Executive branches of government have much larger staffs and resources than those of the legislatures and have therefore taken more and more authority into their own hands. Legislatures, besieged with bills, overwhelmed with duties, and lacking in resources, have done nothing to keep a rein on the growth of executive authority. Recently in both Eastern and Western Europe a few steps have been taken to decentralize authority and to increase local decision making. But only in West Germany, where the Allies set out to prevent another centralization of power similar to that under national socialism, is there an extensive decentralization of authority.

The unprecedented material rewards of the new Europe have undermined unique European life-styles. Europeans speak of a decline of Frenchness, or Germanness, and a rise of the materialism which they equate with the American way of life. Increasingly, Europeans have begun to discuss measures to preserve the European quality of life. At the same time, other Europeans are recommending that Europe adopt many American economic and business practices in order to be able to compete with American companies.

Even a casual observer can note the American influence on Europe's languages even in very middlebrow newspapers and on television. However, there is a distinct difference from country to country in the extent of the use of English. As might be expected, in France the inroads are relatively slight; admitting the reality of "le weekend" was a major step for them. But it is going to be difficult for Europeans to avoid the cultural homogeneity that is a byproduct of economic modernization and the close economic ties among European nations and between Europe and the United States.

The pessimism spawned by the Arab oil embargo, inflation, recession, and currency problems of the early 1970s seems to have been exaggerated. By 1976, West Germany and France were again experiencing accelerated economic growth as world trade began to pick up. There were certainly lingering problems of inflation and monetary instability, especially in Italy and Britain, but even these countries managed to reduce their inflation rate in early 1976 and increase their exports. The recession underscored the interdependence of the European economies as well as their dependence on a healthy U.S. economy and on foreign supplies of oil.

The economic slowdown in the United States preceded and exacerbated the recession in Europe because it meant a sharp cutback in European exports to the United States. But the international efforts to overcome the economic crisis reflected the changed relationship of European nations in the postwar world. Although some nations did try to go it alone during the Arab oil embargo, no European nation ultimately erected huge trade barriers to protect its economy, as had been done in the interwar years. It may well be that this new spirit of international cooperation will in time bring all the European countries out of the recession. Notable are the EEC attempts to extend trade preferences to third and fourth world countries so as to reduce the international imbalance between have and have-not nations. A continuation of this trend may be one of the ultimate tests of Europe's greatness.

Index

Abbas, Ferhat, 113
Acheson, Dean, 14
Adenauer, Konrad, 17, 82–84, 137, 146
African independence movements, 110–117
Agriculture
  in Communist world, 192–194
  developments in Western European, 71–72
Albania, 60, 129–131, 133, 188, 199, 201, 218
Algeria, 66, 87, 107, 112–113
Algerian rebellion, 85–86, 228
Allied Foreign Ministers Conference (1945), 33
Aminoto, Tjokro, 106
Andreotti, Giuillo, 228
John XXIII (Pope; Angelo Cardinal Roncalli), 81
Angola, 233
Antonescu, Marshal Ian, 31
Arab independence movements, 107–110
Arab-Israeli wars
  1948–1949, 108
  1973 (Yom Kippur War), 147
  Sinai campaign (1956), 141
Arab oil embargo, 237–238
Ardagh, John, 159, 178, 183
Aristocracy, 180–181
Asia, end of European dominance in, 98;
  see also specific Asian countries
Attlee, Clement, 46, 49, 90
Australia, 22
Austria
  economic recovery in, 69, 70, 75
  effects of détente on politics of, 224, 231

European unity and, 143
politics in (1945–1965), 58, 91, 93–94
ruling class of, 173, 176, 183
socioeconomic conditions in (1960s), 153, 156, 160
Austro-Hungarian Empire, 26, 137
Awolowo, Obafemi, 115
Azikiwe, Nmandi, 115

Bacilek, Karol, 216
Badoglio, Marshal Pietro, 53
Balewa, Abubaker Tafawa, 115
Balkans, *see* Albania; Bulgaria; Greece; Yugoslavia
Ball, George, 143
Balmiel, Lord, 181
Bao Dai (Emperor of Indochina), 105
Barricades Revolt (1960; France), 86
Basque region, 236
Basso, Lelio, 81
Bay of Pigs invasion (1961), 223
Belgian Congo, 93, 113
Belgium, *see* Benlux countries
Bello, Sir Ahmadu, 115
Ben Barka, Ahmed, 111
Benelux countries (Belgium; Holland; Luxembourg), 6, 44
  in Cold War, 16
  economic recovery in, 62, 65, 66, 69–71, 75
  effects of détente on politics of, 224, 231
  European unity and, 137, 140, 142, 147
  lose their empires, 106–107
  politics in (1945–1965), 58, 62, 66, 92–93
  ruling class of, 176

socioeconomic conditions in (1960s), 153, 158–160, 166
Beneš, Eduard, 34, 36, 38
Benn, Anthony Wedgwood, 230
Beria, Lavrenti, 120, 122
Berlin Blockade (1948–1949), 17, 37
Bevan, Aneurin, 46, 48, 90
Bevin, Ernest, 46–48
Bidault, Georges, 51, 52
Blum, Léon, 52, 138, 160
Bolshevik Revolution (1917), 98
Bonomi, Ivanoe, 53
Bourguiba, Habib, 108, 111
Boxer Rebellion (1900), 102
Brandt, Willy, 79, 83, 146, 225–226
Brezhnev, Leonid, 189–191, 222
Briand, Aristide, 137
Bulganin, Nikolai, 122, 124, 128
Bulgaria, 7, 8, 37, 60
  socioeconomic conditions in (1960s), 188, 192, 194, 198–199, 201
  Sovietization of, 32–33
Burma, 101, 102
Byrnes, James, 12

Caetano, Marcelo, 233
Callaghan, James, 148, 230
Cambodia, 105
Canada, 65
Capitalism, new, 68–70
Carmoy, Guy de, 79
Carvalho, Maj. Otelo Saraiva de, 235
Castro, Fidel, 208, 223
Ceausescu, Nicolae, 219
Ceylon, 102
Chiang Kai-shek, 103–105
China, 102–103; see also People's Republic of China; Taiwan
Chinese Revolution (1950), 4, 13, 21, 37, 64, 99–100, 103
Churchill, Sir Winston, 6, 7, 9–13, 31, 89
  European politics and, 45–46, 49, 59
  European unity and, 137, 138
  Indian independence and, 100
Clementis, Vladimir, 41
Cohn-Bendit, Daniel, 206, 208, 211
Cold War, 4, 5, 9, 12–23, 64, 110, 113
  beginning of, 12–15
  détente, 146, 222–235
  European politics and (1945–1965), 45, 50, 52, 57, 79–81, 90 93 94
  European unity and, 137
  Korean War during, 19–22, 48, 82, 105, 139, 140
  objectives of, 22–23
  Sovietization of Eastern Europe and, 26–43
  widening of, 15–19
Comecon (Council for Mutual Economic Assistance), 38, 60, 132–134, 143

Common Market (EEC), see European Economic Community
Consumer goods, West European ownership of, 158–160
Constantine (King of Greece), 231, 232
Copenhagen Summit (1972), 147
Coty, René, 86
Coudenhove-Kalergi, Count Richard, 137
Council of Europe, 82, 138–139
Council for Mutual Economic Assistance (Comecon), 38, 60, 133–134, 143
Cripps, Sir Stafford, 46, 101
Cuban missile crisis (1962), 89, 133, 218, 223
Cult of personality (Stalinism), 4, 119–121, 123–124, 130–131, 216
Cyprus, 231, 236
Czechoslovakia, 15–16, 224
  coalition government of, 34–36
  in Comecon, 132
  European unity and, 139
  1952 unrest in, 41
  1968 unrest in (Prague Spring), 196, 206–207, 216–220
  socioeconomic conditions in (1960s), 191–196, 199, 202
  sold out (1938), 5, 27

da Costa Gomes, Gen. Francisco, 234
Dahrendorf, Ralf, 179, 188, 199
de Gaulle, Charles, 44, 222, 223, 228, 229, 235
  Cold War and, 22
  dissolution of French Empire and, 104, 108, 116
  economic recovery and, 66, 73
  European unity and, 142, 144–146
  Fourth Republic under, 48–50, 53
  role of, in European politics (1948–1965), 79, 85–90, 95
  student unrest and (1968), 209, 215–216, 220
Denmark, see Scandinavian countries
Détente, 146, 222–235
Deviationism, Eastern European nationalism as, 36–37, 41–42; see also Tito, Marshal; Yugoslavia
Dimitrov, Georgi, 33, 37, 41
Djilas, Milovan, 7, 26, 201
Dogmatism in People's Republic of China, 130–131
Douglas-Home, Sir Alec, 91
Dubček, Alexander, 196, 216–220
Duclos, Jacques, 50
Dulles, John Foster, 140
Dutschke, Rudi (Red Rudi), 208

Eanes, Antonio Ramalho, 234, 235
East Germany, 41, 236

Brandt recognizes, 225
in Comecon, 132
Oder-Neisse line, 10–11, 225
socioeconomic conditions in (1960s), 188, 191–197, 199–200, 202
and unrest in Czechoslovakia, 218, 219
East-West relations during World War II, 6; *see also* Cold War; Soviet Union; United States; *and specific Western European countries*
Eastern Europe, 3, 4, 7–8, 15, 66, 69
economy of (1950s, 1960s), 124, 125, 132, 188–194
German military power and (1930s), 26–27
Sovietization of, 26–43
See also specific Eastern European countries
Economic nationalism, 132–133
Economic recovery, 63–72
characteristics of, 63–64
developments in agriculture and, 71–72
industrial concentration and nationalizations and, 70–71
new capitalism and, 68–70
postwar patterns of, 77–78
stimuli to, 64–68; *see also* Marshall Plan
See also the entry "economic recovery" under specific Western European countries
Economy
Eastern European (1950s; 1960s), 124, 125, 132, 188–194
effects of Arab oil embargo on, 237–238
new capitalism, 68–70
role of, in European unity, 137–140; *see also specific economic organizations*
role of, in politics (1948–1965), 94–96
postwar Soviet, 119, 121, 122
Soviet (1960s), 188–194
Soviet, under Khrushchev, 133–134, 188–190, 192
U.S. and Western European industrial production compared (1901–1955), 2
Western European (1946–1948), 46–48, 53
See also Economic recovery; Nationalizations
ECSC (European Coal and Steel Community), 82, 139–142, 146
EDC (European Defense Community), 140–141
Eden, Sir Anthony, 6, 89
Edinger, Lewis J., 173
Education
in Communist countries, 199–200
of Western European ruling class, 175–180
EEC, *see* European Economic Community

EFTA (European Free Trade Area), 91, 143
Egypt, 107–109, 141
Eisenhower, Dwight D., 22, 105
Eisentein, Sergei, 120
Empires, dissolution of, 26, 98–118, 136, 137, 233
England, *see* Great Britain
Erhard, Ludwig, 84
Euratom, 142, 146
European balance of power
effects of World War I on, 26
effects of World War II on, 1–3
European Coal and Steel Community (ECSC), 82, 139–142, 146
European Defense Community (EDC), 140–141
European Economic Community (Common Market; EEC), 61, 82, 88, 94, 141–147, 156, 238
British entry into, 90–91, 140, 143–147, 228
Comecon as answer to, 132
economic recovery and, 63, 65–66, 71–72, 76
major shipping station of, 93
strength of, 149
European Free Trade Area (EFTA), 91, 143
European Recovery Program, *see* Marshall Plan
European unity, 136–149, 235

Fanfani, Amintore, 81
Farouk (King of Egypt), 108, 109
Feisal (King of Iraq), 108
Fifth Republic (French), 86, 228, 237
Finland, *see* Scandinavian countries
First secretaries (of Communist parties), revolt of, 36–37
Fourth Republic (French; 1945–1958), 49–53, 85–86
France, 1, 3, 6, 8, 11, 27, 29, 44, 94
centralized authority in, 237
in Cold War, 13, 14, 16, 17, 19
economic recovery in, 64–66, 69, 70–73, 75, 76
effects of détente on politics of, 224, 228–229
European unity and, 136, 139–142, 146–149
loses its empire, 104–108, 110–111, 113, 116–117
politics in (1945–1965), 46, 49–53, 60, 84–89, 95
reunification of Germany and, 83
ruling class of, 172, 175–176, 178–179, 181–185
socioeconomic conditions in (1960s), 151, 153–165, 167, 195, 199
student unrest in (1968), 158, 167, 206–207, 209–216, 220

in Suez crisis, 90, 109–110
Franco, Generalissimo Francisco, 56–57, 94, 210, 233, 236
French Guiana, 116
Fring benefits, Western European (1960s), 157–158

Gaitskell, Hugh, 90
Galbraith, John Kenneth, 77–78
Gandhi, Mohandas K., 99–101, 114
Gardner, Lloyd, 22
Gasperi, Alcide de, 54–55, 80, 137, 138
Gaulle, Charles de, see De Gaulle, Charles
General strike, French (1968), 212–216
Geneva Conference (1954), 105–106
German Federal Republic, see West Germany
Germany, 44
  defeated (1945), 2
  Eastern Europe and military power of (1930s), 26–27
  obtaining reparations from or dismembering, 9–11
  occupation of, 11–12
  reunification of, 82–83, 146, 225
  See also East Germany, West Germany
Gerö, Ernö, 126
Ghana (Gold Coast), 112, 114
Gheorghiu-Dej, Gheorghe, 32, 132
Giap, Vo Nguyen, 105
Giroud, Francoise, 156
Giscard d'Estaing, Valéry, 149, 156, 224, 229
Gokhale, G. K., 100
Gold Coast (Ghana), 112, 114
Gomulka, Wladislav, 37, 41, 124, 126, 128, 129, 219
Gonçalves, Vasco, 234
Gottwald, Clement, 36
Gouin, Pierre, 51
Great Britain, 1, 3, 6, 8, 27, 33, 59, 224
  in Cold War, 13, 16, 17
  economic recovery in, 64, 65, 69, 71, 75–76
  European unity and, 136–141, 143–147, 149
  joins EEC, 90–91, 140, 143–147, 228
  loses its empire, 100–102, 107–110, 113–116
  nationalism in (1970s), 235
  in occupation of Germany, 11
  Polish government exiled in, 29, 30
  politics in (1945–1965), 45–49, 53, 60–61, 82, 88–91, 94
  Portugal and, 57
  recession in (1970s), 237
  ruling class of, 172, 175–178, 181–185
  socioeconomic conditions in (1960s), 15, 153–154, 156, 158–161, 163–65, 167, 195, 199

in Suez crisis, 109–110
Greece, 7, 47, 58–60, 77, 222, 231–232
Greek Civil War, 4, 7, 13–14, 37, 39, 47, 59–60, 64
Groza, Petru, 32
Guadeloupe, 116
Guevara, Che, 208
Guinea, 116, 117
Guinea-Bissau, 233, 234
Guttsman, W. L., 173

Hallstein, Walter, 145
Hamilton, Duke of, 181
Hassan II (Sultan of Morocco), 111
Heath, Edward, 143, 146, 177, 229–230
Hegel, G. W. F., 136–137
Hilter, Adolf, 2, 3, 5, 11, 26–27, 49, 104, 137
Ho Chi Minh, 99, 103–105, 208
Holland (Netherlands), see Benelux countries
Horthy, Adm. Miklós, 34
Houphouët-Boigny, Félix, 116–117
Housing of Western European ruling class, 183–184
Hungarian Revolution (1956), 79, 80, 90, 110, 125–128, 130, 136, 142, 220
Hungary, 7, 33–34, 194, 196–198, 202
Husák, Gustav, 220

Iberian peninsula, see Portugal; Spain
Ibrahim, Abdallah, 111
Ignatiev, E., 120
Immigrant labor, 66, 156–157
Income (and wages)
  in Soviet Union (1960s), 194–195
  Western European (1960s), 153–159
Independence movements, 47, 87, 99–117;
  see also Algerian rebellion; Indochina War
India, Alois, 220
India, 47, 100–102
Indochina, 101, 103–106, 111
Indochina War (later Vietnam War), 52, 85, 89, 206, 208–211, 230
Indonesia, 93, 106–107
Iran, 3, 12, 23, 108
Iraq, 107, 108, 110
Ireland, 147, 153, 156, 160
Israel, 109, 194
Italy, 6, 44, 46
  in Cold War, 13, 14, 19
  economic recovery of, 65, 69, 70, 72, 75–77
  effects of détente on politics of, 224, 226–228
  European unity and, 140, 142, 147
  immigrant labor from, 66
  nationalism in (1970s), 235
  politics in (1945–1965), 53–56, 60, 79–81, 95

recession in (1970s), 237
ruling class of, 172, 176, 185
socioeconomic conditions in (1960s), 153, 155, 158–162, 165, 199
student unrest in, 207–209
Ivory Coast, 117

Japan, 1, 2, 9, 21, 22, 75, 77, 90, 101–106
Jinnah, Mohammed Ali, 101
Jordon, 109
Juan Carlos (King of Spain), 232
Jungblut, Michael, 183

Kádár, János, 127–128
Kaganovitch, Lazar, 124, 128
Kahan, Arcadiu, 192
Kang Yu-wei, 102
Karamanlis, George, 231
Kennan, George F., 14–16, 21
Kennedy, John F., 143
Keynes, John Maynard, 68
Khrushchev, Nikita, 38, 42, 83, 93, 121–125, 194, 202
  in Cuban missile crisis, 223
  economy under, 133–134, 188–190, 192
  denounces cult of personality, 119, 123, 216
  Hungarian Revolution and, 126, 128
  ousted, 133–134
  postwar economy under Stalin and, 121
  Poznan riots and (1956), 123–125
  threat of polycentrism and, 128–133
Kiesinger, Kurt Georg, 225
Kolko, Gabriel, 3
Korean War (1949–1953), 19–22, 48, 82, 105, 139, 140
Kostov, Traicho, 41
Kosygin, Aleksei, 189–191
Kreisky, Bruno, 231
Krippendorf, Ehkehart, 208

Labor unions, Western European, 161–163, 165–167
Laos, 105
League of Nations, 8, 107, 108
Lebanon, 107, 108
Lecanuet, Jean, 88
Lenin, Vladimir I., 98, 128, 131
Liberia, 111
Libya, 107
Life-style of Western European ruling class, 173–174
Lloyd George, David, 98
Low Countries, see Benelux countries
Lulchev, Kosta, 33
Lumumba, Patrice, 113
Luxembourg, see Benelux countries

MacArthur, Gen. Douglas, 22
Macauly, Herbert, 114

McMahon, Sir Henry, 108
Macmillan, Harold, 90–91
McNeill, W. H., 6
Makarios, Archbishop, 231, 236
Malenkov, Georgi, 121–122, 125, 128, 132
Malraux, André, 136
Manchuria, 3
Mao Tse-tung, 131, 132, 201, 208
  revolution led by, 13, 27, 37, 99–103
Marshall, George, 14, 15
Marshall Plan (European Recovery Program), 36, 38, 42
  announced, 12
  Congress approves, 16
  OEEC and, 138
  purpose of, 14–15, 63–65
  Western European politics and (1945–1948), 53, 58, 60–61
Martinique, 116
Marx, Karl, 152
Masaryk, Jan, 36, 218
Massu, Gen. Jacques, 86
Mattei, Enrico, 70
Mayne, Richard, 143
Mendès-France, Pierre, 52, 84–85, 111, 141, 214
Michael (King of Romania), 31–32
Middle East, see specific Mideastern countries
Mikolajczyk, Stanislav, 30–31
Mikoyan, Anastas, 120, 124
Mills, C. Wright, 172
Mindszenty, Josef Cardinal, 41
Mitterand, François, 88, 224, 229
Mohammed V (Sultan of Morocco), 110–111
Mohammed Reza Shah Pahlevi (Shah of Iran), 208
Mollet, Guy, 116
Molotov, Vyacheslav, 8, 52, 120, 121, 124, 128
Monnet, Jean, 72–73, 136, 139–141
Morgenthau, Henry, 9
Moro, Aldo, 81
Morocco, 85, 110–111
Moscow Conference (1941), 6
Moscow Conference (1947), 52
Moulin, Jean, 85
Mozambique, 233, 234
Munich Conference (1938), 5, 27
Mussolini, Benito, 53

Naguib, Gen. Mohammed, 109
Nagy, Imre, 34, 125–126
Nasser, Gamal Abdel, 85, 89–90, 109–110, 141
National Communism in Romania, 132
Nationalism
  Comecon and economic, 132–133
  Eastern European, as deviationism,

36-37, 41-42
independence movements and, 47, 99-117
in 1970s, 235-236
post-World War I, 98, 137
Nationalist China (Taiwan), 8, 21, 103
Nationalizations
British, 46, 75, 90
economic recovery and, 70-71
French, 50
Portuguese, 234
of Suez Canal (1956), 89, 141
NATO (North Atlantic Treaty Organization), 19, 21, 58, 82, 83, 89, 141, 228
Nehru, Jawaharlal, 99, 100
Nenni, Pietro, 80-81, 226
Netherlands, *see* Benelux countries
New capitalism, 68-70
New Zealand, 22
Nigeria, 99, 111, 114-115
Nixon, Richard M., 224
Nkrumah, Kwame, 98, 99, 101, 124
North Atlantic Treaty Organization (NATO), 19, 21, 58, 61
North Korea, 3
North Vietnam, *see* Indochina; Indochina War
Northern Ireland (Ulster), 236
Norway, *see* Scandinavian countries
Novotny, Antonin, 130, 216, 217
Nyerere, Julius, 115-116

Oder-Neisse line (German-Polish border), 10-11, 225
OECD (Organization for European Cooperation and Development), 155, 166
OEEC (Organization for European Economic Cooperation), 19, 138, 139
Organization for European Cooperation and Development (OECD), 155, 166
Organization for European Economic Cooperation (OEEC), 19, 138, 139
Orwell, George, 171
Ostpolitik (eastern policy), 146, 222, 225
Ottoman Empire, 26, 107, 108, 137

Pakistan, 101
Palestine, 47, 107-109
Papandreou, George, 231, 232
Paris riots (1968), 158, 167, 206-207, 209-216, 220
Paris Summit Conference (1972), 147
Parri, Ferruccio, 54, 55
Pasquier (Governor General), 104
Patrascano, Lucretio, 41
Pauker, Ana, 32
People's democracies, 37-38; *see also* specific *Eastern European countries*

People's Republic of China, 22, 119, 124, 223
attacks Yugoslavian revisionism, 129
dogmatism in, 130-131
economic nationalism and, 133
proclaimed (1949), 103
Petkov, Nikola, 33
Pflimlin, Pierre, 85
Philippines, 22
Pius XII (Pope; Cardinal Pacelli), 137
Pleven, René, 140
Pluralism
in Communist countries, 201-203
Western European, 172-173
Plutocrats, Western European, 182-183
Poland, 6
coalition government of, 29-31
Oder-Neisse line, 10-11, 225
Poznan riots in (1956), 123-125, 196
socioeconomic conditions in (1960s), 192, 193, 196, 198-199, 202
and unrest in Czechoslovakia, 218, 219
Politics
effects of détente on, 224-235
1945-1948, 44-62
1948-1965, 79-97
See also Unrest
Polycentrism, Soviet domination threatened by, 128-133
Pompidou, Georges, 88, 146, 215, 229
Portugal, 65, 66, 77, 91, 143
dictatorship overthrown in, 222-223
end of empire of, 117
political transition of, 233-235
politics in (1945-1965), 57-58, 94
socioeconomic conditions in (1960s), 153, 159, 168
Postan, M. M., 63, 70
Potocki, Ignacz, 198
Potsdam Conference (1945), 10-11
Poujade, Pierre, 72, 73
Poznan riots (1956), 123-125, 196
Prague Spring (1968), 196, 206-207, 216-220
Profumo, John, 91
Prokofiev, Sergei, 120
Prussian empire, 26

Quebec Conference (1944), 9, 10

Radziwill family, 198
Rajk, Lásló, 34, 41, 126
Rakosi, Matyas, 34, 125-126, 128
Ramadier, Paul, 52, 53, 84
Realpolitik, 7
Réunion (islands), 116
Revisionism, *see* Deviationism
Reza Khan Pahlevi (Shah of Iran), 108
Rhodesia, 117
Romania, 6-8, 31-33, 132-133

coalition government of, 31–32
socioeconomic conditions in (1960s), 191–192, 194, 198–199, 201
unrest in Czechoslovakia and, 218, 219
Roncalli, Angelo Cardinal (Pope John XXIII), 81
Roosevelt, Franklin D., 6–11, 27, 31, 49, 56
Royer, Jean, 72
Ruanda-Urundi, 93
Ruhr, internationalization of, 10, 52
Ruling class
    Communist, 200–201
    Western European, 171–186
Rumor, Mariano, 227
Russian Civil War (1919–1922), 27, 30
Russian Empire, 26
Russo-Japanese War (1905), 98

Saar, internationalization of, 10, 82
Salazar, Antonio de Oliveira, 57, 58, 94, 233
Sampson, Anthony, 174, 178
Saragat, Giuseppe, 55, 80
Saudi Arabia, 107
Scandinavian countries (Denmark; Finland; Norway; Sweden), 6, 8
    effects of détente on politics of, 231
    European unity and, 143, 146, 147
    politics in (1945–1965), 58, 61, 65, 69, 91–92, 95–96
    ruling class of, 173, 176, 180, 182–185
    socioeconomic conditions in (1960s), 151, 154–156, 158–163 165–168, 194
Schmidt, Helmut, 149, 226
Schumacher, Kurt, 17, 83
Schuman, Robert, 53, 72, 136–140
SEATO (South-East Asia Treaty Organization), 89
Sedar-Senghor, Léopold, 117
Senegal, 117
Service class (white-collar workers), Western European, 151–154, 163
Seton-Watson, Hugh, 29
Shostakovich, Dimitri, 120
Sik, Ota, 217
Simeon (King of Bulgaria), 33
Sinai campaign (1956), 141
Sino-Japanese War (1894–1895), 102
Six-Power Conference (London; 1948), 16
Slanski, Rudolf, 41
Soares, Mario, 234
Socioeconomic conditions
    in Communist countries (1960s), 188–203
    in Western Europe (1960s), 152–168, 188–195, 197–199, 200–202
    See also Economic recovery; Economy; Ruling class
Sokolovsky, Marshal, 16
Social class
    in Communist world, 198–200

political attitudes and, 165–166
    Western European, 152–156
    See also Ruling class; Working class
Social leveling, 163–165
South Africa, Republic of, 117
South-East Asia Treaty Organization (SEATO), 89
South Vietnam, *see* Indochina; Indochina War
Soviet Union (U.S.S.R.; Union of Soviet Socialist Republics), 1–6, 44
    de Gaulle and, 88–89
    Eastern Europe under domination of, *see* Eastern Europe
    European unity and, 136–137, 139, 140, 142, 146
    independence movements and, 104, 113
    Korean War and, 21
    nuclear capacity of, 19, 139, 140
    proposes German reunification, 82–83
    socioeconomic conditions in (1960s), 188–195, 197–198, 200, 202
    Western European politics and (1945–1948), 51, 58, 61
    See also Cold War; Khrushchev, Nikita; Stalin, Joseph; *and specific Balkan countries*
Spaak, Paul-Henri, 137–139, 142
Spain, 65, 66, 77
    effects of death of Franco on, 232–233
    nationalism in (1970s), 236
    politics in (1945–1965), 56–57, 94
    socioeconomic conditions in (1960s), 153, 159, 168
Spanish Civil War (1936–1939), 56, 57
Spinola, Gen. Antonio de, 233–234
Springer, Axel, 208
Stalin, Joseph, 3–17, 21, 125, 140, 189, 194
    choosing successor to, 121–122; *see also* Khrushchev, Nikita
    European politics and (1945–1948), 52, 59, 60
    European unity and, 138
    postwar society and economy under, 119–122
    removing body of, from Kremlin, 131
    and Sovietization of Eastern Europe, 26–34, 36–38, 41–42
    at Yalta Conference (1945), 7–8, 30
Stalinism (cult of personality), 4, 119–121, 123–124, 130–131, 216
Standard of living
    in Communist countries (1960s), 194–197
    Western European (1960s), 158–160
Stettinius, Edward, 9
Strauss, Franz Josef, 84
Strikes
    French general (1968), 212–216
    See also Politics; Socioeconomic conditions

Strougal, Lubómir, 220
Student unrest (1960s), 206–220
Suez crisis (1956), 3, 89–90, 109–110, 112, 136, 141, 230
Sukarno, Achmed, 99, 106–107
Sun Yat-sen, 102–103
Superpowers
  emergence of, 1–3
  See also People's Republic of China; Soviet Union; United States
Svoboda, Ludvik, 217, 220
Sweden, *see* Scandinavian countries
Switzerland, 91, 143
  economic recovery of, 65, 66, 72, 76
  socioeconomic conditions in (1960s), 151, 153, 156–157, 159–160, 166
Syria, 107–110

Taiwan (Formosa; Nationalist China), 8, 21, 103
Tanganyika, 99, 11, 115–116
Tanzania, 115
Technocrats, 185–186
Teheran Conference (1943), 6–11
Thorez, Maurice, 50, 51, 84
Tilak, B. G., 100
Tildy, Zoltan, 34
Tito, Marshal (Josip Bròz), 4, 33, 37–39, 41, 59–60, 130
  Hungarian Revolution and, 126, 127
  Khrushchev and, 123
  1960s socioeconomic conditions and, 195
  pluralism and, 202
  ruling class criticized by, 201
  unrest in Czechoslovakia and, 219
Tocqueville, Alexis de, 1
Togliatti, Palmiro, 80
Touraine, Alain, 171, 175
Transjordan, 107
Trotsky, Leon, 208
Truman, Harry S, 11, 12, 14, 16, 21, 22, 47, 105
Truman Doctrine, 12, 14, 15, 42, 47, 52, 60
Tunisia, 85, 107, 108, 111
Turkey, 3, 12–14, 23, 47, 66, 77, 231, 236

Ulbricht, Walter, 12, 130, 219
Ulster (Northern Ireland), 236
Umberto (King of Italy), 53–55
Union of Soviet Socialist Republics, *see* Soviet Union
United Kingdom, *see* Great Britain
United Nations (UN), 21, 78, 86, 109, 110, 236
United States, 1–6, 9, 11, 12, 94, 103, 110
  de Gaulle and, 88–89
  dwindling influence of (1960s), 79, 89
  European economic recovery and, 63, 65, 75, 77; *see also* Marshall Plan

European politics and (1945–1965), 47, 49, 53, 55, 57, 61, 80
European unity and, 136–146, 149
independence movements and, 105–106, 108, 113
ruling class of, 175, 180, 182, 184, 185
socioeconomic conditions in, 153, 158–160, 162–163, 167–168
socioeconomic conditions in Communist countries compared with those of (1960s), 191–194
student unrest in (1960s), 206–207
Suez crisis and, 110
ties between Western Europe and (1970s), 237–238
unrest in Czechoslovakia and, 220
See also Cold War; Indochina War
U. S. S. R., *see* Soviet Union

Vandenberg, Arthur, 14
Victor Emmanuel III (King of Italy), 53
Vietnam War (earlier Indochina War), 52, 85, 89, 106, 206, 208–211, 230
Voroshilov, Marshal Kliment, 34, 120

Warsaw Pact, 218–219
Welfare states
  British, 45–49
  Scandinavian, 91, 92
Werth, Alexander, 44
West Germany, 21, 94, 237
  economic recovery of, 65, 66, 68, 69, 71–76
  effects of détente on politics of, 224–226,
  European unity and, 139–142, 146
  formed, 17
  politics in (1945–1965), 60, 81–84
  ruling class of, 172–175, 179–180, 182–183
  socioeconomic conditions in (1960s), 153, 157–163, 165–167, 195, 199
Western Europe
  industrial production in (1901–1955), 2
  See also specific countries
Westminster, Duke of, 181
Williams, William A., 3, 22
Wilson, Harold, 91, 146, 149, 229–230
Wilson, Woodrow, 98
Wolff, Karl-Dietrich, 207
Women, 156–157, 198
Work week in Western Europe, 160–161
Working class
  Western European, 66, 151–161
  See also Labor unions; Strikes
Wylie, Laurence, 73

Xoxi, Koce, 41

Yalta Conference (1945), 6–11, 30

Yemen, 107
Yugoslavia, 7, 13–14, 33, 128–129
  economic nationalism and, 133
  Greek Civil War and, 60
  influence of, 123–125, 132
  leadership position of, 119
  socioeconomic conditions in (1960s),
    193–197, 199, 202
  splits from Soviet bloc, 4, 37–42
  unrest in Czechoslovakia, 216, 217, 219

Zanzibar, 113
Zhdanov, Andrei A., 15, 120
Zhukov, Georgi, 120, 124